D0480491

Merry Christmas
To: Alan
Love, Morag x

# From Pole to Pole

*This book is dedicated to*

*Captain Roald Engelbregt Gravning Amundsen (1872–1928)*

Master Mariner, Arctic & Antarctic explorer, first through the North-West Passage (1903–1907), first to the South Pole (14 December 1911), First to be awarded a Federation Aeronautic Internationale (Norge) aviators certificate (18 September 1915), third through the North-East Passage (1918–1920), first to circumnavigate the globe above the Arctic Circle (1903–1907 & 1918–1920), furthest North by air (22 May 1925), first to the North Pole (12 May 1926), first to cross the Arctic Ocean (11 May–14 May 1926), innovator, author, lecturer, leader of men, statesman, citizen of an independent Norway.

# From Pole to Pole

## Roald Amundsen's Journey in Flight

**Garth James Cameron**

First published in Great Britain in 2013 by
Pen & Sword Discovery
an imprint of
Pen & Sword Books Ltd
47 Church Street
Barnsley
South Yorkshire
S70 2AS

Copyright © Garth James Cameron 2013

ISBN 978 1 78159 337 0

The right of Garth James Cameron to be identified as the Author
of this Work has been asserted by him in accordance with the
Copyright, Designs and Patents Act 1988.

A CIP catalogue record for this book is available from the British
Library

All rights reserved. No part of this book may be reproduced or
transmitted in any form or by any means, electronic or mechanical
including photocopying, recording or by any information storage and
retrieval system, without permission from the Publisher in writing.

Typeset in Ehrhardt by
Mac Style, Driffield, East Yorkshire
Printed and bound in Malta by Gutenberg Press Ltd.

Pen & Sword Books Ltd incorporates the Imprints of Pen & Sword
Aviation, Pen & Sword Maritime, Pen & Sword Military, Wharncliffe
Local History, Pen and Sword Select, Pen & Sword Military Classics,
Leo Cooper, The Praetorian Press, Remember When, Seaforth
Publishing and Frontline Publishing.

For a complete list of Pen & Sword titles please contact
PEN & SWORD BOOKS LIMITED
47 Church Street, Barnsley, South Yorkshire, S70 2AS, England
E-mail: enquiries@pen-and-sword.co.uk
Website: www.pen-and-sword.co.uk

# Contents

# Introduction

'Victory awaits him, who has everything in order, luck we call it. Defeat is definitely due for him who has neglected to take the necessary precautions, bad luck we call it.'

Roald Amundsen 1927

'I desire to offer your Majesty and the people of Norway my congratulations on the successwhich has attended the bold undertaking of this hardy and intrepid descendant of the Vikings.'

President Calvin Coolidge 1926. Telegram to King Haakon VII

I have written this book because Amundsen's aviation activities were important, interesting and have not been examined in detail from a modern perspective. I knew something of the story and wanted to know more. It was a pleasure to get to know the subject and write about it detail. About halfway through the book I realised that I had grown to like Amundsen very much and my only regret is that of course I will never have the opportunity to sit down with him, have a few drinks and talk about his life. The social, political and technological context of Amundsen's life could not be more different from that of today. In his lifetime every nation had its hero's and it was acceptable to admire and respect people who took risks and achieved. In his lifetime aviation came into existence and developed at a rate that no one had predicted. Explorers found that they could cover in hours what had taken months or years to cover on the surface. It suddenly seemed possible to fill in the blank spots on the maps. Maps became much more accurate due to aerial photography and aerial survey. Airships seemed to be the future, aviators were seen as heroes, governments encouraged 'air mindedness' but few people would do more than have a ten minute flight with a barnstormer. Newspapers published lists of the few passengers who arrived at the new airports. Air navigation was developing and very complex. A long flight required an air navigator to work from take-off to touchdown with the varied tools of his trade. The world seemed to be an exciting place with exciting possibilities due to aviation. Explorers and aviators were celebrities in a way movie stars are today. Most importantly, people had not come to take air travel or recreational aviation for granted. I admire Roald Amundsen for his professionalism, his attention to detail, his courage, his achievements and for being interesting character with a fair share of imperfections which make him that much more likable.

## A note on names (1896–1928) and numbers

### Place Names
The primary sources for this book use a variety of names for the same place. Usually the English language sources used anglicised versions of the place names. The name Spitsbergen was sometimes used for the whole archipelago including the Islands of Spitsbergen, North East Land and many smaller islands. Sometimes Svalbard was used for the group of Islands and Spitsbergen for the main island. The modern convention is to call the whole archipelago Svalbard and Spitsbergen refers solely to the biggest island in the group. Danes Island is Danskoya, Amsterdam Island is Amsterdamoya, Virgo Harbour is Virgohamna, Kings Bay is Kongsfjorden, New Alesund is Ny Alesund, North East Land is Nordaustlandet and Bear Island is Bjornoya.

Norway gained its independence from Sweden on 7 June 1905.

The Norwegian capital Christiania became Kristiania in 1877 and was renamed Oslo on 1 January 1925.

### Names of people
The sources often give two or more spellings of each individual's name. I have chosen the most likely one for each person and referred to him or her by that name throughout the book.

### Dates, Times and Details
The books published immediately after Amundsen's 1925 and 1926 expeditions are valuable but were rushed into print and written by a number of expedition members in parallel. This has resulted in some contradictory statements about dates, times and flight times. I have done my best to reconcile these contradictions.

### Units of Measurement
The sources for this book use a mix of units. For continuity, where the text refers to flight planning and flights, I have converted figures in the sources

to the units now used in aviation; metres for runway dimensions, metres and kilometres for visibility distances, feet for elevations and altitudes, nautical miles for navigational distances, litres for volumes, kilograms for weights and knots (nautical miles per hour) for speeds. Directions are expressed in degrees(°) with a circle divided into 360° eg: due east is 090°, south east is 135°, south is 180°.

The original figures were often round figures. I usually use the exact result of the conversions for the sake of accuracy in narrating the navigational parts of the story. This sometimes gives oddly precise figures. For example the cruising speed of the Dornier Wal flying boat is 150kmph which converts to 81kt. If a figure is rounded in the text I note that the figure is 'about'.

I recommend:www.metric-conversions.org to readers who wish to convert any of the numbers in the text.

In the early twentieth century the indigenous people of the Arctic were usually called Eskimo rather than Inuit.

*Chapter One*

# The Past is a Foreign Country

*Norway–North-West Passage, 1872–1907*

Novelist L P Hartley wrote that 'the past is a foreign country, they do things differently there' and that observation certainly applies to the life and adventures of Roald Amundsen. When he was born there were no airships or aeroplanes and large parts of the Arctic and Antarctic were unexplored. He started out using skis, dogs and ships and then adopted the aeroplane and airship as vehicles. Amundsen was the most successful Arctic and Antarctic explorer of his day and one of the reasons for his success was his willingness to innovate. Amundsen's involvement in aviation started in 1909 and included Arctic flights in 1925, 1926 and 1928. In 1925 he and five others attempted to fly two flying boats from Spitsbergen to the North Pole and back. It was a heroic failure and a near disaster. In 1926 Amundsen lead an expedition in the airship *Norge* from Svalbard to the North Pole and on to Alaska. This was the first undisputed journey to the North Pole, the first journey across the Arctic Ocean and the first flight from Europe to the Americas by way of the North Pole. In 1928 Amundsen joined the search and rescue effort for the crew of airship *Italia* which had crashed on the pack ice north-east of Svalbard. His flying boat with all on board disappeared on the last leg of its positioning flight from Troms in northern Norway to Kings Bay in Svalbard.

Roald Engelbregt Gravning Amundsen (1872–1928) was the last Viking. A mariner by profession, he turned himself into the best known and most successful Arctic and Antarctic explorer of the early twentieth century. His achievements made him one of the most famous Norwegians of his day. He mixed with kings and queens and princes, with presidents and prime ministers. He was a celebrity who earned his fame the hard way, by doing what no one had done before. He was a hero in Norway, which gained its independence from Sweden in 1905 while he was navigating the North West

Passage. He was an innovator in the exploration of the Arctic and Antarctic and this book is about his innovative use of aircraft to explore the Arctic.

Amundsen was every inch the explorer, 180cm tall, deeply tanned with the strong but trim build of a middleweight boxer and a Roman nose. He would stay fit and strong down to the day he died aged 55. He had decided to be an arctic explorer when he was a teenager after reading accounts of some of the many expeditions mounted in the nineteenth century. From these books he learnt which equipment and techniques worked and which did not. He would always be an open-minded innovator. From an early age he worked on developing the physical strength and endurance that would be required for this type of career and he undertook dangerous and demanding cross-country ski trips whenever he could. He wrote with understandable pride that his physique impressed the doctors who examined him before his compulsory military training. His mother wanted him to be a doctor and he enrolled in University for several years but left as soon as she died. He went to sea to acquire the skills and sea time he would need to qualify as a ship's officer and ultimately as a master mariner.

In 1897–1899 he was second mate on de Gerlache's *Belgica* expedition to Antarctica. The ship was trapped in the ice and the crew became the first men to overwinter in Antarctica. Dr Frederic Cook was the ship's surgeon and Amundsen developed a respect for that deeply flawed character which survived Cook's later fraudulent claims to have climbed Mt McKinley and to have reached the North Pole. Cook ended up in prison having been convicted of a major fraud involving oil reserves. Amundsen visited him in prison and demonstrated one of his (Amundsen's) most likeable qualities; he was loyal to his friends. He knew that he would only truly be in control of his future expeditions if he commanded the ship that was used. He therefore qualified for a master mariner's licence at the earliest opportunity. His career as a ship's officer was a key part of his overall plan to be a career explorer. For the rest of his life the one title he valued was Captain.

In 1903–1907 he commanded *Gjoa* on the first continuous voyage from the Atlantic to the Pacific by way of the North West Passage across the top of Canada and Alaska. During that expedition he also made overland journeys to locate and make observations at the North Magnetic Pole. In the process he developed skill in dog sledding and managing expeditions in the snow, ice and deep cold of high latitudes.

Before the 1903–1907 expedition he had decided to innovate and trust to his own judgment how to do what many men and ships had been lost doing:

'What has not been accomplished with large vessels and brute force I will attempt with a small vessel and patience'

Roald Amundsen (L), Master Mariner, with the crew of *Gjoa*. After the *Belgica* expedition to Antarctica in 1897-1899 Amundsen had sailed *Gjoa* from Kristiania in Norway to San Francisco in 1903-1907 by way of the North-West Passage. This was an important 'first' and established him as an Arctic explorer of note. Norway had become independent in 1905 when Amundsen was at Gjoahaven on King William Island. He had reached the North Magnetic Pole and made magnetic observations for two years.

He had faith that a small herring boat like his *Gjoa* could endure the treacherous Arctic Ocean.

During 1910–1912 he commanded the *Fram* on its third voyage; an expedition to Antarctica. On 14 December 1911 he became the first man to reach the South Pole, beating Captain Scott and his party by a month. This achievement consolidated his national and international fame and guaranteed him a place in the history books. It also created an on-going resentment in Great Britain and its Empire that a 'foreigner' and a professional had beaten Scott, the heroic amateur.

After doing well financially during the shipping boom of the Great War (1914–1918) he ordered a new ship for a further Arctic expedition. This was the *Maude*, which he sailed through the North East Passage (from the

Atlantic to the Pacific across the top of Russia) in 1918–1920. The ship would have to be built to survive being trapped in the pack ice of the Arctic Ocean for years at a time. He had a Norwegian naval architect and shipbuilder Colin Archer design a vessel that had a hull almost a metre thick and was curved laterally and longitudinally so that it would rise out of the ice and not be pinched and crushed. This was only the third time a ship had completed this voyage. Amundsen had now completed the first circumnavigation of the world above the Arctic Circle. The *Maude* voyaged in the Arctic for seven years (1918–1925) although Amundsen was not aboard for most of the later years.

In the twenty-first century anyone in the developed world can access high resolution satellite photos of every metre of the earth's surface, talk to anyone anywhere in the world by satellite phone, fly to anywhere in the world in 24 hours and navigate accurately and easily with a hand-held GPS unit, but it was not always so. In the third decade of the twentieth century a state of the art flying boat cruised at about 80 knots and airships at about 40 knots. A strong wind could halve an aeroplane's ground speed or reduce that of an airship's to a crawl or even drive it backwards. Air navigation was developing and was as much an art as a science. The crew of an aircraft flying over the Arctic Ocean without radio was entirely on its own. If they were forced down on the pack ice no one knew where they were and the chances of being found or rescued was zero. Even if a downed crew made radio contact they might well be beyond the reach of available rescue planes. There was no such thing as a comprehensive search and rescue service in the era in which explorers took to the air for the first time.

Large segments of the arctic basin were unexplored. No one was sure whether or not there were land masses in that part of the globe. In the early years of the twentieth century the Arctic Ocean that covers the northern extremities of the globe was largely *mare incognitum* or perhaps *terra incognita*. No one knew how much of the area was sea and ice and how much, if any, was land. Its natural history, weather, and surface conditions were little known but had been the subject of intense speculation for centuries. It follows that attempts to reach the North Pole were of great geographical significance as any successful journey would traverse a significant section of this unknown area. Many attempts to reach the North Pole had been made since the eighteenth century using ships, sledges, dogs and man power. The explorers spent years at a time on expeditions and endured hardships unknown to travellers in more benign climates.

Ships were locked in the pack ice for years at a time and were frequently crushed and sunk. The survivors only stayed alive by enduring the most appalling privations and chance was always a factor. The British Antarctic explorer Sir Ernest Shackleton rightly called such expeditions 'white warfare'. British polar explorers were awarded the Polar Medal which was worn with war medals on ceremonial occasions.

Before Amundsen's 1925 attempt to fly from Spitsbergen to the North Pole there had been two claims to have reached the Pole, both by surface travel. In 1909 Dr Frederick Cook (1864–1940) claimed to have reached the Pole on 22 April 1908 with two Eskimo companions. He arrived back in civilisation in 1909 and, at first, his claim was widely accepted. He had been medical officer with Robert Perry's Arctic expedition of 1891–1892 and he had the same role on the *Belgica* Antarctica expedition of 1897–1899. Shortly after Dr Cook's return to civilisation doubts about the veracity of his claims were widely felt and widely published. Cook maintained his claim for the rest of his life but by the end of 1909 his claim had been rejected by most of those with knowledge of the lack of evidence to support his claim. A few weeks after Cook made his claim Robert Peary (1856–1920) returned from his 1908–1909 Arctic expedition and claimed to have arrived at the Pole on 6 April 1909 with Mathew Henson and four Eskimo. There were doubts about his claim but the authorities accepted it and Peary received the honours due to the first man to the Pole and secured a place in the history books. The majority opinion amongst modern scholars is that he did not reach the Pole.

Even if Peary had reached the Pole his party were surface bound and their observations were limited to only a few miles either side of their route. Other travellers in the Arctic Ocean such as Fridtjof Nansen (1861–1930) who spent 1893–1896 firstly aboard the *Fram* iced into the pack ice in the Polar Ocean and then trekking over the ice in an unsuccessful attempt to reach the Pole had also been limited to observing what could be seen from the highest masses of pack ice and the mast heads of their ships. That meant that much of the polar basin was unexplored and there could be land masses waiting to be discovered.

Aircraft had the dual advantages of covering in hours what could be covered by surface travellers in months or years and the great tracts of the surface visible from high altitude. When visibility is perfect the horizon is 100km away in all directions at the modest altitude of 1000m. Even when the visibility was not perfect the occupants of an aircraft could expect to observe a huge swath of previously unseen surface.

Amundsen wanted to be the first to reach the Pole by air and to make an important contribution to mankind's knowledge of the planet. He was well aware that there had been a number of unsuccessful attempts to fly to the Pole.

*Chapter Two*

# Before Amundsen (Part One): Salomon August Andree

*Sweden–Svalbard–Polar Ocean, 1896–1897*

When Roald Amundsen made his attempt to fly to the North Pole in 1925 he knew that there had been unsuccessful attempts to fly to the Pole in a balloon in 1896 and 1897 and by airship in 1906, 1907 and 1909. The 1896 expedition had not got off the ground; the 1897 expedition had launched only to disappear without trace somewhere in the Polar Ocean. In 1906 the airship had not even been inflated and in 1907 and 1909 the airship had taken off, flown a short distance and then been either; blown ashore by high winds (in 1907) or suffered mechanical failure (in 1909). The airship expeditions had been high profile fiascos.

Salomon August Andree was the leader of the 1896 and 1897 expeditions. He was born on 18 October 1854 at Grenna, Sweden. It was said that he inherited from both of his parents:

'A keen intelligence, strong will, tenacious perseverance, and a rich fund of humour, together with the most upright of characters'

His 'sober intellectualism' showed as he succeeded in gaining entry to the Royal Institute of Technology in Stockholm 1869. He graduated in 1873 and after two years working as a draftsman he travelled to America. During his time in America he met the aeronaut John Wise (1808–1879) who encouraged his existing interest in aviation. In those days aviation meant ballooning. John Wise was a professional who made 463 flights before disappearing on his final flight. Andree had detailed discussions with Wise although he did not start ballooning until the balloon *Svea* (Sweden), which had a volume of about 1050m$^3$ was made for him in France by Gabriel Yon in 1893. It was inflated with hydrogen which is the lightest of all gases but inflammable when mixed with air. By the time he took delivery of the balloon he had been appointed

Chief Engineer of the technical department of the Swedish patent office and was a founder member of the Society of Swedish Inventors. He made nine flights in the *Svea*, the first of them on 15 July 1893 and the last on 17 March 1895. His longest duration flight was 10½ hours and the greatest distance covered was about 200nm. On one of the flights the wind carried him across the Aland Sea (a part of the Baltic Sea) to the Finnish Archipelago. On several of these flights he experimented with a method of steering the balloon. Normally a balloon will be carried along by the wind and the only way of changing its direction or speed is to climb or descend into wind with a different velocity (strength and direction). Without accurate and detailed forecasts of the winds in the upper air (not available in the 1890's) changing direction was a hit and miss affair. Andree believed that by trailing a rope or ropes in the sea he would slow the balloon, this would create a relative wind past the balloon and a sail would cause the balloon to travel up to 30° off the wind direction. Eventually, by using three trail ropes and a spar with a sail attached he satisfied himself that steering was possible and that a balloon especially designed and constructed for the job would be suitable for a flight across the ice of the Arctic Sea to the North Pole. The trail ropes also acted as an automatic ballasting system. If the balloon became lighter because of the sun the ropes would be lifted until the weight of the extra rope lifted equalled the increase in buoyancy. Likewise, if the balloon got heavier because of cooling of the lifting gas (if the sun went down or was hidden by cloud) the balloon would descend until the weight of the length of trail the trail ropes supported by the water would equal the decrease of the lift. If this automatic ballasting worked the balloon would not run out of gas or ballast as conventional balloons did when they encountered night-time cooling (needing ballast to be dropped to lighten the balloon) and day-time heating (which caused a loss of gas due to its expanding). Andree's third idea was to create a balloon envelope which was much more gas tight than existing envelopes and would therefore be able to retain its gas and therefore lift for many more days than conventional balloons. He satisfied himself that the three improvements would enable a balloon to fly over the pack ice of the Polar Sea to the North Pole. He hoped that the balloon would remain airborne for up to 30 days and in that time it would drift to dry land or within reach of it. The balloon would carry three men, provisions for four months and equipment for a surface journey over the ice to civilisation. The equipment also included cameras and film. As fate would have it, our knowledge of the flight is provided, in part, by 30 or so photographs which were developed from negatives which were discovered on a barren Arctic island 33 years after being exposed by Andree and his companions.

Andree chose Dr Nils Ekholm as the second man in the expedition and set about looking for a third. He appointed Nils Strindberg, who was born at Stockholm on 4 September 1872. He graduated with a Bachelor of Arts degree in 1893 after studying at the Universities of Stockholm and Upsala. Strindberg developed an interest in photography as a teenager and won first prize in a photography competition held at Stockholm in 1895. He had a scientific turn of mind and the summer of 1894 saw him doing geodetic work in Norrland in the north of Sweden. When Andree announced his expedition in 1895 Strindberg was working as an assistant in physics at the University of Stockholm. He was given a number of tasks including selecting cameras and photographic equipment for the expedition. He designed a camera especially suited to the Arctic environment and had it built. Strindberg and Ekholm studied materials for the envelope of the balloon because an unprecedented degree of gas tightness was essential if the balloon was to remain aloft for many days. In the spring of 1896 he travelled to Paris and studied aeronautics. He made seven balloon ascents so that the balloon would have two aeronauts aboard instead of just one (Andree).

The balloon *Ornen* (Eagle) was designed and constructed in France by Henri Lachambre to meet Andree's detailed requirements. The Swedish engineer Per Nordenfelt supervised the construction. The balloon was spherical in shape (as was the normal practice) but was changed to a more elliptical shape when the balloon was enlarged to a capacity of about 4,800m$^3$ in the winter of 1896–97. *Ornen* was almost five times the volume of *Svea* . The envelope was made of several layers of Chinese silk coated with several coats of varnish. Instead of a valve at the top of the balloon it had two valves near the equator of the balloon. Rip panels were provided so that the gas could be dumped in an emergency, such as landing in a high wind. Without a rip panel the balloon's envelope would act as a sail and would cause an out of control dragging of the basket until the gas escaped (slowly) through the valves. The envelope was covered by a net which was attached to a load ring which in turn was attached to the basket. Apart from the number and placing of the valves and the construction of the basket the balloon was of conventional design. The basket was designed with a flight of many days in mind. It provided working and sleeping areas and had a number of unique features. One of them was a kerosene fuelled cooker. To avoid setting the balloon on fire it was designed to slide down a rope before the burner was ignited by line attached to it. Before bringing the cooker back on board the fire was put out by one of the aeronauts blowing down a tube which opened on to the flame. A mirror showed the crew whether or not the flame was out.

When Andree's plans became public there were many who thought the flight impossible. No balloon had flown for more than 36 hours or covered more than 1,000km. There was plenty of data about what balloons could and could not do as balloons, including hydrogen balloons, had been flying since 1783 and some aeronauts had made hundreds of flights. The first problem was that even the best balloon envelopes, those made of gold beater's skin, were porous and lost a significant part of their gas, and lift each hour. It seemed most unlikely that the *Ornen* would retain most of its gas for 30 days of flight as Andree believed. The balloon would be inflated and stored in the balloon house until the wind was right. It would lose gas steadily throughout this wait and would start its flight with less lift than it had when inflated. Andree relied on the trail ropes to stop the balloon from rising too high and venting gas. The trail ropes would only work if the flight was over a smooth surface. The flight would be over the sea and then over the ice. They might be lucky and encounter smooth water to the edge of the ice but it was certain that a large part of the journey would be over ice broken up by wind and currents into pressure ridges of considerable size. The ridges would jerk the balloon around and could snag the ropes. A related problem was the use of trail ropes and sails to steer the balloon. Andree had only tested the idea on short flights in fine weather. The flight plan was to fly at low level and that exposed the balloon to icing up in the freezing fogs which were common in the Arctic. A coating of ice would bring the balloon down. The *Ornen* had never been test flown and Andree and Strindberg had only made a handful of flights each and were not experienced aeronauts.

In spite of the hazardous nature of the enterprise money was raised and the party left Stockholm for the Arctic on 7 June 1896 on board the ship *Virgo*. They were seen off by large crowds and the expedition was seen as heroic. Andree chose Virgo Harbour on Danes Island as a base. This small island was located on the north-western edge of the Svalbard archipelago. It was chosen because it was ice free when the pack ice retreated in the northern summer and it was close to the North Pole. On arriving work commenced to build a plant to generate hydrogen gas and a building to house the inflated balloon. Henri Lachambre, the French constructor of the balloon, accompanied the party to assist with the generation of the gas and inflation of the balloon. This was a lengthy process so it had been decided to inflate and store the balloon until favourable winds occurred. The wind was the ideal southerly for a time while the work went on but when the balloon was ready the winds were consistently unfavourable. While they were waiting Nansen's *Fram* arrived, having broken free from the ice of the Arctic sea after its long drift. Nansen was not aboard having left the ship with a companion to try to sledge to the

Pole. When the *Fram* reached Norway they found that the two men were safe having not reached the Pole but had set a new furthest north. Eventually the decision was made to deflate the balloon and return south. On 17 August 1896 the balloon was deflated and three days later the *Virgo* sailed for home.

Several things changed over the winter of 1896–98. The first was that the balloon was enlarged. The second was that Ekholm had realised during the wait at Virgo Harbour that the balloon lost so much gas and lift that the flight plan was not practical. He had the moral courage to drop out and this meant a third man had to be found. Knut Fraenkel joined the expedition. He had been born on 14 February 1870 at Karlstad, Sweden. He qualified as a civil engineer in 1896 and was training to enter the State Engineering Corps when he joined the expedition. He had excelled at all kinds of gymnastics, was a climber and the strongest of the three.

In 1897 the expedition returned to Danes Island aboard the Swedish naval gunboat *Svensksund* and the *Virgo* and set to work repairing the balloon house, generating the hydrogen and inflating the balloon. Andree was 43 years of age, Strindberg 25 and Fraenkel 26. The *Ornen* was leaking so much hydrogen that it was losing nearly 45kg of lift per day. In spite of this they elected to go. On 11 July 1897 there was a strong, steady, wind from the south- south-west. The walls of the balloon house were removed; the net covering the envelope was attached to the load ring and the basket to the load ring. With all parts of the balloon attached the balloon was higher than the balloon house and the balloon surged back and forward in the wind. Andree waited for a lull and then ordered the restraining ropes cut. With a cry of 'three cheers for old Sweden' from Andree the *Ornen* rose into the air and started to drift towards the shoreline. The time was 13:46GMT. Within moments things started to go wrong. The couplings joining the upper and lower sections of the drag ropes came unscrewed and they left the bottom two-thirds of the all-important ropes on the beach. The loss of the guide ropes subtracted about 270kg from their ballast and further reduced their ability to steer the balloon. They were in the lee of the hills to the south and a down draft forced the balloon's basket into the water and they dropped ballast to climb. The climb took them to 1,800ft which in turn caused gas to be lost through expansion and venting through the valves. So at the outset they had no means of steering, a leaky balloon and had lost a large amounts of lifting gas and ballast. Soon after the launch they passed over Amsterdam Island and could have landed on it. A few minutes later the balloon flew over the west coast of Vogelsang and they again chose not to land. Andree had been treated as a national hero in 1896 and again in 1897. It would have taken an extraordinary amount of courage to land and return to Sweden not

On 11-14 July 1897 Andree, Strindberg and Fraenkel flew the balloon *Ornen* from Danes Island in Svalbard towards the North Pole. The balloon was airborne for 65 hours 33 minutes. This photograph shows the balloon on the pack ice of the Polar Sea on 14 July 1897. The trio dragged sledges over the ice to White Island where they died in October 1897. Their remains, equipment, journals and exposed film were not found until 1930.

as a hero but as the author of a fiasco. He declined the opportunities and the balloon passed out of sight to the north.

In 1900 a buoy that had been dropped at 22:00GMT on 11 July 1897 was found. The message in the buoy recorded that all was going well with the flight at about 800ft with the direction of flight north-easterly (about 010°) but later changed more to the east (about 045°). In 1899 a buoy had come ashore in Iceland recording that at 22:55GMT on 11 July 1897 they had been at 1,950ft at position latitude 82° north, longitude 25° east. On 15 July 1897 a sealing vessel shot a bird which turned out to be a carrier pigeon from the *Ornen* with a message timed at 12:30GMT on 13 July in position latitude 82° 2' north, 15° 5' east and saying that they were making a good speed to the east, 10° south.

That was all that was known until 1930. On 5 August in that year a party landed on White Island (the most north-eastern of the Svalbard group) from the ship *Braatvag* and chanced on the remains of all three men. They also found diaries and journals which allowed the flight to be reconstructed in detail. It was even possible to develop some of the exposed film 33 years after the photographers' deaths.

The flight had lasted for 65hrs 33min. Initially they travelled north-east but most of the flight was along an east-west line with little gain to the north. They often bumped on the pack ice and suffered from icing of the envelope and rigging. Eventually they were too heavy to continue and they landed. The *Ornen*'s furthest north was about 82° 20°, well to the south of the 'furthest north' of 86° 13.6° set by Nansen on 7 April 1895.

The three men then made an arduous sledge journey across the pack ice and landed on White Island. All three had displayed the symptoms of some kind of illness on the journey. The last diary entry was made on 17 October 1897. Even though they were inadequately clothed for an Arctic winter this was not the cause of their deaths. The winter of 1897/1898 was a mild one and they should have survived it. A Danish doctor, Adam Tryde, read about the illness that they all suffered. He later chanced upon a report of an epidemic at Disko Island in Western Greenland in which the Inuit suffered the same symptoms reported by Andree, Fraenkel and Strindberg. The epidemic was caused by a parasite which carried by walrus and polar bears. He gained access to the artefacts recovered from White Island. He scrapped some meat from the inside of a polar bear skin and found trichina capsules. It is now thought likely that the explorers died from trichinosis, a malady attributable to having eaten undercooked polar bear meat.

Even by the standards of the late nineteenth century the flight was brave but foolhardy. They might have survived but for their understandable desire to conserve the fuel for their primus stove. If the bear meat had been well cooked they would have survived the winter and been able to sledge across the ice to North East Land.

*Chapter Three*

# Before Amundsen (Part Two):
# Walter Wellman

## *Svalbard, 1906–1909*

The next person to attempt to fly to the Pole was the American Walter Wellman (1858–1934). Wellman was a successful but largely self-educated journalist. He often created the news that he reported. Wellman was fond of having himself photographed in 'heroic' poses with his head raised and looking into the distance. His five expeditions to the Arctic created copious amounts of newspaper column inches but little else. Before he turned to aircraft he made two attempts to reach the Pole by traditional means of surface travel. In 1894 he announced that he would make a 'dash for the North Pole'. He sailed to Danes Island in the *Ragnvald Jarl* and set up a base on the Island. His forward base was in the Seven Islands, a group to the north-east of Svalbard. He intended to travel to the Pole and back using sledges and dogs. A few miles into his journey a messenger caught up with the news that his ship had been nipped in the ice and was in sinking condition so he returned to the ship, saw to the safety of the crew and set out again. A few miles into this journey he decided that the pressure ridges in the pack ice (a normal condition for pack ice) were so high and numerous as to be impassable that he abandoned his attempt and returned to civilisation. The newspapers were unkind and he came in for much derisive comment.

His next go at the Pole was from Cape Flora on Hall Island in the Seven Islands archipelago. He overwintered in 1898–1899 and started the attempt when the weather improved in the New Year. Andree, Strindberg and Fraenkel had disappeared after taking off from Danes Island on 11 July 1898 (the only information was the carrier pigeon message sent early in the flight) and Wellman had a theory that he might find and rescue them in the general area of the Seven Islands. If he did it would be a coup equal to Henry Morton Stanley finding Dr Livingstone. He was right about where the missing balloonists might be found but he did not find them. What he did do was to travel 75nm towards the Pole, declare that conditions were not favourable and give up the attempt.

By 1905 airships were being built and flown in small numbers and Wellman decided that an airship was an ideal vehicle. It was no coincidence that there was great public interest in aviation and every stage of the planning and execution of an airship flight to the Pole would generate much copy for his newspaper. He must have been persuasive (in spite of his record to date) and got his paper, the *Chicago Record-Herald*, to put up $75,000 for the project which became the 'Wellman-Chicago Record-Herald Polar Expedition'. He also got backing from various other organisations including the National Geographic Society, Theodore Roosevelt and Alexander Graham Bell. The total raised was $250,000 and he needed every penny of it. His airship was designed and built in France in 1905–06 by Louis Goddard. It had twin engines; a 55hp Clement forward, driving a tractor propeller, and a 25hp Ford aft, driving a pusher propeller. A 5hp motor was fitted to pump air into the ballonets as

Walter Wellman (1858–1934) (second from the left) was a leading journalist who believed in creating his own stories. He was also the least successful Arctic explorer of all time. After two failed attempts at sledging to the North Pole he turned to airships. In 1906 he established an airship base at Virgo Harbour on Danes Island in the north-east of Svalbard. In that year he returned to America without flying his airship. He returned in 1907 and 1909 with his airship the *America*. On each occasion the airship made a brief flight before weather' (in 1907) and mechanical failure (in 1909) brought them down.

required. The gondola was open and equipment included two motor sleds for use if the machine was forced down on the ice. Directional control was with a rudder. Wellman avoided the expense of building an airship base in Europe by shipping the airship (named *America*) to his base in a dissembled condition.

One of the members of Wellman's expedition was a polymath called Chester Melvin Vaniman (1866–1912). Growing up on an Illinois farm gave both a life-long love of agriculture and much experience with machines. Vaniman studied music and started life as a musician, singer and music teacher. He then trained as an electrician and worked in that field for some time. He taught himself photography and arrived in New Zealand in 1902 and spent a year taking photographs of tourist sites for the Oceanic Steamship Company and for the New Zealand Government. He specialised in panoramas and built himself a camera for that purpose. Moving on to Australia in February 1903 Vaniman developed his techniques for taking photographs from above. If no building or mast was available he used a specially built 98ft tall ladder/ mast, stayed with cables pegged to the ground, which could be dismantled for transport. While in Australia Vaniman constructed an improved camera to take panoramas and ordered a balloon (inflated with hydrogen) to be used for taking panoramic photographs from the air. After some months of experiments with both balloon and camera he took a panorama of Sydney on 27 March 1904 which is famous to this day. Moving to Europe he gave up photography for aviation, met Wellman in France and was recruited as a mechanic and engineer for the 1906 expedition.

Wellman's 'airship station' was built within sight of the Andree memorial and the ruins of the balloon shed built to house Andree's balloon in 1896–97. A site for the hangar was blasted out of the rock a few metres from the shoreline of Virgo harbour and timber from the balloon house was used to make the floor of the hangar which consisted of five wooden arches braced by external cables and covered with sail cloth. It was 85ft tall, 82ft wide and 190ft long. There was also a plant for generating hydrogen gas, a machine shop and a building to house the members of the expedition. The hydrogen plant required 125 tons of sulphuric acid, 75 tons of scrap iron filings and 30 tons of other chemicals and apparatus. Machinists, over twenty mechanics and a doctor, were hired and had to be housed. The De Forest Wireless Telegraph Company equipped the *America*, *Frithjof* (the expedition ship) and a station in Hammerfest, Norway for wireless telegraphy (radio using morse code). A steel life boat, tons of food, malted milk and other items too numerous to list were shipped to Virgo Harbour. Ships visited Virgo Harbour in hope of seeing the airship fly. No sooner had the hangar been completed than the flight had to be abandoned. As soon as the motor, drive train and propellers were tested, they self-destructed. Wellman returned to Europe without even inflating the envelope of the *America*. The open basket-work gondola was left at the site and its remains were still visible in 1993.

Over the winter of 1906–07 he had the airship completely redesigned by Melvin Vaniman with an enlarged envelope, a completely new gondola, a new engine, a Lorraine-Dietrich of 70–80hp driving two propellers, mounted on outriggers, one on each side of the gondola, and stabilisers at the rear of the new enclosed gondola. In 1907 he returned to Dane's Island. The hangar had survived the winter but collapsed in a storm on 4 July 1907. He repaired the hangar and inflated the *America*. The new airship was 184ft long, 52.5ft in diameter and 65ft high. It had a volume of 274,712ft³. The ship had a cruising speed of 15kt, fuel for 120 hours and a novel means of maintaining its cruising altitude of about 250ft. Long before Andree's expedition balloonists had sometimes used a trail rope to maintain height when flying low over water or obstacle-free surfaces. If the balloon became light the balloon would rise until the extra weight of the trail rope equalled the increase in lift. If the balloon got heavy it would sink until the weight of extra trail rope on the surface equalled the reduction in lift. Used carefully the trail rope enabled the balloonist to save gas and ballast and prolong the flight. Wellman planned to use an 'equilibrator' which was a long tube with extra fuel and provisions in it. It was 'armoured' with leather and steel plates so that it would slip smoothly over the pack ice of the Polar Sea and it was intended that it function in the same way as a balloon's trail rope. It would work if the ice was as smooth as a billiard table but it was not. The pack ice in the Arctic Ocean is stressed by the currents beneath it and the winds above. They create pressure ridges and the surface resembles a plain strewn with rocks of all shapes and sizes, constantly growing and vanishing. Wellman must have known this from his reading and from early expeditions. There was no chance that the ice would be smooth all the way to the Pole and back. The airship was also equipped with another novel device which could not work; a 'retardeur'. A device like a trail rope, it was a steel cable fitted with hooks or rings that Wellman hoped would dig into the ice and hold the airship stationary if the wind was strong enough to push the airship backwards. When the wind dropped the airship would proceed on its journey. The airship carried sledge dogs, sledges, a boat and supplies for 10 months, all for use if it was forced to land on the pack. On 2 September 1907 the *America* was towed out of its hangar and over the harbour by the steamer *Express*. It slipped its tow and set course for the North Pole. The airship had never been test flown, its engines had probably never run for more than a few hours at a time, and none of the three men aboard had ever flown an airship (although Wellman and Vaniman had ballooning experience). The *America* had many novel and untested features. It was likely that the engines would fail long before reaching the Pole; the equilibrator was untested and would probably be ripped off by the pressure ridges which would be encountered on the pack ice between the base and the Pole. The retardeur was unlikely to work as planned. Even if the engines did not fail and the equilibrator was not ripped off, the airship was likely to encounter winds which would cause it to run out of fuel before returning. A 10 knot headwind from the north would reduce its ground speed to 5 knots and it would run out of fuel about the time it reached the Pole. A 10kt wind from the west or east would also result in the fuel being used up long before completing the journey. If the airship encountered freezing fog, as was likely to happen, it would ice up and the extra weight would force it down onto the ice. If it encountered bad weather it did not have the ability to fly over or around it. What did happen was that a fresh breeze blew up from the north-west, Wellman could not control the airship and it came down on a glacier about 10nm from the hangar. Gas was valved to bring the *America* down and then the rip lines were pulled to open the envelope and spill the gas so that the envelope did not act like a sail and cause the airship to thrash around and damage itself.

In 1908 Wellman was committed to reporting on the American presidential election and had to postpone his next flight attempt to 1909. In that year Wellman returned to his Danes Island base in the Arctic with a slightly improved *America*. The hangar had collapsed and was rebuilt with the nine arches originally planned for it. On 15 August 1909 he set out again. The airship reached the edge of the pack ice and then the equilibrator lashed left and right as it was dragged over the pressure ridges. After about an hour it was torn off and the airship, relieved of its weight climbed to several thousand feet. Gas was valved to stop the airship bursting as the gas expanded and to bring it down. Without the valved gas and the equilibrator the journey was abandoned and *America* was towed back to its base by the ship *Farm* (not to be confused with the famous *Fram*). As the petrol tanks were being emptied on the shore the airship rose into the air; almost taking one of the crew with it rose to about 6,000ft and burst, showering the harbour with debris. Lightening the airship before deflating the envelope was an error so fundamental as to boggle the mind.

Wellman's fellow journalists had a field day:

'Walter Wellman ought to reach the North Pole on air if anyone can'

*South Bend Tribune*

'Walter Wellman may not find the North Pole, but if he fails he can tell a longer story about it than anyone can'

*Toledo Blade*

'In this [expedition] there evidently is more desire to advertise a newspaper and increase circulation than to achieve a scientific victory.'

*Denver Republican*

On the voyage back to civilisation he heard that both Dr Frederick Cook and Robert Peary had (independently of each other) claimed to have reached the Pole by surface travel. Cook's claim was soon proven to be fraudulent. Some doubted Peary's claim but he was awarded the honours due to the first man to reach the North Pole and a place in the history books. It is now generally agreed that Peary did not reach the Pole. In any case Wellman announced that he would not try again. In 1910 Wellman set off in a new *America* to try and fly the Atlantic from west to east. The airship was airborne for over 60 hours and covered about 1,000 miles, most of it drifting with the wind back towards the American coast, after multiple engine failures. If they had been blown ashore in Florida they would have been a laughing stock but they were rescued by the steamship *Trent* and were briefly famous. Wellman wrote a book about his aeronautical adventures and the future of aviation. It was readable and persuasive and got almost every prediction completely wrong. Although he lived until 1934, never flew again.

Did Wellman really think he could reach the Pole by airship? His arctic journeys of 1894 and 1898–99 exposed him to the realities of the pack ice, its freezing fogs, gales, pressure ridges, and leads that opened and closed and froze over. He must have realised that the airships of the 1906–1909 were immature technology and that engines were highly unreliable. The airships of the time had a high accident rate when flown short distances in fine weather. The famous Norwegian explorer Nansen described him as a 'humbug' and that is probably a fair assessment.

Reviewing Wellman's expeditions, the modern reader is left with the impression that their primary goal was to generate copy for a flamboyant journalist rather than make a serious attempt to travel to the North Pole and back.

Vaniman stayed in aeronautics and designed airship hangars with a wooden frame and canvas covering. He claimed they could be rigged, de-rigged and transported quickly and several were purchased and put into service. He designed and built the airship *Akron* and attempted a transatlantic flight in 1912. The airship took off with a large crowd watching and exploded a few minutes into the flight and Vaniman and his crew of four were all killed.

*Chapter Four*

# A Sailor Struck by Lightning

## *Kristiania-San Francisco, 1909–1914*

I n 1909 Roald Amundsen flew in (or under) a quaint and almost forgotten type of flying machine, the man-lifting kite. A photograph shows Amundsen suspended below a train of kites at about 30 feet above the ground. He is dressed neatly in a suit and tie with his usual bowler hat on his head. Always dapper when in the civilized world, he turned 37 on 16 July that year.

He had completed the first ever continuous voyage through the North West Passage from the Atlantic Ocean to the Pacific Ocean (across the northern coasts of Canada and the United States) in 1907 and had thereby established himself as an Arctic explorer of note. He was already planning an expedition to the North Pole which would evolve into a successful journey to the South Pole. 1909 was also the year he first considered aviation as a tool in his explorations.

A grainy but unique photograph of Roald Amundsen airborne under a train of man-lifting kites in mid-1909. The kites were designed for him by Einar Sem-Jacobsen (1878–1936) who was a pioneer of Norwegian military aviation. Photographs of the kites show that they bore a striking resemblance those built by Anglo-American S. F. Cody Britain. The system consisted of a small pilot kite, from two to six lifter kites (depending on the wind strength) and a carrier kite with a seat, canvas sack or basket underneath it for the passenger(s). The system could lift an observer to from 1500 to 2000 ft depending on the conditions.

Aeroplanes had been evolving since the first flights of 1903 but the event that caught his attention was Louis Bleriot's flight across the English Channel on 25 April 1909. The flight from France to England covered only 27 miles and lasted 37 minutes but it captured the imagination of the world as the most significant flight to date. The British saw it as ending their geographical isolation and thoughtful observers realised that aviation had somehow started to come of age. Up to that moment aviation had seemed to be more of a stunt than a practical enterprise. The Channel flight suggested that there might be civil and military applications. Amundsen thought that aeroplanes might now provide the means to reconnoitre proposed routes for his future explorations. In 1925 Amundsen wrote:

> 'As I learned of Bleriot's flight, I knew at once that the time had come to think of using the air to help the Polar expeditions. Certainly human power and skill had overcome and conquered vast tracts of this mighty unknown whiteness, but enormous tracts remained unexplored, tracts that now could be reached from the air. My thoughts turned especially to the enormous area in the arctic which until now had withstood every attempt [to explore]….When I, in the year 1909, equipped *Fram* for a trip to the Arctic; I had a conference with one of the most esteemed aviators of the day. He declared himself ready as willing to go with me. But it never came off.'

This discussion was just the most recent example of his openness to new ideas. The *Gjoa* expedition through the North West Passage was an earlier example. He decided to use a small vessel with a small crew rather than the large ships and large crews used by the earlier unsuccessful expeditions. The *Gjoa* was the first motor ship used in such an expedition. The paraffin fuelled internal combustion engine enabled the ship to shift from sail to power at a moment's notice. This ability saved the ship from being wrecked on more than one occasion and saved fuel because (unlike a steam engine) it did not have to be kept running on the off chance that it might be needed. The discussions about aeroplanes came to nothing, probably because aeroplanes were then unreliable and clearly too fragile and low performance to successfully operate in the harsh environment to be expected in high latitudes.

Amundsen needed some way of extending his vision from his ship so that he could navigate the arctic pack ice with more certainty and safety. An observer at 1,000ft altitude can see 27nm in clear conditions, far further than from the masthead of a ship. An airborne observer could be expected to be able to observe ice conditions and help the ship navigate around impassable areas to shorten journeys through pack ice and make them safer.

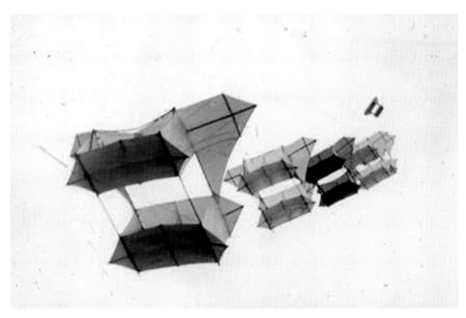

A photograph showing the lifter kites and a pilot kite of the man-lifting system designed by Einar Sem-Jacobsen for Amundsen. All kites were attached to the same cable and were reeled in and out by a winch. The Cody system included controls for the passenger/pilot who could change the angle of attack of the carrier kite and go up and down the cable on rollers. In a strong wind the passenger/pilot could be marooned in the air until the wind dropped or the ground crew winched him in.

Two expeditions to the Antarctic had used captive balloons for ice reconnaissance. On 4 February 1902 Scott, leader of a British expedition, had used a balloon inflated with hydrogen to obtain a view of the Ross Ice Shelf. The indentation where the flight had taken place was named Balloon Bight. On 29 March 1902 Drygalski, leader of a German expedition, flew in the same type of balloon to identify areas for study and possible routes out of the ice where his ship was beset. Both of the balloons were standard spherical types as used for free flights and not adapted in any way for the role of tethered observation platforms. Amundsen probably considered captive balloons and would have known that they had been used by British and German expeditions. However balloons had a number of major defects. They were inflated with hydrogen which is the lightest gas but is inflammable and even explosive when contaminated with air. It was not practical to transport balloons long distances when inflated. They were transported in a deflated state. When needed the balloons were inflated. The process was slow and the balloon vulnerable to bad weather, particularly to high winds. The gas was either generated on the spot, which required a bulky generator and tons of acid, zinc and sulphuric acid, or provided by a large number of heavy high pressure gas bottles. The most important limitation was that the tethered balloon became unstable in high winds. Observation became difficult and a tethered spherical balloon could not be flown in winds over 15kt. The balloons used by both the German and British expeditions were standard spherical type used for sport and scientific flying. The spherical shape was ideal for free flights as the shape gave the maximum ratio of volume to surface area. In flight the balloon moved with the wind and there was no airflow past it. Flight in high winds was not a problem although inflating, launching and landing could be dangerous. When the balloon was tethered the wind became a problem as it then flowed around the balloon. The military spherical balloons used for observation while tethered to the ground used modified rigging which improved their stability in a wind but they were still unusable in a moderate wind. They swayed dramatically which made observation impossible and the flight dangerous. An example of how dangerous this could be is the experience of E T Willows, the British airship pioneer and manufacturer of airships and kite balloons. On 23 August 1926 he and his passengers were killed, when flying in a tethered spherical balloon, when a high wind caused the balloon to escape from its net. The Parseval-Sigsfeld streamlined kite balloon developed in Germany in the 1890s was a great improvement as it could cope with much stronger winds but they were expensive, more complicated to rig, required a winch to control their ascents and descents, and needed more gas and therefore more chemicals or gas bottles. Balloons could not be kept inflated for long periods of time or in gales and so would have to be inflated each time they were needed, making them more trouble than they were worth.

In 1909 Amundsen decided that man-lifting kites might fulfil his requirement for a light and compact device for reconnaissance. Samuel Franklin Cody (1867–1913) in England and Jacques-Theodore Saconney (1874–1935) in France developed systems of kites which lifted a payload into the air. This could be a camera, meteorological instruments or one or two observers. These systems were designed for military use but had obvious civil applications for explorers. When not in use the kites could be dismantled until each kite was a compact bundle of sticks and folded fabric. Stable in a high wind, they could also be flown in light winds or no wind when towed by a ship which provided enough relative wind speed to loft the kites and the observers. The Cody system used a type of winged box kite. The front and rear of each kite was strengthened by diagonals which projected beyond the box. To each of these diagonals a wing-like projection was added. It was long on the front upper diagonals and short on the other six projections. The upper 'wings' had dihedral and the lower ones anhedral. The structure was designed to enable the crew to make the covering taut and therefore more efficient. A pilot kite raised a light line into the air. Then a number of larger, 'lifter kites' were attached to raise a cable into the air. Extra lifters were slid up the cable until a cableway was established in the air. The number of lifter kites used varied from two to six depending on the wind strength and the load to be carried A carrier kite was then attached with a basket for one or two observers. The observers were carried in a seat or basket and were constructed so as to minimise the chance of someone falling out. The kites made for the Royal Navy sometimes used a breeches buoy which resembled an over-sized pair of trousers. A compact fabric seat could be used but was not for the faint hearted. The carrier kite was attached to a small trolley which slid up and down the cable and was controlled by system of lines operated by the pilot. The carrier kite had a means of raising and lowering the front and rear of the kite to increase or decrease lift. The crew could also control a brake acting on the cableway to stop the movement of the trolley at any altitude. In strong wind it was possible for the crew to be stranded aloft until either the wind dropped or the ground crew managed to winch in the whole assembly. A well trained ground crew and pilot made the system reasonably safe. If the pilot kite suffered damage in flight the whole train of kites would start to sway from side to side and descend in a most alarming manner. The usual result was a shaken but uninjured crew. A similar system was built for Amundsen by the Norwegian army officer and aeronautical engineer Einar Olaf Sem-Jacobsen (1878–1936). Sem-Jacobsen was the most important early pioneer of flight, especially military flight, in Norway. In 1909 he co-founded the Norwegian Society for the Promotion of Aviation and qualified for an FAI (Fédération Aéronautique Internationale) balloonist's certificate in 1910. On 21 July 1912 he became the first Norwegian to pass the test for an FAI aeroplane pilot's certificate. He was the head of the Norwegian Army Aircraft Factory from 1916 to 1922. He travelled widely in search of knowledge of all types of flying machines, from balloons and airships to aeroplanes and man-lifting kites. Photographs of the Sem-Jacobsen kites show that they closely resembled the Cody kites. The kites were constructed at the Horten naval base. The pilot kite had an area of 5m$^2$; each lifter had an area of 13m$^2$ and the carrier an area of 20m$^2$. The carrier could lift up to 300kg. The ground crew operated a winch and paid out or reeled in the cable as required. The system constructed for Amundsen differed from the Cody system in that the chair or canvas sack for the observer hung below the lifter kite by about 10 metres. This implied that the system was controlled from the ground rather than controlled by the flight crew and ground crew as in the Cody system. Trials were carried out by Captain Sem-Jacobsen, Lieutenants Presterud, Opheim, Thommesen, and sail maker Ronne. The plan was to fly the kites from a ship so that an airborne observer could spot routes through the pack ice and conditions for men, dogs and sledges. Later experience showed that the observer would have been able to see leads (ice free channels) in the ice of use to the ship but not ice conditions for surface travel.

The Cody system had routinely raised the observers from 1,000 to 2,000ft and a similar performance could be expected from the system trialled by Amundsen. The flight trials took place on the small island of Vealos in Christiania fijord. On 26 July 1909 Amundsen's second in command; Ole Engelstad (1876–1909) was electrocuted by a lightning strike on the cable retaining the kites. They were being flown unmanned and Engelstad was attempting to winch them down during a storm. The kite experiments continued over the winter of 1909–1910 but Amundsen's enthusiasm for them declined. It is said that the kites were aboard *Fram* during the 1910–1913 Antarctic expedition but they were not used.

One unexpected result of the trials was that Amundsen meet Martin Ronne at the Horten shipyard and recognised that he had skills that were needed in preparing for and carrying out Arctic and Antarctic expeditions. Ronne (1861–1932) was a seaman who had had served on both civilian and naval ships. At the age of 40 he took up the trade of sail maker and was working at this trade at Horten when Amundsen was there because of the kite trials. He sewed some of the 'sails' (fabric panels stretched over the kites' framework) and a canvas seat for the pilot/passenger. Because Ronne was light he took part in the test flying of the kites. His ability to produce any fabric item (from clothing to the tent left at the South Pole) made him a key member of Amundsen's expeditions from then on. He went to Antarctica with the *Fram* during its 1910–1912 South Pole expedition and was aboard the *Maude* during its voyage through the North East Passage in 1918–1920. In 1925 he was at Kings Bay to support the Amundsen-Ellsworth North Pole flight and the next year he was back at Kings Bay during the Amundsen-Ellsworth-Nobile airship expedition of that year. Ronne was one of those skilled tradesmen whose essential skills made it possible for men like Amundsen to function. Without the Martin Ronne's of this world, the Amundsen's could not have achieved what they did.

Sem-Jacobsen and Amundsen stayed in touch and Amundsen relied on him for advice and training during his (Amundsen's) continuing efforts to make use of this new technology.

Amundsen wrote that he was the first serious explorer to make use of aviation and history records that, if not the first, his was one of the early efforts

Amundsen's first flight in an aeroplane was with Danish-American aviator Christeffsen in April 1913. The machine was a Curtiss style open floatplane with a central float and tip floats. Amundsen is wearing a life-belt.

to adopt aviation for purposes of exploration above the Arctic Circle (66° 33° north latitude). Amundsen kept aircraft in mind and in 1913, when he was on a lecture tour of America to raise funds, he had his first flight in an aeroplane. This flight was at San Francisco and the pilot was Danish-American aviator Christeffsen. This was in a floatplane which was, or resembled an early Curtiss design with a central float and tip floats. Pilot and passenger sat side by side with dual controls. They sat in the open in front of the engine. Amundsen was in his usual mode of giving lectures about his last expedition (Antarctica and the South Pole in

Amundsen in April 1913 about to fly in a floatplane from San Francisco Bay. The aeroplane is either a Curtiss or a copy of a Curtiss.

1910–1912) to pay off the debts of this last expedition and raise money for the next one. He was planning to use the *Fram* again. This time he would enter the Polar Sea by way of the Bering Strait, be frozen into the pack ice, and drift with the ice for several years. He hoped to do what Nansen had not quite done in 1893–96 and drift across the North Pole. He was so impressed by the floatplane that he ordered two small flying boats at a price of $7,000 each. He also visited Germany that year. Germany was very air-minded and the flying he saw impressed him and kept his interest alive. He encountered his usual money troubles and either sold the flying boats or cancelled the order before taking delivery. He certainly never flew in either aircraft.

Amundsen was not the only Norwegian to recognise the aeroplane as having potential for exploration in the Arctic. *Flight* for 17 May 1913 noted that Lieutenant Gjertsen proposed to explore the North Pole with the aid of a Deperdussin monoplane and was attending the Ecole D' Aviation Deperdussin. This was Hjalmar Fredrik Gjertsen (1885–1958) who had been Amundsen's second mate in *Fram* on the Norwegian Antarctic Expedition of 1910–1912. Gjertsen learnt to fly in France, had the government pay the course fees and trained as a naval aviator in Norway. He served as Captain of the minelayers *Glommen* and *Froya* in 1915–1918 although he does not appear to have served as an aviator after his training.

Aeroplanes were developing rapidly. By the outbreak of the Great War in July 1914 the endurance record was over 24 hours; the altitude record more than 26,000ft and the speed record over 110kt. Aeroplanes had flown across the Mediterranean from France to North Africa; in stages from Madrid to Moscow; and across the United States in stages. Floatplanes and flying boats were in widespread use. Aeroplanes were being built and tested for flights across the North Atlantic. In Russia Igor Sikorski had successfully flown the Grand, a four-engined aeroplane and then a bigger four-engined type, the Ilya Mouromets. On 30 July 1914 the Norwegian pilot Tryggve Gran (who had been to Antarctica with the Scott South Pole expedition of 1910–12) had flown his Bleriot XI-2 aeroplane from Cruden Bay, Scotland to Jaeren, near Stavanger, in Southern Norway in four hours 10 minutes.

During his preparations for his expedition to the Polar Sea he decided that he would learn to fly and purchase an aeroplane to take with him. He recognised that contemporary aeroplanes were not capable of long flights in the Arctic. He intended to carry a machine on board the *Fram*, replace its wheels with skis, and use it for short flights from the ship. The machines of the day were strictly fine weather machines. Their use would be restricted to fine summer weather with good visibility and light winds or no winds. Aeroplanes were (usually) built as light wooden frames, braced with wire or cables and covered

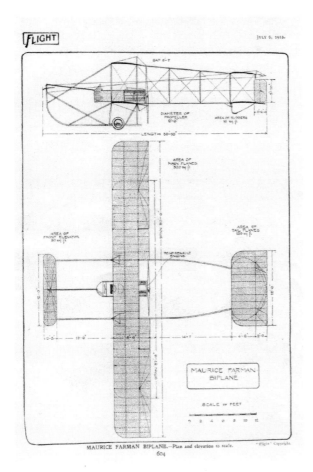

FLIGHT

JULY 6, 1912.

MAURICE FARMAN BIPLANE.—Plan and elevation to scale.
604

Farman aeroplanes saw widespread use and were in service in Norway from 1912 to the late 1920s. This drawing of a Farman MF 7 'Longhorn' was published in Flight on 6 July 1912. Amundsen learned to fly and took his test for an aviator's certificate in this type of aeroplane. He bought a Farman and intended to take it on his North Pole expedition. The Great War broke out in 1914 and caused the cancelation of the expedition. Amundsen donated the aeroplane to the Norwegian government for use by the armed forces.

in doped fabric. They were not durable and needed regular maintenance even when hangared and flown in temperate climates. Careful pilots checked the airframe and adjusted the rigging at frequent intervals. Amundsen would not have kept his aeroplane on the deck of his ship and exposed to the elements so his aeroplane would have spent most of its time dismantled in the hold. When it was required it would have been assembled and flown. An aeroplane like a Farman 'Longhorn' would have had a radius of action of about 60nm. This could be increased radically by fitting an enlarged fuel tank. Navigation would be a major problem for the pilot. Magnetic compasses were unreliable in high latitudes close to the Magnetic North Pole. The only reasonably safe way to navigate such an aircraft would be to pick a day with settled weather and exceptionally good visibility. A departure from a well mapped land mass would one way to do it. Another would be for the *Fram* to keep a fire burning, causing a plume of smoke visible from far away. Attention to detail

Amundsen (L) and Einar Sem-Jacobsen
(R) ca 1913-1914.

would be important. If there was a
temperature inversion the smoke
plume would flatten out not and
not be visible from a distance.

Amundsen obtained permission
to receive instruction from Captain
Sem-Jacobsen in Army aeroplanes.
It was a great privilege for a civilian
like Amundsen and only his status
as a national hero made it possible.
The flight instruction was given
in Farman 'Longhorn' aeroplanes.
This machine was a biplane with
the tail supported on outriggers to
allow the engine and 'pusher' propeller to be positioned behind the pilot and
passenger who sat in a small nacelle. The name 'Longhorn' was applied to the
machine because it had a second elevator mounted on outriggers in front of
the nacelle. It had two wheels (which were replaced by skis in the Norwegian
winter) attached to each of the two landing skids. Farman's of this type saw
widespread service both as combat aeroplanes early in the Great War and
then as trainers. The British aviation weekly *Flight* reported on 9 August 1913
that Amundsen was receiving flying instruction in Norway in anticipation of
receiving two 'waterplanes' presumably the two Christofferson flying boats that
were destined not to be delivered. He may have started to learn to fly in 1913
but he was certainly doing so in early 1914. Amundsen flew with Sem-Jacobsen
every chance he got and spent about 20 hours in the air. The controls look
quaintly amusing to the twenty-first century eye, although they worked in the
conventional sense. The ailerons and elevators were operated by a handlebar
which had loops at both ends. Tilting the bar to port or starboard caused the
machine to roll to port or starboard. The handlebar was attached to a vertical
tube. Pushing the handlebar forward or aft caused the Farman to pitch down or
up. There were two rudder pedals. Pushing the port pedal caused a yaw in that
direction and pushing the starboard pedal caused a yaw to starboard. Responses
to control inputs were sluggish, partly due to the low airspeed and partly due to
the lack of refinement of contemporary aircraft. A British pilot who trained on
a Farman with the same control set up wrote this about the experience:

Einar Sem-Jacobsen and Amundsen in a Farman. The aircraft was not fitted with dual controls and Amundsen was wedged between the instructor and the fuel tank. He had to reach over the instructor to grasp the 'handle bars' which operated the ailerons and elevators. Amundsen probably could not reach the floor mounted rudder pedals.

'[It was] a queer sort of bus like an assemblage of birdcages......Flying with their antiquated controls was a mixture of playing the harmonium, working the village pump, and sculling a boat'

The Farman Amundsen trained on had only one set of controls and he sat behind Sem-Jacobsen and reach over his shoulders to grasp the wheel which controlled the elevators and ailerons of the biplane. He could not reach the rudder pedals.

In the midst of his training he travelled to France with Sem-Jacobsen and purchased a Farman of the type that he was learning to fly in. Sem-Jacobsen then set out to fly it from Paris to Christiania. This would probably be the longest cross-country flight to be carried out by a Norwegian at this time. In 1914 cross-country flying was an adventure. In Western Europe visibility was often poor, even in good weather, because of the haze caused by factory chimneys. Aircraft compasses were of limited reliability and tended to rotate very unhelpfully even when the aircraft was flying wings level on a constant

Amundsen (second from the left), about to receive flight instruction on a Norwegian Army Farman 'Longhorn' in late 1913 or early 1914. The figure in uniform on the left may be his instructor Einar Sem-Jacobsen.

heading. It was normal practice to follow line features like railway lines, canals or coastlines. Cruising speed was about 42kt and endurance three hours 15 minutes giving a still air range of about 135nm with no reserve. The low cruising speed meant that winds had a major effect on the ground speed. Winds of 20kt were common and a head wind of that strength would almost halve the aircraft's range. The aircraft's rate of climb was modest and made the aircraft vulnerable the type of down drafts encountered in unstable conditions. An aircraft flying in the lee of a ridge in windy conditions could find itself descending in spite of trying to climb at full power. Flight in turbulent air was a challenge with coarse use of the controls needed to keep the aeroplane under control and the pilot understandably anxious about the structural integrity of the machine. Turbulence could also cause the aeroplane to descend because of the extra drag caused by the frequent control inputs. With an aeroplane flying at only a few knots above the stall speed the nose had to be lowered to compensate for the extra drag caused by the control inputs.

Einar Sem-Jacobsen (1878-1936), pioneer of military aviation in Norway. He designed a system of man-lifting kites for Amundsen in 1909. In 1913-1914 he taught Amundsen to fly on Farman 'Longhorn' aircraft operated by the Norwegian Army. In 1914 Amundsen bought a Farman in France and Sem-Jacobsen attempted to fly it back to Norway.

The flight from Paris to Christiania was to be made in stages and on 20 May 1914 Sem-Jacobsen flew from Paris to Reims in two hours and then set off across the Ardennes. A forced landing was made which resulted in some damaged struts. Repairs were made and they set off again. *Flight* for 29 May 1914 reported that the flight from Rheims to Liege had been completed with stops at Roequigny and Namur. Weather was a problem on the leg from Liege in Belgium to Krefeld in Germany. He set off but encountered strong headwinds at the Belgian-Dutch border and returned to Liege to wait for better weather. The bad weather persisted until 25 May when Sem-Jacobsen's commanding officer ordered him to dismantle the aeroplane and ship it to Norway.

On 11 June 1914 it was arranged for Amundsen to take the test for the issue of a Federation Aéronautique Internationale aviator's certificate. He was in his forty-second year. Three flights were required for the issue of an aviator's certificate, all of them solo. The first and second flights were identical. On them the candidate had to cover 5km over a closed circuit. There were two turn points marked out on the ground 500 metres apart and the aeroplane was flown in continuous figures of eight with the markers in the centre of each loop of the figure until 5km had been covered. After each of these two flights a normal landing had to be made, with the engine shut off at or before the moment of touchdown, with the aeroplane finishing its landing roll within 50 metres of a point designated before the flight. On the third flight a climb to at least 100 metres was required. The candidate was then required to switch off the engine and glide down to a normal landing. The aeroplane was flown solo and the examiners viewed the flights from the ground. The spot landings were perhaps the easiest part of the test as, due to its light weight and high drag, the Farman's glide angle was steep and a steep approach is easier to

On 11 June 1914 (the day of the flight test for his aviators certificate) Amundsen was receiving dual instruction from Sem-Jacobsen when there was (what looks like) a heavy landing which seriously damaged the aircraft. Amundsen took and passed his test on another Farman. He received a telegram of congratulation from King Haakon VII. On 18 September 1915 he was issued with Federation Aéronautique International (Norge) Aviator's Certificate number one.

judge than a flat one. Amundsen would have pointed the nose of the Farman at the mark and let gravity do most of the flying. When he flattened out from the glide the speed would wash off rapidly and the aeroplane would have no tendency to 'float', it would sit down and stop in a short distance.

On the day of the flight test Sem-Jacobsen was giving Amundsen some last minute dual instruction when the Farman suffered severe damage in an accident. The sources disagree on the cause of the accident. An engine failure may have occurred, or some kind of structural failure or there may have been a handling error. A photo of the wrecked machine shows damage consistent with a heavy landing. This damage could have been caused by flattening out too late, or by flattening out too high and stalling on to the ground. Whatever caused the accident, Amundsen was not put off flying and later that day he took his test in another Farman. He passed the test and became the first Norwegian civilian to qualify as an aviator in Norway. He received a telegram from King Haakon VII congratulating him. On 18 September 1915 he received Federation Aéronautique Internationale (Norge) aviator's certificate number one. In the future journalists would sometimes write, or imply that Amundsen would be flying the aeroplanes he bought for his expeditions but this was not the case. It is probable that the flight test was the only time he flew solo and he certainly was not interested in acquiring more flying time and skill. He would be an aviation enthusiast for the rest of his life but this enthusiasm was for aircraft as vehicles rather sporting equipment. To put his achievement in perspective his total flying time was about 20 hours, some of it away from the airfield but not far away. He passed no written exams, never took a passenger flying with him, had flown in daylight and in fine weather, had never flown at night or in bad weather or over long distances. An aviators certificate meant, in 1914, that recipient had demonstrated the most basic of handling skills and would then have to teach himself the rest of the skills required for applied flying such as cross country flying and air navigation.

At about this time an extraordinary situation arose in Russia and it would provide the opportunity for that nation to be the first country to use aeroplanes in the Arctic. In 1913 three separate expeditions were missing in the Russian Arctic. Georgiy Yakovlevich Sedov was making an attempt to reach the North Pole. His ship *Svyatoy Foka* and crew had last been reported in June 1913 when they were iced in for the winter on the north-west coast of Novaya Zemlya and had run out of coal and had limited supplies of food and winter clothing. Geogiy L'vovich Brusilov and his ship *Svyataya Anna* had intended to sail through the North East Passage from the Atlantic to the Pacific and had last been seen on 16 September 1912. Vladimir Aleksandrovich Rusanov with his ship the *Gerkules* did some important geological field-work on Svalbard and then set off along the North East Passage. On 31 August 1912 he called at a settlement on Novaya Zemlya reported that he was heading around the northern tip of the island to the Kara Sea and had not been heard of since.

It was not until the spring of 1914 that public pressure forced the government to purchase two ships, charter two more and send them to look for the three missing ships and their crews. One of the expeditions was equipped with an aeroplane, a pilot and a mechanic to aid the searches. Yan Iosifovich Nagurskiy was a 26 year-old Polish (then part of Russia) army officer and had qualified as a military pilot in early 1913. He kept up his flying privately and studied naval engineering, qualifying in July 1913. He went to Paris to purchase and test fly a Maurice Farman with a 70hp Renault air-cooled motor, a cruising speed of around 40kt and fuel for five to six hour's flight. It would be transported in a disassembled state. It was fitted with floats for the search flights. After test flying it 18 times it was shipped to Kristiania where Nansen and Amundsen had been consulted by the Russians about how to go about searching for the three lost expeditions. The Farman, its pilot and Yevgeniy Kuznetsov, a naval aviation mechanic, were aboard *Pechora* and were tasked with an aerial search of part of the coast of Novaya Zemlya. *Andromeda* had already found a cairn with a note from Sedov dated 21 August 1913. The Farman, which had been painted red to make it more conspicuous if it was forced down, was assembled on the beach at Krestovaya Guba with help from the crew of *Pechora*. At 03:00 Nagurskiy test flew the floatplane. After refuelling and loading survival equipment and food he took off with Kuznetsov aboard and flew north following the coast. The weather was clear for a start and they flew at about 2,500ft with the thermometer reading −5°C. The weather started to deteriorate, only the mountains were visible above the fog and the compass failed. A boat compass was carried as back-up and the pilot stayed on course until the fog started to clear. On the way back south a planned landing to refuel at a cache left by *Andromeda* could not be made because of a lack of open water and no level area of ice. They kept on flying south until at 08:50 they found open water near Mys Borisova and made a perfect landing. This was the first flight in the Arctic and had covered about 240nm in 4hrs 20min. Taxiing to the shore a float was holed by a rock but the water was shallow and they waded along and got the aeroplane to shore. It was 36 hours since they had slept so they built a fire, had a quick meal, a cup of tea and went to sleep on the shore by the beached aircraft.

When the men awoke they repaired the float with some tin and a rubber patch. A polar bear showed a close interest in them and had to be shot. *Andromeda* appeared and landed fuel and oil. Captain Pospelov marked the first flight with a bottle of cognac and requested an ice reconnaissance around Ostrov Zayach'iy where he had been instructed to leave an emergency food depot. On 22 August the aviators flew north up the coast in clear weather and noted a number of errors in the chart and that the coasts and straits were still ice covered. After one hour 45 minutes they spotted a hut and landed safely on a level strip of snow covered ice. They slept in sleeping bags until late in the evening *Andromeda* appeared at the ice edge. The hut turned out to have no sign of Sedov's expedition. A storm threatened to tear the Farman from its tie-downs and Kuznetsov was sick until 25 August. On that day the Farman made a flight which showed that the ice had been cleared by the storm. They landed in the open water and pulled the machine onto a sheltered spot. Captain Popov was passenger that evening when the engine failed causing a forced landing within sight of the ship. Repairs and a wait for fine weather meant they did not fly for the next two weeks. A note was found saying that Sedov had died on an attempt to reach the North Pole. A flight was made on 12 September out over the sea to the west-north-west about 60nm from land looking for the *Svyatoy Foka*. On landing he reported that the ice was drifting south and both *Andromeda* and *Hertha* weighed anchor and headed south. On 13 September the airmen made a flight of three and a half hours over low cloud. A westerly wind drifted the aeroplane over the glacier covered interior of Novaya Zemlya and they could clearly see the Kara Sea to the east of the island. They returned to Krestovaya Guba to find *Pechora* anchored there. The Farman was dismantled and loaded aboard the ship.

*Svyatoy Foka* arrived at the port of Rynda on 4 September 1914 so although Sedov had perished his ship and crew had survived. No trace of Rusanov or the crew of *Gerkules* was ever found. Geogiy L'vovich Brusilov and his ship *Svyataya Anna* was frozen in the Arctic Ocean in 1913–1914. A party of men left the ship and two survived a gruesome march to land. The captain and the rest of crew perished with the ship some time in 1914–1915. No trace of the ship was found until 2010 on Franz Joseph Land.

While Nagurskiy was making his successful flights another Farman was at sea on the ice-breaker *Tamyr* operating out of Vladivostok at the eastern end of the north-east passage. It was damaged badly on its brief first flight. A sled was made and the engine and propeller turned into a successful aerosled which could and did slide over the snow pulling a sledge at up to 22kt.

Nagurskiy had made five major flights totalling 10 hours 40 minutes and flown more than 570nm. The first aeroplane flights in the Arctic had been a major success and Nagurskiy was decorated with the Order of Sv. Anna, third class after the Tsar read the Naval Minister's final report.

Nagurskiy had succeeded because of his training and attention to detail. Amundsen could have supplied the attention to detail but his training had been of the most elementary kind and he would have been stretched to acquire the rest of the skills while on expedition in the Arctic.

By the time the Russian search ships returned most of the European powers were at war. Norway remained neutral but Amundsen was obliged to cancel his plans for the Polar Drift expedition and on 9 August 1914 he wrote to the government offering his Farman for use by the Norwegian military. His offer was accepted so he was again without an aeroplane.

Amundsen remained convinced that aircraft had potential as tools for Arctic exploration but it would be more than a decade before he put the theory into successful practice.

*Chapter Five*

# A Flight to the North Pole?

## *New York–Seattle–Wainwright–New York, 1922–1924*

T he outbreak of war in August 1914 created a shipping boom. Neutral countries like Norway found their ships in great demand and freight rates high, although it was a dangerous business and many neutral seamen were killed or wounded by German U-boats, surface raiders and mines. Norway lost 50 per cent of its fleet of merchant ships and 1,892 Norwegian seamen were killed. Amundsen accepted that seamen would die but did not accept that Germany was entitled to sink merchant ships with no attempt to safeguard the lives of the passengers and crew. He felt so strongly about the Norwegian seamen killed after Germany embarked on its second campaign of unrestricted submarine warfare in February 1917 that he returned his German medals to the German ambassador to Norway. He is quoted in *Flight* for 1 November 1917 as writing:

> 'As a Norwegian sailor I beg to return my German decorations as a personal protest against the German murders of peaceful Norwegian seamen in the North Sea on 17 October 1917.'

The incident alluded to was a raid on a convoy by two German cruisers. Two Royal Navy escorts were sunk (this was a legitimate act of war). Nine neutral merchant ships were sunk without any opportunity to abandon ship first and many Norwegian seamen were killed. Amundsen invested heavily in shipping and made a large profit. He may have doubled his money and the profits enabled him to order a ship designed to survive years locked in the ice. He planned to set out on his polar drift expedition as soon as the political situation allowed. In 1903–1907 he had had to settle for a small vessel not designed for Arctic voyaging. In 1910–1912 he had to go cap in hand to obtain use of *Fram*. He had planned to use the *Fram* for his projected 1918–1920 voyage. The ship was famous for having been used on three major voyages in polar regions; Nansen's of 1893–1896, Otto Sverdrup's of 1898–1902, and Amundsen's of 1910–1912. It turned out that the *Fram* was suffering from deterioration in its wooden hull, possibly as a result of a lengthy stay in tropical waters after the 1910–12 expedition and sheer old age as the ship was over 20 years old and had seen much use amongst the Arctic and Antarctic ice. Now he could afford to build a ship he would own and he would be free to use it as he saw fit. Amundsen ordered a new ship to be named the *Maude* in honour of the Norwegian Queen. *Maude* had a hull which had a pronounced curve both in cross section and fore and aft. This meant that the ship would be forced upwards when locked in the pack ice rather than being crushed as a ship of conventional shape would. Its hull was almost three feet thick for the same reason. The *Maude* was launched on 1 July 1917 and was then fitted out and equipped for a long drift locked in the pack ice of the Polar Sea. Amundsen was still keen to use aircraft for exploration and the 28 December 1916 issue of the journal *Flight* noted that he would be taking an aeroplane with him on his next expedition. The same report said that he would be taking an American type that was under construction for him. When Amundsen departed Tromso on 15 June 1918 there was no aeroplane on board. America came into the war in April 1917 and it is possible that this occurrence prevented the export of a machine for a civil expedition by a citizen of neutral Norway. Amundsen's intention was to sail north-east along the northern coast of Russia and allow the *Maude* to be frozen in the pack ice of the Polar Sea. Earlier expeditions had done this but they had drifted around the North Pole rather than across it as Amundsen hoped to do. Peary's claim to have reached the North Pole in 1909 meant there was no distinction to be gained by simply going there but a prolonged drift through unexplored parts of Arctic would produce scientific data including meteorological information important to weather forecasting, and there was always the possibility that new lands would be found. Amundsen was taking a chance because he departed when the Great War was still being waged and the Imperial German Navy operated U-boats in the White Sea which Amundsen had to traverse on his way to the top of the Eurasian landmass. The *Maude* failed to drift north as hoped although he completed a transit of the North East Passage in 1918–1920 and by the spring of 1921 *Maude* arrived in Seattle for repairs and a refit before re-entering the ice for another try. The ship's voyage from Tromso to Seattle by way of the north coast of Russia was only the third transit of the North East Passage. The voyage of the *Gjoa* through the North West Passage in 1903–1907 added to the voyage of the *Maude* in 1918–1920 meant that he had circumnavigated the globe above the Arctic Circle and was the first man to do it. It is a striking fact that surface expeditions in the Arctic were measured in years while aerial expeditions in the same areas are measured in hours. The ability of aircraft to cover ground quickly and provide a view of a wide swath of previously unexplored territory accounts for Amundsen's enthusiasm for aviation and his willingness to take risks with a technology that was improving rapidly but was not yet mature.

Amundsen had the use of an aeroplane for the next stage of the *Maude* expedition. The aeroplane was a Curtiss Oriole biplane, which had two open cockpits and a water-cooled motor of 160hp. The Curtiss was had a distinctive appearance as the fuselage had a rounded and streamlined appearance and the radiator was placed vertically on top of the fuselage just in front of the top wing. The Oriole was on loan from the Curtiss Company and normally retailed for $3,000. Aeroplanes like the Oriole were hard to sell in the early 1920s because of the glut of cheap war surplus aeroplanes like the Curtiss JN 4 'Jenny' which were available new out of the crate at a few hundred dollars. Amundsen took delivery of the Oriole on 6 April 1922 at Mineola, Long Island, New York. There was a handover ceremony including a young woman breaking a bottle of champagne over the prop boss. Photos of the event show

Curtiss Oriole *Kristine* with Oscar Omdal and Roald Amundsen. Amundsen took delivery at Mineola, Long Island on 6 April 1922. The Oriole was to be carried aboard Amundsen's ship *Maude* and used for short range reconnaissance in the Arctic.

Amundsen dressed in flying clothing and the name *Kristine* painted on the fuselage in large letters in honour of Amundsen's friend Kristine Elisabeth Bennet. The machine carried the Norwegian colours of red, white and blue stripes on the wings and rudder. The Curtiss was to be carried aboard the *Maude* and used for short range flights from the ship and back again to check on ice conditions.

He had a much more ambitious plan for a second aeroplane he wished to acquire. He read about a new type of aeroplane that had set an endurance record of almost 27 hours. On 29–30 December 1921 Edward A Stinson and Lloyd Bertaud had stayed aloft for 26 hours 19 minutes and 35 seconds. The aircraft was a Junkers F 13 designed and built in Germany and marketed in the United States as the Junkers-Larsen JL 6. It was an advanced aircraft for its day, being of all metal construction with a cantilevered monoplane wing and an enclosed cabin for four passengers although the two pilots were housed in an open (sometimes characterised as a semi-enclosed) cockpit. This was at a time when most aeroplanes were open cockpit biplanes of wood and fabric construction with the wings braced by struts and internal and external wires. The machine was streamlined and had a futuristic look. The cabin was lined and the seats for the passengers were upholstered. The seats had seat belts and the cabin upholstery provided a degree of soundproofing. Everything about the Junkers was in marked contrast to the slow, two-seater, open cockpits of the war surplus Curtiss JN 4 Jenny (in North America) and Avro 504K (in Great Britain and its Empire) that aviation minded people were most likely to encounter. Amundsen believed that the all metal structure was suited to Arctic conditions. The American agent for the type was the Danish-American businessman John A Larsen. Larsen had obtained the agency and a licence to construct the type in the United States. Although he imported 23 F13s he did not use the manufacturing licence. In 1920 he sold eight aircraft to the US Post Office. In 1920–21 three of the Post Office aircraft caught fire in the air and all three were destroyed with the loss of at least seven lives. Amundsen may not have been aware of the accidents. The US Air Service investigated the accidents and came up with modifications that cured the problem. In the Air Service report it was noted that the aircraft was promising but its handling required suitably trained pilots. The aircraft seemed to have the range to make a non-stop flight from the north coast of Alaska to the North Pole and on to Kings Bay, Svalbard. The distance to be covered was about 1,835nm and the Junkers cruised at 75kt giving it a still air range of about 2,000nm. There was, of course, a huge difference between staying aloft for over 26 hours near an airfield in fine weather, with no navigation issues and the option of landing if the weather changed or a fault developed, and the flight Amundsen wished

Amundsen and Omdal about to fly the Curtiss Oriole, probably at Mineola on 6 April 1922.

to make. He was always an optimist and he decided to procure a Junkers and attempt the flight. He intended to divert to Cape Columbia in north-west Greenland if circumstances prevented him from reaching Svalbard.

Amundsen needed pilots and his first choices were two of his countrymen. Odd Dahl (1898–1994) was not only a pilot but a mechanic, a motion picture cameraman and radio operator. Amundsen also hired Norwegian naval aviator Oscar Omdal (1895–1927) to be one of his two pilots. Omdal was both a pilot and a mechanic. When he was hired he had military and civilian flying experience and had served in the Norwegian Navy. The 1922–23 expedition was the first of three of Amundsen's expeditions he would take part in. Omdal was present at Long Island when the Oriole and F13 were handed over in April of 1922. Amundsen and Omdal familiarised themselves with the aircraft by making flights in both of them. The Curtiss and the Junkers each had distinctly different features and handling characteristics. The Curtiss was a conventional strut and wire braced biplane with a light wing loading, a low stalling speed and a steep glide with the throttle closed. The F13 was a streamlined monoplane with no external wires or struts, a high wing loading and a high stalling speed. Its glide without power was shallow compared to the Curtiss. Omdal had to adapt to the characteristics of both machines. The J13 was named *Elisabeth* (in large letters on both sides of the fuselage), painted grey overall with a black engine cowling, Norwegian colours on the wings and tail and the distinctive Junkers-Larsen logo on both sides of the fuselage. The metal skin of the machine was corrugated in a very distinctive way and Junkers aircraft used that type of covering for 25 years. The modern appearance, the luxurious seating in an enclosed cabin and it's relatively high performance made the F13 the 1920s equivalent of an executive jet. Amundsen decided to fly from New York to Seattle in the Junkers. The flight would be in stages and he would then have the machine dismantled and loaded aboard the *Maude* to be carried to Point Barrow on the Arctic Coast of the Territory of Alaska. The flight would give Omdal valuable experience of the F13 and of navigating on long cross-country flights. Amundsen had always stressed the role of careful preparation in achieving successful expeditions. On 10 April 1922 Amundsen and four companions took off from an airfield at Long Island, New York bound for the first stop at Cleveland. Near Clarion, Pennsylvania they encountered trouble of some kind and the Junkers turned over when landing in a field. The pilot and passengers escaped with bruises but the aircraft was badly damaged. The cause of the accident is not clear and reports suggest that bad weather (a hail storm), or a shortage of petrol, or an overheating engine caused the unplanned landing. The *Pittsburgh Press* for 12 April 1922 reported that 'Tuesdays hail storm forced him to land'. The most likely scenario is that bad weather caused the pilot to make a precautionary landing in a field which turned out to be soft. The undercarriage sank into the soil causing the aircraft to flip onto its back. The Junkers's streamlined airframe, high wing loading and high stalling and approach speeds would have made it a challenging machine to fly for pilots used to the high drag and light wing loading of the biplanes typical of the day. A pilot unfamiliar with the Junkers might have found it more difficult to judge the approach and flare out for landing. Omdal was on board but it is not clear if he was flying the machine on the first leg of the journey. The aeroplane was dismantled at the scene and returned to New York. Within days Amundsen had acquired a second Junkers and this was crated and sent to Seattle to be loaded aboard the *Maude* for the voyage to northern Alaska.

At some point Amundsen hired a Canadian pilot to fly the Junkers on the great flight to the North Pole and Svalbard, with Omdal and Dahl as back-ups. The Canadian pilot was Elmer G Fullerton who arrived in Seattle on 30 May 1922 to join the expedition. He had been a pilot in the Royal Flying Corps and the Royal Air Force during the Great War and had experience of flying the F 13. Imperial Oil purchased two Junkers F 13s from Larsen in 1920 and had them flown from New York to Edmonton, a distance of over 1,600nm. This delivery flight was a notably long one for the era and made good sales copy for Larsen. Imperial Oil named them *Rene* and *Vic* and employed the aircraft

Oscar Omdal, Roald Amundsen and John M Larsen with Junkers F 13 *Elisabeth*. Larsen was the Junkers agent for North America and imported more than 20 F13s. He also had a licence to manufacture the Junkers design but did not do so. Amundsen took delivery of an F 13 in April 1922. This was damaged on the first leg of a delivery flight from New York to Seattle. He was loaned a second F 13 which was shipped to Seattle and loaded on the *Maude* to be taken to Point Barrow on the Arctic Ocean coast of northern Alaska.

to support the survey of oil reserves discovered in the North West Territory of Canada where surface travel was difficult, particularly during the winter. One of the pilots dropped out at Edmonton and was replaced by Fullerton. Fullerton and George Gorman flew the aircraft up to the McKenzie and Fort Norman areas of the Territory. The pilots were pioneers of bush flying in

Omdal and Amundsen boarding a Junkers F 13 in cold weather gear. If the planned flight Alaska–North Pole–Svalbard had been attempted they would have spent up to 30 hrs flying and navigating in sub-zero temperatures in the aeroplanes open cockpits. A 75 kt slipstream awaited the navigator while leaning out of the cockpit to take sun sights with a sextant.

remote areas during the winter and had many mishaps and adventures as a result of a demanding operational environment and a lack of experience of this type of flying. At one point one of the Junkers was flown with a locally produced propeller. Fullerton had flown the Junkers on wheels, skis and floats and was familiar with flying from ice and snow in an Arctic winter. He was aboard the *Maude* when the Oriole was flown on skis. The pilot was Odd Dahl with Captain Oscar Wisting (Captain of the *Maude*) as observer. After the second flight the Curtiss was damaged on landing and could not be repaired locally.

The Junkers had been loaded aboard *Maude* at Seattle and transported to the north-west coast of Alaska. It was then transferred from the *Maude* to the schooner *C S Holmes*, a trading vessel, to be carried to Point Barrow. Ice conditions were not favourable and the crated aircraft plus a prefabricated hut and supplies for the winter were unloaded at Wainwright. In 1926 Alaska was sparsely populated and America's last frontier. Alaska had been a territory

The Curtiss Oriole *Kristine* on the sea ice by the *Maude* off the northern coast of Alaska. It was intended for short range ice reconnaissance. It was flown by Odd Dahl with Captain Oscar Wisting as a passenger. It was damaged on landing from its second flight and was not used again.

since 1912 and would not become a state until long after Amundsen's day (it became the 49th state of the United States on 3 January 1959). The population of the territory in 1920 was just over 55,000. By the time they arrived at Wainwright conditions were not suitable for an immediate flight to the Pole and beyond. They erected the hut, named it Maudheim and stored the Junkers for the winter. Omdal stayed with the Junkers while Amundsen left for Nome for the winter. The plan was to make the attempt on 21 or 22 June 1923 when the sun would be at its highest. Fullerton had elected not to stay with the expedition and dropped out of the story at about this time. Omdal was assigned to the Junkers for the great flight and Dahl would stay with the *Maude*. Dahl's skills included those of radio operator. He had been trained in radio at Marconi's in Great Britain.

The flight was taken seriously in Norway with *Flight* reporting on 31 May 1923 that the Norwegian government had voted 60.000 kronor for two seaplanes to be taken to the ice edge north of Svalbard to meet and escort the Junkers to Kings Bay. It may be inferred that the real reason was for them to conduct a search and rescue flight if Omdal and Amundsen did not arrive. Amundsen's flight plan included diverting to Cape Columbia on Ellesmere Island (the most northerly point of Canada) if the weather on track was too bad. There was also a plan to use the Curtiss and Junkers to lay down a fuel cache about 400 miles to the north. How the aviators would find the cache without a radio beacon (not available in 1923) on the drifting ice pack was never explained. Amundsen sledged to Nome for the winter, returning to Wainwright in 1923 to find that Omdal had assembled the Junkers. The expeditions gear included wheels, skis and floats for the F 13. A photo dated 27 April 1923 shows Amundsen and Omdal, dressed in cold weather gear, about to board the F 13 which has *Christine* painted on the port fuselage side, just behind the cabin door. The aircraft is on wheels and is resting on a grassy surface with no sign of ice or snow. The photo may be mis-dated and may have been taken in New York before the F 13 was shipped to Alaska. If it was taken in 1923, it appears the aircraft was flown on wheels in Alaska. The aircraft was fitted with skis by the start of May and on 11 May 1923 Omdal flew the Junkers on a test flight from the frozen lagoon at Wainwright as a movie camera rolled. The camera operator caught the action when the Junkers port undercarriage leg and ski was damaged on the first landing. A photo taken at Wainwright shows Amundsen and Omdal standing beside the Junkers which has floats fitted but is minus its wings. It is not clear whether it was flown with the floats but Amundsen did write that they were 'unserviceable'.

He abandoned the flight at this point but it is not clear whether the damage was the reason or that he had re-assessed the situation and decided that it was just too risky. One author has written that Amundsen had now calculated that the Junkers could carry no more than 18 hours fuel when operating on skis. The skis would also produce more drag than the wheeled undercarriage and lower the cruising speed and therefore reduce the range available on whatever amount of fuel could be carried. Amundsen had planned to make flights out on to the frozen Arctic Ocean to lay down fuel caches. Amundsen's business manager Haakon Hammer offered to operate an F 13 from Svalbard to lay down further caches from his end. The whole idea was clearly unworkable as the ice moved miles per day in unpredictable patterns. Without radio beacons and precise navigation (this was the 1920s) there was no chance of finding a fuel cache on the ice en-route and a safe landing and take-off from the ice was unlikely if they did find it. This meant they would have to take off from Wainwright with fuel for about 30 hours. This would require a long and smooth runway. The length required would have to have been determined by a series of test flights with the load increased on each flight. Assuming they took off safely they would have navigate accurately and control the aeroplane in conditions of poor visibility and the technology required was simply not available to them in 1923. Historian, pilot and air navigator admired Amundsen but wrote:

> 'This was the most unimaginative plan ever put forward by Amundsen, whose extensive knowledge of the ice was not matched by his understanding of aircraft operations.'

Hammer had gone ahead with his part of the plan and when he received a telegram from Amundsen saying that he (Amundsen) would not be making the flight in 1923 was faced with a decision about what to do. He had obtained a Junkers F 13 on floats registered D 260 and named it *Eisvogel* (Kingfisher). After doing some joy rides for notables at Bergen it was being shipped north to Tromso when Hammer received Amundsen's telegram. Hammer decided to continue on to Svalbard and make a photo survey of northern Spitsbergen. His expedition included pilot Harold Neumann, photographer Walter Mittelholzer, scientist Kurt Wegener, reserve pilot Duks, mechanic Holbein and Junkers service representative Lowe.

The aircraft was assembled at Green Harbour and operations were commenced. They started with a 2hrs 12min flight and followed this with flights lasting 2hrs 45min and 6hrs 40min. The flights covered much of Spitsbergen, and still and movie pictures were taken. On the last flight Neumann had pressed on in spite of one of the magnetos failing and the engine developing less than full power and running roughly for the entire

Haakon Hammer's Junkers F 13 floatplane at Green Harbour, Svalbard in July 1923. Hammer is second from the left standing on the float. He had planned to co-ordinate with Amundsen on Amundsen's flight from Alaska to the North Pole and Svalbard. Hammer was already on his way when Amundsen cancelled his flight and Hammer decided to continue. The F 13 was flown by Harald Neumann and made some notable flights exploring and photographing Svalbard. The result was a book of photographs of Svalbard from the air.

Pilot Harald Neumann with Haakon Hammer's Junkers F 13 floatplane during the 1923 Svalbard Expedition.

flight. The passed over Danes Island at one point and could see the remains of Andree's and Wellman's buildings clearly from 7,000ft. On return it was found that the magneto was burnt out. There were no spares so that was the end of the flying. The photosand motion picture film were outstandingly beautiful due to Mittelholzer's skill and the exceptionally clear atmosphere. With the engine running rough they were lucky to get up to over 7,000ft and 80° north on the final flight. This expedition returned to Germany having made the first photographic flights above the Arctic Circle.

In the meantime Amundsen had been pondering the lessons of the failed North Pole flight expedition. He later wrote:

'I had now become convinced, from our experience at Point Barrow, that the Junker plane could not make the flight, and that the only hope of success lay in getting flying boats. In other words I had concluded that efforts to land on the very rough Arctic ice with skis or similar devices was not practical. We must have airplanes specially designed to light on and take off from the water, snow and ice'

The only aircraft that would meet his requirements was the Dornier Wal designed by Claudius Dornier in Germany and manufactured in Italy.

'At this point I ran full steam into a series of events that led to the most distressing, the most humiliating, and altogether the most tragic episode of my life'

Amundsen was planning new expeditions and trying to sort out his finances and pay off his debts. His brother Leon had been his business manager for many years and served Amundsen well. However in 1923 he calculated that Roald owed him $25,000 and feared that the total debts owed would mean he would be unlikely to get his money. Leon resigned and tried to have Roald's house sold to satisfy the debt. In 1921 Roald had asked Hammer to act as his agent and gave him a power of attorney to conduct all kinds of business in his (Amundsen's) name. Hammer was an American of Danish origin and was carrying on business in Seattle as a ship broker. This appointment turned out to be a mistake as, just when Amundsen needed a conservative approach to his financial affairs, Hammer took some great financial risks in his name. Amundsen latter described Hammer as being 'a criminal optimist' and the facts support that assessment. Hammer committed him to the purchase of three Dornier Wal flying boats at $40,000 each when there seemed to be no real chance of raising the money. Amundsen had often taken financial risks but this time it appeared as if he was never going to work his way back to solvency. Amundsen consented to an order declaring him bankrupt. He toured the United States writing articles for the newspapers and lecturing to raise money but audiences were thin and profits low. Late in 1924 he was in a hotel room in New York feeling gloomy and thinking that it would take him 60 years to pay off his debts when the phone rang and an acquaintance from seven years before offered to change his life forever.

The man on the phone was the American Lincoln Ellsworth. He had meet Amundsen in France in 1917 and he had a proposition for him, Ellsworth would supply the bulk of the money for a flight to the North Pole if he was allowed to fly with it. He had always wanted to be an Arctic explorer, although he started late in life. Amundsen had started his career as an explorer in 1897, at the age of 25. Ellsworth was 44 years old when he and Amundsen went into a partnership with the aim of being the first men to fly to the North Pole. Ellsworth had arranged an interesting life for himself. He always preferred to work outdoors at activities which required powers of endurance. These included some years with the United States Geological Survey and time in France during 1917–1918. In March 1917 (just before the United States declared war on the Central Powers) he joined an ambulance unit and sailed for France. During the voyage his ship dodged a torpedo from a surfaced German U-boat and engaged it with gunfire. He arranged a discharge from his unit, enlisted as a private in the French Air Service and was sent to Tours to train as an aviator with other Americans who would form Franco–American units. He was 37 in 1917, 14 years above the age limit for pilots. He passed his medical as fit for duties as an observer, but not as a pilot. Initially his training was conducted by the French but later the Americans took over. As the truck carrying the trainees entered the grounds of the airfield, two aeroplanes collided overhead, killing one of the pilots. The recruits were given the job of clearing away the wreckage and removing the body. Surprisingly, his training included piloting, and after instruction in a dual-controlled Caudron he was sent solo to make several take off attempts and a landing during which a wing-tip brushed the ground and the impact broke a strut. He persevered and a week later he was awarded his 'eleve' pilots insignia and promoted to sergeant. He continued flying at Tours for three months and while he was there Eddie Rickenbacker learned to fly and was sent to the front to become America's most successful fighter pilot of the Great War. Probably because of his age, Ellsworth, who wanted a combat assignment, was sent to Paris to undertake clerical work. One day in March 1918 he heard an explosion and, on investigating, found a crater, caused by a shell from the Paris Gun which was bombarding Paris from more than 100km away. He never got to the Front

Line but, importantly, met Roald Amundsen, who was in Paris preparing for the voyage of the *Maude*. Ellsworth had arranged a meeting and asked to be included in the *Maude* expedition which was due to sail in mid-1917 and would involve a drift embedded in the ice, hopefully across the North Pole, and might last for many years. Amundsen had listened politely but smiled, noted that it was a bit late in life for Ellsworth to start exploring, and said no. It was this meeting that Ellsworth reminded Amundsen of and they were soon deep in discussions of an expedition to be mounted in the spring of 1925. Ellsworth's proposal was simple: he would make a major contribution to the next expedition and his only condition was that he went along with it.

Ellsworth did not have to work because he was the son of a multi-millionaire industrialist, James W Ellsworth, and was in receipt of a generous allowance. Ellsworth Snr had wanted Lincoln to take part in running the family businesses but Ellsworth Jnr had preferred to indulge in his outdoor activities. These activities had left him lean and fit and up for adventure. He was a little shorter than Amundsen and photographs show a tanned, confident man with a ready smile. Ellsworth admired Amundsen for his many achievements in the Arctic and Antarctic and Amundsen respected Ellsworth for his courage and willingness to endure any hardship. The professional relationship between Amundsen and Ellsworth blossomed into a friendship which would endure until they were separated by the death of Amundsen in 1928. Lincoln Ellsworth negotiated with his father for an $85,000 advance on his inheritance and his father agreed but insisted that Lincoln give up smoking.

There was a curious footnote to the negotiation between father and son for money with which to make the flight. Ellsworth senior insisted that parachutes be purchased and carried for each of the six air crew. Ellsworth junior agreed to make his father happy. Reliable parachutes for civilian and military airmen had only become generally available since the end of the Great War. There were regular reports of their successful use in newspapers and magazines and it would make perfectly good sense to a non-pilot to insist that they be carried. However this was not the case if the big picture was considered. Only structural failure or fire in the air would require escape by parachute. If they jumped they could not take any survival equipment with them. If they survived the descent they would either die in minutes in the frigid Arctic sea or in days on the pack ice. It follows that it would be better if they left the parachutes behind and carry the equivalent weight in fuel which would increase the range and endurance of the aircraft and increase the safety factor.

*Chapter Six*

# Towards the North Pole

*Marina di Pisa–Tromso–Kings Bay–Arctic Ocean,*
*25 February 1925–21 May 1925*

At about 17:10 on 21 May 1925 two Dornier Wal flying boats took off from the ice of Kings Bay, on the island of Spitsbergen, in the Svalbard archipelago. They flew in a loose formation and shaped a course for the North Pole. The crews consisted of Amundsen, Riiser-Larsen, Dietrichson and Omdal from Norway, Ellsworth from the United States and Feucht from Germany. In the days of sailing ships a ship was said to be sailing 'towards' rather than 'to' its destination and this seems an appropriate was to describe this flight. They were aware that the machines did not have the range to fly to the Pole and back non-stop. Their sextants were useless if the horizon was hazy or invisible. Without the observations the sextants navigation would be approximate rather than precise. They had no radios and would be on their own the moment they crossed the southern boundary of the sea ice which lay just to the North of Svalbard.

Amundsen and Ellsworth had chosen Ny Alesund, a settlement on the southern shore of Kings Bay as their base. There were several reasons for this decision. It was close to the Pole, 665nm away, and although it was isolated by the Arctic pack ice during the winter, it was accessible early in spring because of the warm Gulf Stream current. The expedition was planned to take place in the months that the sun was above the horizon 24 hours per day. In 1916 Peter S Brandal had started a coal mine at Ny Alesund and mining was in full swing when the Amundsen-Ellsworth expedition arrived in 1925. The settlement consisted of a wharf, machine shops, barracks, bathhouse, hospital, houses and a narrow gauge railway operated by horses. The machine shops and man-power were particularly valuable and might be needed for unloading and assembling the aeroplanes.

They had chosen Dornier Wal flying boats for the expedition. Their requirement was for a machine that could take off and land on water, ice or packed snow and be durable enough to survive in the Arctic environment. Amundsen had visited Marina di Pisa in Italy during 1924 and inspected the all-metal Dornier Wal flying boats that were manufactured under licence from Dornier in Germany. Germany was prohibited from manufacturing large aeroplanes by the provisions of the Treaty of Versailles which had terminated the Great War of 1914–1918. Italy allowed Germany to circumvent this provision even though it had fought against Germany in the war.

Amundsen was favourably impressed as the all metal structure seemed ideal and the bottom of the hull was almost flat and the machine used sponsons, (which looked like a small wings attached to each side of the hull beneath the wing) rather than tip floats, to keep the aeroplane from capsizing at low speed, or stationary, on the water. The large monoplane wing was placed on struts well above the fuselage and the two engines were mounted on the centre section of the wing, in tandem, where the propellers were as far away as possible from the spray which was part of every take-off and landing on water. The placing of the engines also had the advantage that if one failed the remaining engine

The two Dornier Wal flying boats were shipped to Kings Bay in six enormous packing cases as deck cargo aboard *Hobby*. They could not dock at Ny Alesund. They were unpacked aboard ship and the components were lowered on to the ice. The engine nacelle is being mated to the fuselage of N 24.

was on the centre line and did not cause yaw and extra drag. The Wal was made in civil and military versions. They chose the military version as its empty weight was lower than the civil and it was easier to convert to a long range machine with extra fuel tanks located in the fuselage, below the engine nacelles. A significant factor in the choice was probably the Rolls-Royce Eagle engines of 380hp each. The name Rolls-Royce was synonymous with quality and reliability. The plan was to have a crew of three in each aircraft. The navigator would occupy the open cockpit in the nose, the pilot in the open cockpit behind the navigator and the mechanic managed the fuel and engine in an enclosed position in the fuselage below the engine nacelle. The Wal was an advanced design and would prove to be exceptionally robust on the 1925 Arctic flight and on other pilot's long distance flights over water and ice. The Rolls-Royce engines on Amundsen's Wal started up time after time.

They chose to ship the aircraft to Kings Bay and assemble them there. There were conflicting reports of their intentions; at one point it was reported that they intended to fly from Spitsbergen to the North Pole and on to Alaska. Each aircraft carried fuel for 16 hours flight. The only way they could fly to Alaska would be to land on the ice at the Pole after flying for about eight hours and transfer the remaining fuel from one aircraft to the other. They would then load all six crew members to one aircraft and take off with 16 hours fuel and fly on to Alaska. Eventually they decided to fly from Kings Bay to the North Pole and back to Kings Bay. In late 1925 (after the flight of that year), Amundsen wrote:

'Our hope to get right along to the Pole was very small, for that, our radius of action was too limited. Apart from that I had not any great interest in reaching the Pole, as I had always regarded Peary as being the first on the spot.'

The general understanding of the aims of the flight was that it was to be to the Pole and back. There is no evidence that they intended, when they took off, to fly to a point South of the Pole and then turn around with enough fuel for a non-stop return. They aimed for the Pole but were shy about how they were going to do it. The explorers always gave the impression that they might have to land and transfer fuel from one aircraft to the other but in fact this would be inevitable. The realities of endurance, range, navigation weather made it so. The Wal had an endurance of 16 hours at an airspeed of 81 knots giving a range in still air of 1,296nm. The distance from Kings Bay to the North Pole and return is 1,330nm. The figures are not far apart but in reality the endurance and range required to fly to the Pole and back were far in excess of the aircraft's capability. With no wind and perfect navigation the Wal could not complete the flight before running out of fuel. The true situation was even worse because flight planning for long distance flights have to assume some adverse wind. In 1925 air navigation was an evolving art and some inaccuracy in navigation was to be expected. A five per cent allowance for adverse winds plus a further five per cent for small cumulative errors in navigation and five per cent for a reserve increase the range and endurance required to 1,530nm and 19 hours. It followed that there was no chance of a return flight without landing to transfer fuel and crew and abandoning one of the Wals on the ice. This basic fact would make the flight a near death experience for all concerned.

Amundsen appointed Hjalmar Riiser-Larsen as the expedition's second in command and relied on him to arrange the technical matters. After going to sea in merchant ships as a teenager, Riiser-Larsen had entered the Norwegian Naval Academy at Horten, near Christiania, as a 19 year-old cadet in 1909. He was commissioned into the Royal Norwegian Navy in 1912 and was promoted to First Lieutenant in 1915. He joined the Royal Norwegian Naval Air Service 1915 and ultimately became proficient in flying both land planes and seaplanes. He was inspector at the Naval Aircraft Factory 1916–1919 and had flown in Great Britain and Germany to broaden his experience and select aircraft for Norway. On 13–14 July 1922 he flew a Hansa-Brandenburg seaplane from Kristiania to Kirkenes near the Finnish border and back, a distance of around 1,950nm in less than 48 hours.

Riiser-Larsen's first airship flight took place in 1919 in the German civil Zeppelin *Bodensee* and in 1921 he was sent to Great Britain to train as an airship pilot. His training included flying in captive balloons (kite balloons), non-rigid and rigid airships and ground school covering the theoretical aspects

Riiser-Larsen with the Goerz drift meter fitted to both Wals. When there was a clear view of the surface it could measure both drift and groundspeed. The navigator used the information to update his dead reckoning.

of lighter-than-air flight. He should have made flights in free balloons but none were available. He had been sent to Great Britain because the British government were planning an airship airline to link London with Stockholm and Copenhagen and Norway wanted Oslo to be included in each round trip. They also wanted Oslo to be the first stop on the flight from London. His superiors instructed him to lobby General Edward Maitland (who was playing a major part in the project) while he was receiving instruction. Brigadier-General Edward Maitland had joined the British Army in 1900, served during the Boer War (1899–1902) in South Africa and taken up ballooning in 1908. He was aboard the balloon *Mammoth* in 1908 when it flew from England to Russia, covering 970nm in 36½ hours. In September 1911 he was awarded Federation Aéronautique (British Empire) airship certificate N.8. He served in the Air Battalion, the Royal Flying Corps, Royal Naval Air Service and the Royal Air Force. He was aboard R 34 during its double transatlantic crossing in 1919. Maitland was a keen golfer and Riiser-Larsen agreed to receive golfing instruction so that he would have time alone with Maitland. He produced meteorological records which supported his contention that Oslo would be an appropriate port of call and that Oslo should be the first stop but the service was never started. Maitland was one Riiser-Larsen's instructors. When Maitland wished to get back to the office he would direct the airship back over the landing ground and parachute from it. An enthusiasm for parachuting was a very rare thing in the early 1920s. Maitland was killed when the new rigid airship R 38 broke up in the air and burnt on 24 August 1921. Another instructor was Major Scott. Major George Herbert Scott was a major contributor to the British airship programme as both engineer and pilot. Scott trained as an engineer and worked in both Great Britain and Spain before the Great War. He joined the Royal Naval Air Service in 1914, trained as an airship pilot and flew non-rigids before being appointed as Captain of HM Airship No. 9, the first British rigid airship to fly. After the war he commanded R 34 on its double crossing of the North Atlantic which took place 2 July to 13 July 1919. The east to west leg was flown on 2–6 July 1919 against the prevailing westerly winds and took 108 hours. On 10–13 July 1919 the west to east leg was flown in 75 hours. R 34's average groundspeed west bound was less than that of the fastest contemporary ocean liner over the same track.

In the early days of aviation in Norway it was common for military pilots to do some civilian flying from time to time and Riiser-Larsen was no exception. He was probably the most experienced aviator in Norway at the time of his appointment by Amundsen. Riiser-Larsen was tall (6' 4°) and strongly built and aged 35 in 1925. His combination of physical strength, endurance and piloting skills saved his life and those of his companions during the 1925 expedition. He had visited the aircraft factory at Marina di Pisa to liaise with the manufacturers and inspect the Wal flying boats during their construction. He had to return home when Amundsen went bankrupt but returned to the factory when Ellsworth's money became available. He played a crucial role in organising the expedition by liaising with Amundsen, SCMP (Societa di Costruzioni Meccaniche di Pisa; the aircraft manufacturers) at Marina di Pisa in Italy and the Norwegian Luftseiladsforening which was in overall charge of the expedition. As well as supervising the construction of the specially modified Wals, he had to select the flight and navigational instruments which were to be installed in the flying boats. Amundsen wrote this about Riiser-Larsen:

'Hjalmar Riiser-Larsen had already taken part in the spring attempt to get the expedition going, so he quite familiar with everything. It was therefore both with gladness and with trust that I was able to telegraph to him the $85,000 – James W, Ellsworth's [Lincoln Ellsworth's father] gift – asking him to order the two seaplanes. From this moment Riiser-Larsen got permission for leave and was able to give himself up entirely to the expedition. As a flying man he is so well known by every person in the land that it is superfluous and stupid to mention more. But he has dozens of other notable qualities which I need not enumerate and which made him specially qualified to fill the post he has. With such a second in command a difficult trip becomes for the leader a pleasant and light effort'.

The other pilot was Leif Ragnar Dietrichson who had attended the Naval Academy in 1908–11 before going to sea as a mate with the Bergens Steamship Company and serving in the Navy from 1914 onwards. He transferred to the Royal Norwegian Naval Air Service when it was established in 1915. He learnt to fly in 1916 and took further instruction in Great Britain in 1918, being appointed Chief of the flying boat base at Kristiansand in that year. He continued in that position, surviving a crash into Portør harbour in 1919. Amundsen wrote this about him:

'His skill as a flyer is recognised by all. His bravery and resolution will stand out clearly......With his light outlook on life, his glad smile and happy nature, he was an invaluable comrade on the flight.'

A third naval aviator was appointed although he flew as a mechanic and reserve pilot. This was Oskar Omdal who had been with Amundsen in the United States and Alaska during the expedition of 1922–23. And Amundsen wrote:

'If things went with him or against him it was all the same. Nothing seemed to depress him. He stood beside me in my two unhappy attempts in 1923 and 1924, and you can believe that it took a real man to show courage and keenness in a third attempt, but Omdal did not disappoint me'. "So long as you don't give in", he said to me, "you shall always find me ready". He is a marvellous being; he seems to have several limbs more than the rest of us. He moves slicker and thinks quicker. It is impossible to depress him'.

In the book Amundsen wrote (with contributions from other members of the expedition) in 1925 he defined the expeditions aim as being to:

'Trek in as far as possible over the unknown stretch between Spitsbergen and the Pole to find out what **is** there or what **isn't** there'.

Harald Sverdrup was still aboard the *Maude* in the summer of 1924 and he had sent a telegram to Amundsen indicating that his tidal observations indicated that it was unlikely that there were any large tracts of land north of Alaska.

It is reasonable to assume that before the flight a major aim was to make the first flight to the Pole as well as well as put a swath of the Polar Ocean on the map. If, as seemed likely, there was no land to be discovered, they could at least confirm its absence.

Amundsen meet up with Riiser-Larsen at Marina di Pisa where Riiser-Larsen oversaw the preparation of the aircraft for the flight. One of Amundsen's biographers wrote that:

'The lieutenant was the expert, the polar explorer the fantasist'

This is fair comment given that Riiser-Larsen's experience and expertise in aviation was in marked contrast to Amundsen's. Riiser-Larsen was a man whose professionalism in all aspects of aviation equalled Amundsen's in all aspects of Arctic exploration by surface travel. The problem was that Amundsen was expedition leader whose decisions were final while Riiser-Larsen was second in command and this may account for some of the shortcomings of the plan they acted on. On 25 February 1925 the two men left Italy by train having left instructions that the Wals were to be crated and sent north by ship. After a stop in Berlin the explorers arrived near the Norwegian capital (now called Oslo) on 4 March. Riiser-Larsen travelled on alone to deal with the crowds. The fact that Amundsen was constantly plotting to avoid crowds of curious citizens and journalists is testimony to his fame and the intense interest in his expeditions. The fact that the expedition would use leading edge technology (aeroplanes) only added to the interest. Amundsen would have acknowledged that he sought fame, as it helped him raise money for his expeditions, and that he enjoyed the limelight most of the time. He would not have been human if he thought (like the English playwright and wit Oscar Wilde) that 'the only thing worse than being talked about is not being talked about'. On 11 March a telegram was received advising that the planes had left Marina by ship on that day.

On 30 March Ellsworth arrived in Oslo by ship and on the day before their departure he and Amundsen attended a dinner held in their honour. At 18:30 they were seen off from the East Station by a large crowd of well-wishers and journalists. On 9 April 1925 the Expedition and its equipment departed Tromso bound for Ny Aalesund on Kings Bay. The ships were the motor ship *Hobby* (carrying the aircraft as deck cargo in six huge crates and 21 smaller containers) and the naval vessel *Farm* (not to be confused with the famous *Fram*) which had been placed at Amundsen's disposal. It was early in the season and Amundsen had some anxiety over the dangers of the voyage including ice and bad weather. After a stormy voyage, during which the ships had lost sight of each other, the ships arrived at Ny Aalesund to find the bay iced over. Another ship cut a channel through the ice so that the expedition ships could approach the shore. They moored near the coal company's jetty and began unloading the aircraft. With the expedition were Schulte-Frohlinde (director of SCMP), his two mechanics Feucht and Zinsmayer, and Rolls-Royce mechanic Green. All of them helped to get the crates ashore and the Wals assembled and ready for flight. There were two meteorologists with the expedition and they collated radio reports of the weather information from places around the margins of the Polar Sea and prepared weather forecasts. Amundsen particularly appreciated the work of sail-maker Ronne who prepared everything from trousers to sleeping bags and tents. Ronne gave Amundsen a large knife which proved to be invaluable when the ice runways were being prepared on the ice at 88° north. During the stay at Kings Bay the Expedition made itself comfortable and looked forward to Fridays when they could use the bath house with its boiler fired by coal from the mine. Amundsen biographer Tor Bomann-Larsen wrote of Ny Alesund that it was 'entirely taken up with Pole fever' for those few weeks in the spring of 1925.

Sea ice was still a problem this early in the season and on 29 May *Farm* had to turn back when it attempted to sail to Green Harbour (on Spitsbergen about 50nm south of Kings Bay) to deliver and pick up mail.

Amundsen also had decisions to make about an expedition to be mounted in 1926. Riiser-Larsen had the information that the Italian semi-rigid airship

A fuselage being towed across the ice of Kings Bay from the *Hobby* to land at Ny Alesund.

The two Dornier Wals were assembled in the open at the mining settlement of Ny Alesund as photographers took still and motion pictures for the book and documentary film about the expedition.

N1 could be purchased for $100,000. It had always been assumed that a large airship would cost more than they could raise. Ellsworth offered to put up the money and it was decided to negotiate the purchase and organise the expedition as soon as the 1925 flight was completed. The 1925 flight now became less important and was represented as reconnaissance towards the North Pole rather than attempt to fly to the Pole and back.

The preparations were marked by the attention to detail that Amundsen applied in all of his expeditions with a precise plan for food for each man for each day and the contents of each man's rucksack. It was intended that each man would have equipment and food for about a month on the ice. There were pistols and rifles to shoot game and for protection if they encountered polar bears. They carried gear for a surface journey across the ice including skis and collapsible sledges and boats. Riiser-Larsen and Dietrichson had to allocate time to instruct Amundsen and Ellsworth in air navigation as they (the pilots) would be fully occupied with flying. Amundsen taught Ellsworth to ski as this would be an essential skill if they had to trek out from a landing on the ice. Amundsen and Ellsworth each had three chronometers and checked them against the radioed time signal from the Eiffel Tower every day for 14 days because their accuracy was essential for accurate navigation. There were

Feucht, Riiser-Larsen and Amundsen aboard N 25 just before take-off on the flight towards the North Pole.

three chronometers so that they could be checked against each other. Another essential for navigation were sextants to measure the angle between horizon and the sun. An aircraft sextant should have an artificial horizon built into it so that it could be used if the horizon was indistinct or invisible. The sextants they had were defective in that this feature did not work. They had ordered radio sets for each aircraft but they had not arrived. The radios could have been used to supplement the onboard navigation by taking bearings on the radio stations afloat and ashore at Kings Bay. Amundsen and Ellsworth elected to go in the knowledge that navigation would be problematical and that they could not summon help if they could not make the return flight.

On 9 May the N 25 was ready and taxied on the ice of the bay although neither aircraft was flown before they departed for the Polar flight. The day of

Amundsen in the front cockpit of Dornier Wal N 25 shortly before departure from Kings Bay late on the afternoon of 21 May 1925. From left to right are; the windshield of the pilots cockpit, sun compass, airspeed indicator and venturi which was used to drive the gyroscopic instruments used in blind flying. The sun was low throughout the flight and 'blinkers' were placed behind the clear windshields of both cockpits as soon as they reached cruising altitude. The two Dorniers would have the sky to themselves and so there was no risk of collision as long as the Wals kept to a loose formation with a clear view of each other.

Dietrichson and Ellsworth in their cockpits waiting to take-off late on 21 May 1925.

departure for the Pole would be the first and only time that the Wals would take off with a full over-load. Amundsen met with Ellsworth, Riiser-Larsen and Dietrichson in late April and announced that he intended to over-fly the Pole and fly in to Alaska. Ellsworth's aircraft would return to Kings Bay. In this he was re-enacting his famous announcement at Madeira in 1910 that *Fram* was not going to the Arctic Ocean and the North Pole but on to Antarctica and the South Pole. The difference here was that he did not possess the expertise to assess the risks the journey would involve. The distance from Ny Alesund to the North Pole and on to Wainwright, Alaska was over 1,800nm and the range of a Dornier Wal was about 1,300nm, even if no allowance was made for wind, navigational issues and a reserve. Riiser-Larsen and Dietrichson vetoed the plan (for perfectly good technical reasons) and Amundsen had to agree, grumbling in his diary:

'I ask myself so often, where are the guts? If they are the slightest bit uncertain, they pull in their horns'.

On 21 May 1925 the aircraft and the men were ready and the weather and ice conditions were suitable for the take-off. The plan had always been dependent on the ice in the Bay being strong enough for the flying boats to take off from. The machines were overloaded and if the Bay had been ice free they would have been so low in the water that they could not have accelerated enough to get 'on the step' and could not have taken off. The normal maximum take-off weight was 5,700kg and the Wals were loaded to 6,660kg, and overload of almost 1,000kg.

At 17:00 they were ready for departure with the engines warmed up and the final details attended to. The crew members donned or made ready the special clothing and footwear that was necessary for long flights in open cockpits in sub-zero conditions. The mechanics were protected from the slipstream in their enclosed positions and needed to move around to manage the fuel and engines and so were less warmly clad than the observers and pilots. The sun compasses were set going final goodbyes made and the machines taxied down the ramp and onto the ice of the bay. In N 25 were expedition leader and navigator Amundsen, pilot Riiser-Larsen and mechanic Feucht. In N 24 were Ellsworth, pilot Dietrichson and mechanic Omdal.

The N 25 made its take-off first with the ice bending beneath its weight and the sea water surging up as it made its run with both engines running flat

Amundsen biographer Tor Bomann-Larsen wrote of Ny Alesund that it was 'entirely taken up with Pole fever' for those few weeks in the spring of 1925. The two Dornier Wals surrounded by onlookers at Ny Alesund just before take-off on 21 June 1925.

out at 2,000rpm. After a tense 40 or 50 seconds Riiser-Larsen eased the wheel back and the machine took to the air. Dietrichson in N 24 had a more eventful take-off. In turning through 90° on to the slipway (with the help of some of the men watching the departure) the pilot heard a sound like a row of rivets popping and, sure enough, when he slowed down in the middle of the Bay so the crew could don their cold weather gear, the ice sank beneath machines weight and the hull started to fill with sea-water. They hurriedly finished dressing and made a full throttle dash across the ice with Dietrichson letting the air speed rise to 65kt before pulling back on the wheel to rise into the air. The take-off had taken 1,400m.

The two Wals flew in loose formation up the western coast of Spitsbergen, passed Danes Island and Amsterdam Island off the North Western point of Spitsbergen and made their departure for the North Pole. The mean temperature during the flight was about –13° and the airspeed was around 80kt giving a substantial wind-chill factor if they had to expose any part of their bodies to the slipstream. The clothes and footwear had been carefully chosen and cold was not a problem. They were facing the low sun and even dark sun glasses did not make for comfortable vision. They had anticipated this

The expedition was the most exciting event in the history of the mining settlement which had been operating at Ny Alesund since 1916. The miners show a close interest in one of the Dornier Wals as it waited to take-off. When Amundsen returned to Kings Bay in 1926 he found a monument to the men of the 1925 flight.

The Dornier Wals were overloaded with three crew, survival gear and fuel and oil for 16 hours flight. The also carried both still cameras and motion-picture cameras to document the expedition. The Dorniers were able to take-off and land on water, ice or packed snow. Here N 25 gets a push from the onlookers as it slides down the ramp onto the frozen surface of Kings Bay. N 25 was crewed by Amundsen as navigator, Riiser-Larsen pilot and Feucht as mechanic. Feucht was a last minute choice and had no experience in the Arctic.

problem and they installed shields called 'blinkers' behind the windscreens in the bow and pilots cockpits in each machine. As long as they kept the formation loose there was no risk of collision.

As they flew north Amundsen tried to take a sun sight with his sextant. The horizon was indistinct. This should not have been a problem because they had 'bulb sextants' which provided an artificial horizon. They had discovered at Spitsbergen that these sextants did not work and had chosen to depart knowing that, if the horizon was indistinct, they would not be able to determine longitude. Latitude was easier to calculate and Amundsen kept track of it without too much trouble. They were over cloud cover so they could not use the drift-meter to determine their drift or ground speed. The horizon was indistinct so the sextants could not be used. Dead reckoning gave them a general idea of their position but could not provide a fix. Wind was probably drifting them to the west or east of their track. The sun compass and the magnetic compasses gave them a reliable heading and they continued to maintain a heading of due north.

Early on in the flight cloud 'thick clouds and fog' made them climb to over 3,000ft to stay in the clear air. Shortly afterwards Dietrichson noticed the engine radiator temperature gauge showing a rising temperature and rang the bell which summoned Omdal. He later wrote:

> 'The indicator had passed 100°, and I felt sure that we would have to make a forced landing. Through small holes in the fog we could see the drift ice below us where a landing would certainly mean a wrecked plane. The temperature rose higher and the last I saw was, that it indicated 115°, when the thermometer burst, and my hopes sank to zero. I rang again for Omdal, but a little time elapsed before he came, and I judged that he was busy. Meantime I was astonished to see that the engines still went as well as ever. I had throttled them down to 1600 revolutions, but expected to hear a crack any minute; and how goes it with the forward motor?'

The engines continued to run and the flight continued with the Wals flying in a loose formation. As he flew Dietrichson thought about the conflicting advice they had received about whether or not they would find places suitable for landing both the Dorniers:

> 'Nobody had so far observed the conditions from a flying man's point of view. This we were quite clear about, but we depended on the material at our disposal, namely our flying boats, which if the worst should happen, ought to be able to take us back home without our making a landing.'

This is a curious observation to make because a return without landing and with a small reserve of fuel and endurance could only happen if they had agreed, before take-off, to turn around at some defined point short of the Pole. They had taken off without agreeing to do this. By default, they set out knowing that landings would have to be made and that they were hostages to fortune. At about 82° north they flew out of the fog belt and could again see the surface. They flew at altitudes varying from 3,000ft to 10,000ft (about the service ceiling of a Dornier Wal) and looked carefully for land. Of land there was no sign. Their view of the surface was not reassuring. Dietrichson noted:

> 'The ice looked quite different to what I expected. Instead of the big kilometre ice plain, we saw ice plains which through cracks or bergs had been divided into small, irregular pieces, where it was impossible to land. And open water lanes? These were reduced to small snake-like cracks, following a winding

course, on which it was impossible to land....Hour after hour passed without
the conditions below use changing to any noticeable degree.'

After about eight hours, when they should have been in the vicinity of the
Pole, depending on the wind direction and strength (they had been unable to
get a fix on their position during the flight) they saw blue water rippling in the
sunshine, the first seen since leaving Spitsbergen. They had planned to land
on the ice if at all possible but the ice was broken and quite unsuitable for a
landing so N 25 descended towards a lead. As Riiser-Larsen reduced power
the rear engine started to back fire and loose power. He was obliged to land
in a lead full of slush and small pieces of ice which at least slowed N25 down.
Amundsen saw one of the wing-tips pass over the top of an iceberg close
enough to blow off some loose snow:

'We zig-zagged along in a manner which was most impressive and alarming...I
expected every moment to see the left wing destroyed. The speed now slackened
in the thick slush, and we stopped at the end of the arm-nose up against the
iceberg. It was again a question of millimetres. A little more speed and the nose
would have been stove in.'

The lead was too small for both machines so Dietrichson found another one
and landed. As soon as he throttled the engines back the rear engine stopped
but he was able to land safely. As soon as he was down he taxied to a small
berg, and as far up it as he could, so that the N24, with its sprung rivets,
would not sink.

Conditions on the ice were fluid. Ellsworth later wrote:

'The danger of being crushed became apparent...a north wind tended to open
the leads. On the second day, though, it shifted to the south, and we could see
the ice closing in. The whole field was alive with inert motion. Ice cakes in the
lead would disappear, as if sucked under; others would emerge to the surface.
The edges of the lead drew imperceptibly closer to each other. The implacable
jaws were shutting on us, and we all felt that our plane would soon be caught
in them'.

Soon after landing Dietrichson and his crew saw a seal, the only sign of life
that they would see during their stay on the ice. They would soon regret not
having shot it for its meat.

## Chapter Seven

# A Merciful Deliverance from the Ice

*Arctic Ocean–North East Land–Kings Bay,*
*22 May–18 June 1926*

Dietrichson 'took the sun' with his sextant and found that they were at about 87° 50' north. Amundsen and N25 were close to N24 but out of sight. Amundsen also checked his position and calculated that they were at 87° 43' north latitude and 10° 20 west longitude. As he had suspected, they had encountered an easterly wind which had set them 53nm west of track. They were 130nm from the Pole and 528nm from Kings Bay. Amundsen, Riiser-Larsen and Omdal tried to move N25 up on to the ice but the three men could not defeat the gluey ice-slush. Eventually they settled for moving all food and equipment on to the ice

It is difficult not to overestimate the peril the six men were in. They had no radio and there was no chance of an air search finding them. If long range aircraft were sent to Kings Bay to conduct a search they would have no idea where to look as the Wals could be down anywhere in the 665nm between Ny Alesund and the North Pole. And they could be anywhere within 100nm east or west of the direct track. The ice was in constant motion with ice ridges being formed and leads opening up and closing. N24 was in sinking condition, because of the rivets popped just before the take-off, and would do so if the ice opened up beneath it, which was a distinct possibility. The aircraft was partly in the water of the lead and needed regular pumping, the leak getting worse as time went on. The rear engine was damaged and when they tried to move the N24 on to firm ice using the engines and man-power they found that the front engine would not start and the rear engine and three men did not have the power to move the aircraft. They had been awake for 24 hours and needed a rest and food. They made hot pemmican soup, coffee (with some alcohol in it) and lit their pipes. Even the sun could be an enemy in the Arctic and Dietrichson suddenly went blind with snow blindness. They bandaged his eyes and put him in a sleeping bag in the aircraft.

N24 would not fly again and, until the crews of the two flying boats were re-united, they only had three men and one engine to work the Wal away from sinking or being pinched in the ice and then sinking. It was essential that the N24 be protected until they could transfer fuel and supplies from it to N25. For a time some of the men thought that they would be able to continue on to the Pole. All thoughts of reaching the Pole were abandoned as soon as the facts of their predicament became clear. The only possible plan was to fuel up N25, dump all equipment not essential for flight, find a lead long enough and wide enough for a take-off or find or create a runway on the ice, load all six men, and fly back to land.

Standing on top of an ice hummock, Dietrichson was able to see the tips of a wing and a propeller blade of N25, and thought that it was about three-quarters of a mile away. Omdal worked on the damaged engine and Ellsworth and Dietrichson attempted to walk to N25 carrying the canvas boat. They failed after hours of labouring up and down the jagged ice.

At midday on 23 May the N24's crew noticed that the N25 was visible again having drifted closer and communication was established by semaphore with flags. It was a tedious and time consuming business as none of them was expert and two men were needed at each end. Sending was easy enough but receiving required one man to observe the flags through binoculars while the second noted the message down, letter by letter. Ellsworth wrote that 'It took us two or three hours to exchange the simplest message.' Amundsen requested that they walk to N25 carrying as much gear as possible. Several attempts were made to do this until Dietrichson and then Omdal sank through the ice slush and the strong current tried to drag them under the ice edge. They were saved because they had life belts on (a last minute purchase in Bodö), had their skis unfastened and so could kick them off, and Ellsworth acted decisively. He crawled towards Dietrichson and managed hold out his (Ellsworth's) skis close enough for Dietrichson to grasp the tips and be dragged up on to firm ice. Omdal was shouting 'I'm gone, I'm gone' in English. Ellsworth crawled towards him, spreading his weight as much as possible to avoid falling through himself. Ellsworth got his skis out in front of him, close enough for Omdal to grab the tips and be hauled out, gasping for breath and spitting blood from his front teeth, five of which had been broken off as he struggled to cling to the ice as the current tried to drag him under. They were close to N25 and could be heard shouting but were too far away to be any help. Ellsworth's skill and strength saved not only the two men in the water, but all six of the expedition members. If Omdal and Dietrichson had drowned the remaining four men would have been unable to prepare a runway for take-off and would have died of starvation on the ice. Forty minutes later the six men were glad to be reunited at the N25. Ellsworth noted that Amundsen seemed to have aged years in the few days since he had last seen him.

> 'Five days had brought a shocking change in Amundsen. Sleepless toil and anxiety had graven in his face lines that seemed to age him ten years. In all his many adventures in the Polar Regions, I doubt if he had ever been in such peril as this or under such a strain. Yet in his manner he was the same old self, cool, clearheaded, resourceful.'

Amundsen was not an experienced aviator and it may have been that he had not quite appreciated the risks of the flight until they were down on the ice. Whatever his state of mind he displayed his professionalism and leadership skills in the ordeal which was about to begin. The first task was to move N25 on to a level, thick, piece of ice. It had been impossible for three men and was easy for six.

They had only two choices; attempt to walk out to on the ice to Greenland or transfer fuel and food from N24 to N25 and attempt to fly home. At the time they reunited there was no lead in the ice and the ice surface was ragged and totally unsuitable for a take-off. It followed that they would have to cut a runway out of the ice surface and reposition the N25 from time to time to

Dornier Wal N 24 on the ice of the Polar Ocean at 87° north 43° west. This Wal was abandoned and all six men flew back to Svalbard in N 25 flown by Riiser-Larsen. The expedition book (*My Polar Flight*) implied that N 24 was abandoned because of irreparable damage to the rear engine. In fact one of the Dorniers had to be abandoned because the only way to make the return flight was by transferring fuel from one to the other.

stop it from being pinched and crushed by the ever changing ice. An attempt to walk out was unattractive for a number of reasons. Firstly they only had food for a month or so on full rations. The region seemed to be empty of game that could be killed for its meat. Secondly the condition of the ice was most unfavourable for a surface journey as it was covered with ridges, areas of thin ice and gaps where they would have to launch their boats and ferry men and supplies across. The journey of less than a mile, from N24 to N25, had taken several exhausting attempts and had almost resulted in two men being swept under the ice and being drowned. On the plus side, Amundsen, Riiser-Larsen, Omdal and Dietrichson were experienced skiers and Ellsworth was physically strong and an experienced out-doors man. They had collapsible boats and sledges and ski and other carefully selected survival equipment. In Riiser-Larsen they had an experience and skilled pilot. Most importantly, they had Amundsen's experience and skill as a traveller in the Arctic and his leadership skills. Feucht was relatively young but appears that he did not have any experience relevant to survival in this most hostile of all environment. Feucht was uniquely challenged as he was the only one of the five who was neither an explorer nor a naval officer. He worked alongside the others and made a major contribution to the expedition's escape from the ice. They decided that their best chance was to try to fly out although they revisited this decision as the days turned into weeks.

In addition to the human resources the expedition had this material to work with:

- N25. A serviceable flying boat capable of carrying all six men to safety
- Petrol for about eight hours flight stowed on N25
- Petrol for about eight hours flight stowed on N24
- Navigational equipment to fix their take-off position accurately and their progress on the flight home approximately
- Two collapsible sledges and boats
- Rucksacks and ski for each man
- Shotguns, rifles and pistols and ammunition for hunting and for protection from polar bears
- Enough provisions of salt beef, chocolate, biscuits, dried milk and malted milk to give each man 1,000gr each day (when on full rations) for a month
- Cooking gear including a Primus stove and Meta stove
- Miscellaneous equipment selected by Amundsen as being useful

Although the expedition was, in many ways, well planned and equipped, there were some surprising omissions. Although a landing and preparation of a take-off runway were inevitable, they had no special tools with which to shift ice and snow. The last minute gift of a bayonet, by sail-maker Ronne to Amundsen, was crucial as this was the best tool that they had. Amundsen soon established a routine as they prepared for take-off. The first decision to make was to reduce the daily ration to make the most of their limited supplies of food. From time to time, as the days and the unsuccessful take-off attempts, mounted up they revisited the ration to be allocated to each day, and it was further reduced several times. By the end of the stay on the ice the ration provided only a small fraction of the 5,000 calories per day required by men carrying out hard physical labour in the cold of the Arctic. At the end of each working day the men were exhausted and steadily lost both weight and strength. In time the prospect of a walk over the ice to Greenland became more attractive. In summer the coast of Greenland was ice-bound on its west coast to Washington Land in 80° north and its east coast Kong Oscar Fjord in about 73° north and so they could get there without having to cross any sizable bodies of water. If they were to attempt to walk out, the earlier they made the decision the better. The longer it was delayed the less food they would start with and the greater the risk of failure. Greenland was about 400nm away. Calculations of their position, taken at regular intervals, showed that the currents were carrying the ice to the south-east.

In the midst of the hard labour and peril they remembered to take still and motion pictures for the expedition documentary (should they live to send the exposed film to the organisers) and their scientific obligations. They had a device that exploded a charge and they measured the time taken for the echo to return with a stopwatch. On 28 May they used the device twice and the time suggested that the sea was about 3,750m deep. This was further evidence that there no landmasses to be discovered in the Arctic Ocean.

They set to work creating a runway on the ice. Amundsen insisted establishing a routine. Each day started with breakfast of a cup of chocolate and three oat cakes. At 13:00 they stopped work for a meal of pemmican soup and in the evening three biscuits. They soon ran out of tobacco and were forced to smoke Riiser-Larsen's foul black chewing tobacco. When they were not working they lived aboard the N25, managing to squeeze all six men into the cramped compartments located from nose to tail. They even managed to dry their clothing by hanging it up inside the flying boat. All of this happened while the temperature aboard was well below zero.

Preparing a runway wide and long enough was brutally hard work but they knew their lives depended on it. For tools to shift and level the ice they used knives, axes and an ice anchor. The work involved filling in cracks and ditches, levelling and compacting the surface and cutting down icebergs so they would not damage the wings as they passed on the take-off. A petrol tank was removed from N24 and dragged across the ice. Every possible drop was required because, not only did they need enough for the return flight, they also used fuel every time they started the engines to shift the N25 or to make a take-off attempt.

From the day work started down to the morning of 14 June they made five take-off attempts, all of them unsuccessful. On each occasion they started and warmed the engines and set the sun compass going. Riiser-Larsen was the most experienced pilot so his place was in the cockpit with the throttles, instruments, control wheel and rudder pedals in front of him and the runway before him. Amundsen, Dietrichson, Ellsworth, Omdal, and Feucht climbed into the central compartment where they could see nothing but could hear the engines and the sounds of the ice against the hull and the slipstream made by the propellers and the air rushing by. Each time they were keyed up and then bitterly disappointed when Riiser-Larsen judged that they would not reach flying speed and cut the throttles in time to prevent an overrun and damage. If he had misjudged it they might have been killed but they would, as a minimum, have lost the machine and have had to attempt a surface journey to Greenland.

8 June 1925 brought fog, drizzle and a reduction in the rations down to 300g per man per day. They worked in damp snow and made a place to turn the machine through 180° to line up for the take-off. On 9 June the rations were down to 250g and they were working on their fifth runway which was to be 500m long by 12m wide. They were using up the last reserves of physical energy a mental courage. On 11 June Omdal realised that it would be quicker and more efficient to stamp the snow down until it was firm enough to support the flying boat and they adopted this method. By 14 June Amundsen estimated that they had shifted 500 tonnes of ice since work began on 24 May. That day they made their sixth and seventh unsuccessful attempts at taking off. A key problem was that the temperature, which had been at −12°C, rose to 0° and the resulting slush clung to the hull and would not permit acceleration to take-off speed. The next day the temperature had dropped and the runway was hard frozen, there was even a light head wind to shorten the distance required for take-off. In poor visibility they laid out black strips of film to mark the runway. They had dumped everything on board except:

- Petrol and oil for eight hours
- One canvas boat
- One tent
- Two shotguns

- Six sleeping bags
- Cooking gear and food for about two weeks
- A minimum amount of clothing for each man
- The exposed still and movie film

They started and warmed the engines. The clockwork mechanism of the solar compass was started. Amundsen made a last inspection of the runway and everyone except Riiser-Larsen climbed into the central compartment of the Wal.

At 22:30 on 15 June 1925 Riiser-Larsen opened the throttles wide and the machine slid along the ice, up a slight slope, over several small cracks and accelerated with each engine delivering its full 2,000rpm. After 30 or 40 seconds the vibrations ceased as the machine took to the air for the first time in almost a month. Dietrichson moved into the bow compartment to take up the navigator's position and Riiser-Larsen turned on to a heading which would take them home to Spitsbergen. The flight was a difficult one but seemed an anti-climax to the exhausted crew who had lived with hard labour, short rations and uncertainty for so long.

For eight hours the N25 flew south at an airspeed of about 80kt. During those eight hours the crew did not see one place big and smooth enough for a landing or a take-off. For two hours they flew through fog without being able to get under it or over it. They were not tempted to land and wait it out. Nothing but an engine failure would have brought them down. Dietrichson made drift observations as often as possible so Riiser-Larsen could adjust his heading to allow for any wind across their track. Each observation required a descent to about 100ft and was a risky business.

After more than seven hours flight Feucht sighted land and it was identified as Spitsbergen. With safety in sight the famished explorers wolfed down the chocolate and biscuits they carried as survival rations. Riiser-Larsen had been experiencing some kind of problem with the controls (Amundsen wrote that the aileron control had stiffened up) and elected to land a mile or so off shore and they taxied the rest of the way through rough seas which drenched him and drove the others back into shelter in the central area of the fuselage. Ellsworth was violently ill from a combination of rich food, a shrunken stomach and sea sickness. N25 taxied into a bay and they dropped anchor. It was about 08:00 on 16 June 1925 and they were in a bay on the northern coast of North-East Land, the second largest of the islands that made up the Spitsbergen Archipelago, and about 135nm north-east of Kings Bay.

They had survived because of Amundsen's leadership, Riiser-Larsen's skill and airmanship, Ellsworth's quick thinking and courage when Dietrichson

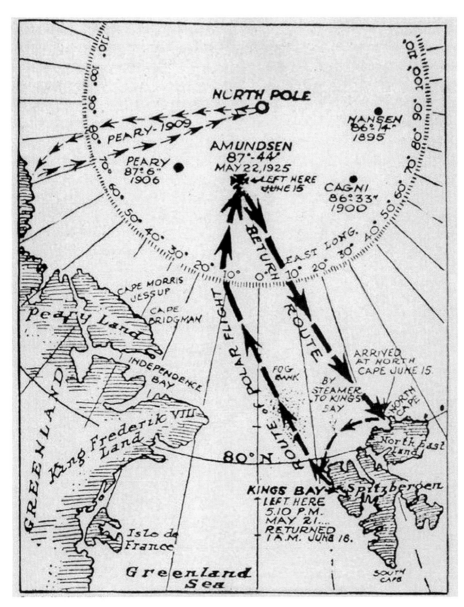

Map of the attempt to fly from Svalbard to the North Pole and return. On the outward flight both Dornier's drifted well to the west of track due to an easterly wind and problems obtaining a position line with sextants that could not measure a precise angle between sun and horizon in hazy conditions. On the return the Dornier N 25 drifted to the east of track but made a landfall on the northern coast of North-East-Land in the Svalbard archipelago.

and Omdal had fallen through the ice, hard work by them all and a good measure of good fortune. John Grierson, pilot, air navigator and historian of Arctic and Antarctic aviation wrote of Amundsen and his comrades:

'Surely there has never been a more merciful deliverance from the ice'

They went ashore and Ellsworth lay on a flat rock while the sun warmed his face. They had 30 litres of petrol left, enough for about 30min of flight.

*Chapter Eight*

# Svalbard

## *21 May–18 June 1925*

When the last sound of the Wal's engines had faded Schulte-Frohlinde walked out on to the ice of Kings Bay and inspected the tracks cut by the two flying boats and found that they had both broken through at the start of their take-off slides and left tracks 1,400 metres long. The tracks became fainter as the aircraft accelerated and the wings started to take the load. The onlookers searched the sky to the north for a few hours in case the aircraft returned and then started the wait for the return.

At 09:30 on 21 May 1925 there was no sign of the aircraft returning and the non-flying members of the expedition knew that the flying boats had landed somewhere between Kings Bay and the Pole. They had taken off with 16 hours fuel in each machine and 09:30 was just over 16 hours after take-off. At first there was no concern and it was simply assumed that, in due course, the machines would return having landed on the ice for a time. Alternatively, one machine would appear with both crews aboard, having landed on the ice, transferred fuel, made scientific observations, and then taken off for the return. At Ny Alesund, the ground party, after six weeks' hard work preparing for the take-off, had nothing to do except wait. The sun shone high in the light blue Arctic sky, the glaciers 'scintillated with lovely colours'. They packed up *Farm* and *Hobby* ready to depart for Danes Island as planned. Acting on Amundsen's instructions they cruised between Danes Island and Amsterdam Island in case there had been an early force landing but there is nothing for them to see except the 'abundance of sea birds…filling the air with their screaming and chattering'. The ice edge was examined as far to the east and north as they could reach without entering the pack. To fill the *Farm*'s fresh water tanks they tied up to an ice berg and hacked off chunks which fell into the tanks. Sailors shot two seals for meat and brought them aboard.

There is an element of danger in all sailing close to the ice in the Arctic and at one point *Farm* anchored in ice-free water but became surrounded overnight. An iceberg drifted alongside and they could see a tongue of ice under the ship. The captain decided to shift into Virgo Harbour to avoid damage. The intense public interest in the flight was reflected in the pessimistic reports in the media when there was no sign of the adventurers after six days although Amundsen had instructed the ground party not to be concerned until 14 days had elapsed. James Berg had taken movie footage of the preparation and take-off and sailed with the ground party in the hope of recording the return of the Wals. As they waited, some of the men found the continuous daylight and the absence of night difficult to deal with.

On 31 May several members of the expedition sailed from Ny Alesund for the outside world in the ice breaker *Pasvik*. In early June the Norwegian Navy decided to send aircraft to assist in the search. Two Hansa-Brandenburg W 33 floatplanes were shipped from the naval base at Horten, in Southern Norway, to Spitsbergen aboard a collier. *Farm* went to Advent Bay to coal and to meet the ship with the floatplanes. While the *Farm* was away, and the *Hobby* was again patrolling the edge of the ice to the north and east, the journalists spent some days at Pike's House at Virgo Harbour. The house had been built by the Englishman Pike in the 1880s. While they were waiting the journalists searched through the many items left behind by Andree and Wellman in 1896–1909. There was a monument to Andree and his companions and timbers from the Balloon House built by Andree in 1896 and the hangar built and rebuilt by Wellman in 1906–1909. The addresses were still visible on some of the packing cases and materials used in the generation of hydrogen gas were strewn about. On 16 June the collier with the float-planes arrived at Advent Bay and the naval patrol boat *Heimdal* was designated mother-ship for the aircraft. The two aircraft, F 18 piloted by Lutzow-Holm and F 22 piloted by Styr, flew in from Advent Bay and moored at the buoys that had been prepared for them. Another naval officer involved was Bernt Balchen who would be a major player in the use of aircraft in the Arctic and Antarctic. Later that day the *Heimdal* arrived to support the aircraft. The plan was for the *Heimdal* and the two aircraft were to be based at Lavöen on the western coast of North East Land. The floatplanes had a comparatively short radius of action and it made sense to base them as close as possible to the search area. The next day would be 18 June 1925, exactly four weeks since Amundsen, his five companions, and the two flying boats, had departed for the North Pole. Most of the watchers now believed that the Wals had been damaged in landing on the ice and the explorers were now attempting walk out to Cape Columbia in Greenland. Amundsen's instructions had included a time limit.

The search was to be continued for six weeks and there were only two weeks left. The *Heimdal*, *Hobby*, the two float-planes and their crews intended to search for the next two weeks.

The *Heimdal* was alongside the *Hobby* at the pier at Ny Alesund with steam up on the morning of 18 June 1925 when *Sjöliv*, a small sealing vessel tied up and on its deck were the missing aviators. Amundsen, Ellsworth, Riiser-Larsen, Dietrichson, Omdal and Feucht were dirty, bearded, gaunt from starvation and darkened by the sun but were back from the dead, happy, and very much alive. The excitement at Ny Alesund was mirrored in the headlines in Norway and around the world.

In 1925 there was intense interest in aviation and in exploration. The 1925 Polar Expedition had all the hallmarks of an activity in which public interest and adulation was inspired and maintained. A famous leader, leading edge technology (the flying boats), a brush with death, the tension and uncertainty of a month long wait without any news and finally a last minute escape. Amundsen was a hero and a celebrity and his survival, when many thought him dead and lost without trace, added just the right frisson to the story.

Headlines from the *New York Times* from 22 May to 22 June 1928 give some idea of the world wide interest in the story, the concern at his disappearance and the joy at his survival:

**AMUNDSEN PLANES HOP OFF ON FLIGHT TO THE NORTH POLE**
*Leaves Kings Bay Spitsbergen At 5.15 PM*

**LONDON EAGER FOR NEWS**
*Great Interest Is Aroused Here By News That Amundsen Has Started Flight For North Pole*

**AMUNDSEN MISSING 112 HOURS IN ARCTIC**
*Our Navy May Act*

**GUSTAV AMUNDSEN EXPRESSES NO FEAR**
*Says His Brother Could Not Make The Trip To The Pole In Less Than Ten Days*

**WASHINGTON NOT WORRIED**
*Sees No Reason to Act On Appeal Made By Hammer*

**NO WORD OF FLIERS ON TRIP TO THE POLE**
*Ships Move North; Planes Of Amundsen Are Now Overdue*

### SAYS AMUNDSEN ERRED IN TAKING TWO PLANES
*English Explorer Holds Doubled Chance Of Accident*

### TRUST AMUNDSEN'S SKILL
*Philadelphia Scientists Say There Is No Reason To Fear For His Safety*

### COOLIDGE FAVORS AMUNDSEN RELIEF SHOULD HE NEED IT
*President Would Approve Naval Plan*

### NORWEGIAN PLANES TO HUNT AMUNDSEN
*Government Decides To Send Ship North With Two Aircraft to Search*

### BELIEVES AMUNDSEN IS WALKING BACK
*Thinks The Explorers Airplanes Have Been Forced Down*

### GIVES PLAN TO NAVY TO HUNT AMUNDSEN
*Captain Lansdowne Of The Shenandoah Would Use Spitsbergen As Base*

### NORWEGIANS SAIL TO HUNT AMUNDSEN
*Seven Men With Two Seaplanes Leave Christianiafjord*

### AMUNDSEN RELIEF SHIP REACHS ADVENT BAY
*Norwegian Fliers Prepare For First Flight To Kings Bay*

### AMUNDSEN'S PERIL NOW FULLY SEEN
*Details Of Adventure Reveal A Terrible Fight To Return From Arctic*

### AMUNDSEN IS FLOODED BY CONGRATULATIONS
*Prominent Norwegians Start Move To Raise Funds*

### NORWAY PREPARES TO HAIL AMUNDSEN
*Oslo Will Give An Enthusiastic Welcome*

They had gone ashore on the morning of 16 June grateful to be on dry land but uncertain of their location. A sight with the sextant had established that they were on the latitude of Svalbard, and they were waiting to take a further sight to provide a cut which would give them longitude as well as latitude when a small vessel motored into the bay. This was the sealer *Sjöliv*. The crew were pre-occupied by the pursuit of a wounded walrus and did not see the flags the six men waved. They rowed out the N25, started the engines

Dornier Wal N 25 over Oslofjord on 5 July 1925. On board were; Amundsen, Riiser-Larsen, Ellsworth, Dietrichsen, Omdal and Feucht. They were on their way to a hero's welcome in Oslo.

and taxied after the ship. The vessel had finished its trip and was returning to Kings Bay.

An attempt to tow the aircraft was thwarted by a head wind so they beached it in a bay near North Cape and sailed for Kings Bay with the ship. On the way they learnt of the efforts made to find them including the Norwegian naval seaplanes and Soviet ice breakers further east. Back at Ny Alesund they shaved, bathed, dressed in fresh dungarees, eat and slept. For three days they surfaced only to eat.

Ellsworth heard that his father had died at Florence on 2 June 1925, not knowing that his son would survive. They received telegrams of congratulation on their survival from the Norwegian government and news that they had made the headlines in all the big newspapers around the world.

They remained at Kings Bay for a week so that N25 could be recovered and then put her aboard the freighter *Skollern* for the trip to Horten naval base near the Norwegian capital Oslo. On 5 July 1925 the six men flew the flying boat to Oslo harbour for the official welcome. They were escorted up the fjord by flights of navy and army aeroplanes. In the harbour were many warships of several navies and all were dressed all-over with flags and the crews manned the sides to cheer them. Officials dressed in formal frock-coats greeted them and they rode in open horse-drawn carriages through streets lined with cheering people. At the official reception Amundsen and Ellsworth were accompanied by Riiser-Larsen, Dietrichson and Omdal who dressed in their dark blue naval uniforms with gold braid and their gold naval aviators' wings on the right breast of their jackets. Feucht was with them to receive his share of the adulation. That night they were honoured by a formal dinner attended by King Haakon VII and his Queen, probably the greatest honour that Norway could offer.

On 7 July 1925 Amundsen received this telegram from King George V, King of Great Britain and Northern Island and Emperor of India:

'My heartiest congratulations upon your safe return from your flight to the Polar region. I trust that you and your companions have not suffered privations during your heroic flight

George R.'

Ellsworth was awarded a gold medal by King Haakon for saving Dietrichson and Omdal when they fell through the ice. The King and Queen were present at a lecture given by Amundsen at Oslo on 14 August 1925. During the lecture Amundsen said:

'…When Lincoln Ellsworth saved Dietrichson and Omdal from drowning, he saved the whole expedition; and I, therefore, deeply appreciate the King's act in conferring on Ellsworth, without whose generosity the expedition would never have taken place, the gold medal for the saving of life.'

The carefully preserved motion picture footage exposed during the ordeal on the ice was included in a documentary film produced to help pay the expedition's outstanding bills. After each expedition Amundsen had to write up the expedition to profit from the publicity and interest in it. The 1925 Polar flight was no exception and there was a deadline so that the book was on the shelves before the reading public had lost interest. The 1925 book was to be around 70,000 words long and Amundsen, Dietrichson, Ellsworth, Riiser-Larsen and Fredrik Ramm (who had been part of the ground party and had participated in the search) contributed to the book. The resulting book was 292 pages long and was published late in 1925. It included a meteorological section by an un-named author and, given that it was thrown together in only few months, is a fresh and interesting account of the expedition. There are details of the flight and navigational instruments as well as the carefully chosen survival equipment and food. Amundsen's attention to detail shines through in the details of the rations and packs, sledges and ski, collapsible boats, firearms and ammunition.

The book is almost silent on the flight plan and navigational issues. They had survived to become heroes in the eyes of the world. They had nothing to gain by advertising the fact that the plan had flaws which almost had fatal consequences.

## Chapter Nine

# Oslo–Rome

## *1925–1926*

As well as writing the book Amundsen, Ellsworth and others had to get down to organising the 1926 expedition which would use the Italian semi-rigid airship N.1. Amundsen, Ellsworth, Riiser-Larsen and Dietrichson had had a meeting at Ny Alesund just before the flight towards the Pole and agreed to return to Kings Bay in 1926 with an airship. They would fly to the Pole and then across the Polar Sea to North America. They would have used the airship in 1925, if it had been available at that time.

The advantage of airships had over aeroplanes (in the mid-1920s) was range, endurance and safety. The overloaded Dornier Wals had an endurance of about 16 hours at about 80kt, which gave them a range of just under 1,300nm in still air with no reserve. If one engine failed on a Wal, it would have to descend as it could not maintain height on one engine while overloaded. The modified N1 would have an endurance of about 75 hours at about 40kt giving it a still air range of about 3,000nm. If there was engine trouble on an airship the faulty engine could be shut down and worked on in flight. If the fault could not be fixed the airship would continue at a reduced speed. If all the engines failed (it had happened in other airships) the airship could made to free-balloon without power. Another safety feature of airships was that they could fly in cloud or fog safely (as long as the crew knew where they were and the altimeter was accurately set with the ambient pressure). An airship was stable in three dimensions but aeroplanes were not. In the mid 1920s blind flying instruments were experimental and pilots flying with no sight of the horizon would become disoriented and spin or spiral out of control to the ground. Airships had certain disadvantages. Their cruising speeds were low compared to with aeroplanes. A 100kt aeroplane flying into a 25kt headwind would still have a groundspeed of 75kt. Its range would be reduced by 25 per cent. A 50kt airship would have its groundspeed and range reduced by 50 per cent in the same wind.

Another limitation was that they needed well equipped facilities at each place they visited. It was not safe to simply tie the airship down. The minimum requirement was a mooring mast and large supplies of hydrogen, petrol, oil and spare parts. The masts were topped by a metal cone which fitted neatly over the tip of the reinforced nose of the airship and was free to swivel around a complete 360° circle. When docked, the airship would weathercock around to face into wind, whatever direction the wind would come from. A very large hangar and a large number of men to control the airship when it was on the ground were highly desirable. The reason was that an airship was vulnerable to wind when on the ground. An airship displayed a large side area to any wind while on the ground and one the size of the N1 could drag hundreds of men back and forwards as they tried to control it. The normal ground handling party at its base at Ciampino, near Rome, numbered about 200.

When the airship was at the mast part of the crew had to remain on board and 'fly' the ship. Ballast had to be dropped if the ship became heavy and gas-valved off if it was light. Airships were sometimes torn from their masts in squalls and the crew would be expected to attempt control and repair it in flight and fly it back. The ideal set up was a mast and a hangar. If the airship landed when there was a strong wind across the axis of the hangar it was not safe to try and walk it into the shed. In that case it was good practice to dock the airship to its mast and wait until the wind had died away before returning it to its shed. The larger the airship, the greater was the vulnerability to wind when being handled on the ground. The German Army and Navy operated numbers of very large rigid airships during the Great War. The problem of getting the airships in and out of the hangars in a cross wind was so great that several rotating hangars were built so that they could be aligned parallel to the wind.

The flight to Kings Bay was in stages by way of Pulham in south-eastern Britain, Oslo in southern Norway, Leningrad (now St Petersburg) in the West of the Soviet Union and Vadso in Northern Norway. The exploration flight was to be non-stop from Kings Bay the North Pole and on to Nome in Alaska. They also had to obtain the consent of the French government for the use of an airship base in northern France to be used if headwinds made a direct flight from Ciampino to Pulham marginal. Airship masts had to be built at Oslo, Vadso and Kings Bay. A mast was also built at Rome so the crew could practise the docking procedure. They also had to build a hangar at Kings Bay to house the airship while they waited for good weather for the great flight.

They could have by-passed Oslo but the expedition was made with major support from Norway and a stop at Oslo would be politically desirable.

They wanted to be at Kings Bay with the airship as soon as the summer melt of the southern part of the sea ice made it possible for ships to reach Spitsbergen. This meant that work on the masts at Oslo, Vadso and Kings Bay, and the hanger at Kings Bay would have to start as soon as possible. For the construction work at Kings Bay to be ready in time the contractor, his workers and the wood, steel, canvas and concrete would have to be delivered there before the sea ice blocked navigation. More importantly it meant that construction work would have to continue throughout the sub-zero temperatures, snow, ice, wind and the days of permanent darkness experienced in mid-winter at this high latitude.

Amundsen started the ball rolling for the 1926 flight by telegraphing Colonel Umberto Nobile to come to Oslo to meet with him and with the other Norwegians involving in planning what was to be a very complex and time consuming expedition. Nobile was an officer in the aviation branch of the Italian Army, a designer of advanced semi-rigid airships and an experienced pilot who regularly flew the airships he designed. Nobile had graduated from the University of Naples with degrees in electrical and industrial engineering. After working for Italian State Railways on the electrification of the system he became interested in aviation and in 1911 took a one-year course in aeronautics with the Italian Army. Italy was the first nation to make full use of military aircraft in a war and had used airships, kite balloons and aeroplanes in combat in Libya during the Italo-Turkish war of 1911–12. Italy entered the Great War on the allied side in 1915 and Nobile was commissioned in the air branch of the Army and worked on the production and improvement of airships for the rest of the war. He also worked on his own designs although none of them flew until after the war.

He formed a partnership with three other engineers in July 1918. The others were Giuseppe Valle, Benedetto Croce and Celestino Usuelli. The partners believed that semi-rigid airships were superior to either the small non-rigids or the large rigids. The core belief may have been that the semi-rigid could combine the relatively low capital cost of the non-rigid with much of the range and endurance of the rigid. In the early 1920s airships seemed to have important advantages over aeroplanes; greater range, endurance and safety. Few aviation people expected the aeroplane to develop rapidly and become superior to the airship in all but a few specialist roles. The company built a large semi-rigid called the T-34. It was 125m long; 25 metres in diameter and the envelope contained 33,810m³ of hydrogen. It was sold to the American Army who fitted it with six 400hp liberty engines and renamed it the *Roma*.

On 21 February 1922 the ship was flying over Norfolk, Virginia under the command of Captain Dale Mabry and experienced control problems with its complex tail fins and rudders. It hit high tension wires and crashed in flames, killing 34 and injuring eight. Only three of the crew escaped unharmed and Captain Mabry was among the dead. The accident was not necessarily caused by a design fault. One commentator has noted that experience in ship handling was measured in years but flight experience was measured in hours. In the 1920s every pilot was inexperienced by modern standards. One of the reasons that aviation has got steadily safer is that all concerned in the operation of aircraft have got more experienced over time and have benefited from the lessons learned from the mistakes of their predecessors.

Nobile went to the United States in 1922 and worked for Goodyear in Akron, Ohio. After returning to Italy the N1 was built to his design and first flew in March 1924. Nobile had one or two eccentricities including his practice of taking his dog Titina with him when flying, including his Arctic flights with the *Norge* and *Italia*. Another notable trait was his driving. Amundsen devoted more than a page of his autobiography to describing how terrifying was his practice of accelerating into corners and jamming on the brakes at the last moment. Riiser-Larsen and Amundsen were notably courageous men but Nobile's driving had them both trying to persuade him to slow down and be more careful. Writing after falling out with Nobile, Amundsen said that he saw the driving as evidence of an erratic nature and extreme nervousness. Riiser-Larsen persuaded Amundsen that these characteristics on terra-firma did not mean that Nobile would behave that way when flying the airship. Nobile would be 41 years of age in the year of the great flight. In 1927 Amundsen wrote:

> 'Nobile on several occasions during the actual flight across the Arctic revealed exactly the same qualities he had exhibited at the wheel of the motor car, and more than once put us in peril of disaster.'

Whatever Nobile may have done in Amundsen's presence, the record shows that he successfully piloted *Norge* from Italy to Alaska in stages, a flight that took 169 hours flying, spread over several weeks. This was one of the most notable achievements with an airship in this era.

Nobile responded to the invitation and when he met with Amundsen and Riiser-Larsen he not only answered all the technical questions but was empowered by the Italian government to negotiate the terms of the contract which would make the N1 available for the flight. He told them that the expedition could have the airship free of charge if it flew the Italian flag during the flight. This was the first hint of the controversy which would cause a public rift between Amundsen, Nobile and their respective nations after the successful flight. There is a saying that failure is an orphan but success has a thousand fathers and there was to be a classic illustration of this saying in the unseemly grab for the credit. Amundsen answered in the negative; the airship would be registered in Norway, fly the Norwegian flag, be under the control of the Norwegian Aero Club and be named the *Norge*. Amundsen would be the expedition leader, Ellsworth the co-leader and Riiser-Larsen the co-pilot and navigator. The expedition was to be named the Amundsen-Ellsworth Polar Flight. There were political and social reasons for this insistence that primary credit be given be given to Norway. The first half of the twentieth century saw nationalism reach its peak in often bloody ways. Amundsen would not live to experience the second Great War (1939–1945) but he had experienced the First (1914–1918) in which developed nations seemed to lose all sense of proportion and moderation. Expeditions like the one being planned were a way of bolstering a nation's sense of identity and pride without resorting to armed force. Norway had only been independent since 1905, took great pride in the achievements of men like Amundsen and Nansen, was going to provide much of the money and support for the flight, and did not intend to share the credit any more than they absolutely had to. They could not do it without Ellsworth's money but he was only one man, was popular in Norway and acknowledging him was not a problem.

Italy was also a new nation which had only come into existence in the 1860s with the unification of the many nation states on the Italian peninsula and Sicily: any achievement that reflected well on the country as a whole tended to bring the sections closer together. There was also a specific political force at work. The fascists, led by Benito Mussolini, had come to power in 1922 and the success of an Italian flight and the international acclaim it generated would help him consolidate the

Amundsen mixed with Kings and Queens, Presidents and Prime Ministers. Here he is with Italian Prime-Minister Benito Mussolini at Ciampino in 1926. Mussolini was a pilot and aviation enthusiast and was also Air Minister.

power of the fascist party. There were also social forces at work. Aviation was new, modern and highly technical. Prominent aviators were national and international heroes and there was widespread public interest in successful flights. The 1920s and 30s were the age in which aviation developed rapidly and societies became air-minded. Countries like Italy, Germany and the USSR put great emphasis on bringing aviation to the people. Flying, gliding and parachuting had a military value and a nation's achievements were a source of great national pride. Successful aviators helped their societies to become technologically advanced. In Germany, Italy and the USSR aviators were seen as role models. The aviator was could be seen as the fascist or socialist or communist superman (or, to a limited extent, superwoman). So negotiations on who got the credit were fraught with powerful feelings of national pride. Benito Mussolini (himself a pilot), the Italian fascist dictator, wrote this in November 1923:

'Not everyone can fly…..Flying must remain the privilege of an aristocracy; but everyone must want to fly, everyone must regard flying with longing. All good citizens, all devoted citizens must follow with profound feeling the development of Italian wings.'

Amundsen came to understand the forces at work and made this comment about the negotiations in his autobiography published the year after the great flight:

'I did not understand the significance at the time, but it is now clear that it was a deliberate effort on the part of the government to gain for the present political regime [ie the Italian fascists] in particular, and for the Italian people in general, a world-wide advertisement. My idea of a trans-polar flight was thus subtly to be appropriated as their own by the Italians, and my skill in Arctic exploration was to be utilised as the means of a dramatic achievement for which the Italians would take the credit.'

Another factor mentioned in the autobiography was that Riiser-Larsen, Dietrichson and Omdal were to contribute to the flight and share the honours. One of the most positive features of Amundsen's character was his ability to choose the right men for the job and his loyalty in seeing they shared in the credit for a successful expedition. Without Amundsen's prestige and leadership skills and Ellsworth's money and Nobile's airship design and piloting skills and Norway's national Aero Club, there would have been no flight. More than 85 years after the event it seems clear that the credit should have been equally divided, but in 1925–26 it was impossible for the parties to be as dispassionate and objective.

Nobile agreed to sign on as captain of the airship and to supervise the modification from a short-range passenger carrier suitable for flights in the relative warmth and settled weather of the Mediterranean to a long-range vehicle suitable for long flights including the one from Spitsbergen to the North Pole and on to Alaska. The price for the ship was agreed to be $75,000, $25,000 less than the $100,000 that Ellsworth had agreed to provide. Agreement on purchase was quickly reached and the discussion turned to technical matters.

The N1 had a soft nose as it did not have to use a mooring mast in its Italian flights. When not in use it was housed in a hangar and a large force of men to handle it on the grounded walked it in and out of its hangar. It had to be modified to use the masts to be built for it at Oslo, Vadso and Kings Bay. Nobile agreed to design and have fitted a reinforced nose-cone which could lock in to a cone on the top of the masts. Airship masts were unknown in Italy and Nobile visited Great Britain to study the masts developed by the airship pioneer Major Scott. He then produced the design from which the three masts were constructed.

Another big modification was to reduce the size of the control car mounted under the forward part of the ship. The old car had housed passengers as well as the captain, helmsmen, navigator and radio-operator. The new car would be much shorter and lighter to house only the operating crew and Amundsen and Ellsworth as observers. Wherever possible the structure was to be lightened to produce the lightest possible airship and therefore the greatest possible usable lift. The aim was to produce a ship that could carry about 16 crew and passengers, fuel and oil for about 75 hours flight at around 43kt, plus survival gear carefully chosen by Amundsen, always the total professional in these matters.

Amundsen was not just an explorer. Even when not in the Arctic or Antarctic he spent a lot of his time away from Norway. He gave lectures on his expeditions in many countries. As a man who spent his life either preparing for his next expedition, on the expedition, or raising money to pay off the debts of the last expedition, he was a great traveller. This was long before cheap air travel made the world accessible. He spoke a number of languages and was worldly in every sense of the word. In 1924 he had visited Italy and had taken a flight in N1 which was based at Ciampino. Riiser-Larsen had flown with Nobile in a small airship called the *Mr*. This was said to be the smallest semi-rigid airship built down to that time. It was powered by a single radial engine driving a two-bladed, wooden-pusher propeller. It had a boat-

Nobile and Riiser-Larsen flying Nobile's 1000 m3 semi-rigid airship *Mr*. Said to be the smallest semi-rigid ever flown, Nobile used it for experimental and recreational flying and often made water landings in it.

Nobile and Riiser-Larsen in the cockpit of *Mr* which was powered by a small radial engine driving a two bladed wooden propeller.

shaped, water-tight car with a pneumatic shock absorber. It could land on water and Nobile did this from time to time. A flight in 1928 demonstrated how manoeuvrable the little airship was by landing in downtown Rome.

Riiser-Larsen went with Amundsen for part of his lecture tour of Europe. When Amundsen went to the United States, Riiser-Larsen and Dietrichson continued the lecture series, each covering a different list of cities. Interest varied from place to place and in one city Riiser-Larsen gave his talk to an audience of 60 in a hall with seating for 3,000. In Berlin the impresario paid him 1,000 Reich Marks not to give the talk as he would have lost more if the lecture had taken place. His final lecture was at Stettin where the hall was sold out and in the final accounting the 1925 flight made a profit. Riiser-Larsen was entitled to a payment of 30,000 kronor but he chose to donate this amount to the 1926 expedition.

The commitments that Amundsen and Ellsworth had in the United States prevented them from taking part in the complex task of attending to the details that had to be sorted out in the months leading up to the flight. Amundsen then brought the Norwegian Aero Club into the venture and the Club agreed to do what was necessary to turn the preliminary arrangements into concrete agreements. The President of the Club was Dr Rolf Thommessen who was also the owner and editor of *Tidens Tegn*, a paper published in Oslo and which had one of the largest circulations of any daily in Norway. While the organisation was called (in the English language sources) the Norwegian Aero Club, it was not an aero club in the modern sense of an organisation, which trained pilots and made aircraft available to them. Its purpose was to promote aviation in Norway and get the population interested. These were the early days of manned flight and long before aircraft were everywhere and affordable air transport was taken for granted. The leaders of all developed nations realised that aviation had, potentially, great things to offer and that populations had to be encouraged or persuaded to accept aviation as part of their lives. The Aero Club took on the job of negotiating with the Italians in general and Nobile in particular. Negotiations about the conditions under which the *Norge* would make her flight, and who would be aboard continued for several months. An objective observer can see that the Italians had a strong hand when they negotiated. They had the airship and the pilot and crew and Amundsen and Ellsworth needed them more than they needed Amundsen and Ellsworth.

Nobile had asked that five Italian airshipmen be aboard the *Norge* during the flight as they were experienced in operating an airship. This was agreed to as there was a dearth of Norwegians experienced in the operation of an airship. Early in January 1926 Nobile travelled to Oslo to sign his contract.

Amundsen wrote that Nobile signed a contract which confirmed that his fee for piloting the airship would be 40,000 kroner and the very next day asked for 15,000 kroner more. The reason he gave was that he had to give up a lucrative contract with the Japanese in order to make the Polar flight. If it happened exactly as stated Nobile was being a bit slippery as, of course, he must have known about this when negotiating the lower figure. The Aero Club agreed and so Nobile's remuneration was increased to 55,000 kroner. Amundsen criticised them for it but a contract is only as enforceable as both parties want it to be. If Nobile had then backed out a law suit would have been a spectacular irrelevancy. Nobile then asked that he be allowed to contribute to the expedition book. It was normal practice for a book to be written and published as soon after an expedition as possible, to contribute to the financing of the expedition. If Nobile contributed, and was named on the title page, there would be a reasonable inference that his part in the expedition had been especially valuable. At this stage Amundsen and Ellsworth were attempting to have a say in commercially important matters by telegram and there was a limit to what influence they could have at a distance. Dr Thommesen agreed that Nobile could contribute and the final agreement allowed Nobile to contribute a section on the technical *and* aeronautical aspects of the flight. This went further than Amundsen was prepared to go but since his agent, the Aero Club, had agreed there was nothing he could do about it.

The preparation of an airship base at Kings Bay was started. Joh Höver was assigned the task of locating suitable sites for the hangar and mast and surveying them. The *Sörland* was the last boat of the year and sailed for Ny Alesund on 4 October 1925. Höver, cement, steel poles and steel bolts for the mast were aboard. The bolts were specially forged and were two metres long and 23.5cm in circumference. Bad weather slowed the passage and it took 13 days instead of the normal six and the ship arrived on 17 October after navigating through calf ice (from the glaciers) which littered the bay. The day before arrival the passengers and crew had the privilege of seeing the aurora borealis and stars reflected in the (now calm) sea. The settlement at Ny Alesund was built by the coal company which operated mines at the site. Höver consulted with Engineer Sherdal who had been at Ny Alesund for six years, particularly about the prevailing winds. After several days of exploration sites for the mast and hangar were found and surveyed in with an assistant, theodolite and measuring tape. The hangar was to lie SE by NW and was 110 x 34m and was 30m high.

Master Builder Arild and Forman Andresen were to supervise the construction. On 23 October the *Alekto* arrived with Arild, some of the men, 600m³ of timber, 50 tonnes of iron and food and equipment for 32 men for three months. There was a narrow gauge railway (operated by horses) and a spur was laid to the hangar site. The mining company had a power plant which provided electricity and enabled the work to go on under lights through the 24-hour a day darkness of the winter months. Two hundred metres[3] of concrete had to be prepared and poured for the anchoring blocks of the hangar and mooring mast. The sun went down for the winter on 26 October 1925 although the moon was above the horizon permanently and provided some light to assist the builders.

Höver departed on the last boat of the season on 30 October and left the builders to their work. The winter snow made finding the materials at the site difficult but the work continued on schedule. The mooring mast was triangular with a six metre base and a 40 tonne block of concrete at each corner. The concrete mix had to be heated in the winter cold but sand and stone were available locally and there was 30,000 tonnes of coal on site so obtaining hot water was not a problem. By February 1926 the hangar had risen to seven metres. On 15 February the framework of the walls was in place and the flag of Norway was raised over the building in celebration.

The hangar at Kings Bay was constructed during the winter of 1925-1926.The workers had to work in the cold and snow and under lights because it was dark 24 hours a day for most of the time they were there although the moon was above the horizon 24 hours a day. The hangar frame is almost completed. The walls were clad with green sailcloth panels and had no roof. The 'doors' were massive sheets of canvas winched up into place.

Snow, sub-zero temperatures, wind and darkness had not stopped the work. The hangar was a skeleton with no roof or doors. In fact it was designed to be a windbreak as protection from the wind was its main purpose. Early in 1926 the *Hobby* arrived from Trondheim with a cargo including 10,000m² of French sailcloth to cover the trestles of the hangar. Sail-maker Houdan supervised the covering of the trestles which made up the hangar walls. The sailcloth consisted of 22 patches of sailcloth each 30 x 32 x 5 metres and each furnished with bolt ropes, eyes and hanks. The patches were laced onto the wall trestles. The 'doors' of the hangar were made up of sailcloth sheets which had to cover an opening of about 30 x 24 metres and were pyramidal in shape, with part draped onto the ground. This shape reduced the strain on the walls in a gale. The doors were raised with a winch at each side. Looking back many years later Riiser-Larsen had this to say about the building of the hangar through an arctic winter:

'If there is anyone to whom I raise my hat, then it is for those fellows who, in the winter of 1925–26, built the hangar, but without a roof, at Kings Bay using canvas covered timber.'

The wooden framework of the hangar, almost finished but without the green sailcloth covering or the canvas doors. The frame was of wood and the hangar was 110 m long by 34 m wide and 30 m high. The covering was 10,000 m 3 of French sailcloth. A 30 m high mooring mast was manufactured in Italy and erected not far from the hangar.

Amundsen wrote:

> 'All who have seen the hangar at Kings Bay have been impressed and astonished; it is a great work, accomplished under more difficult conditions than such a building was ever erected under. It was built in the darkness and the cold of the Arctic night. The head carpenter, Arild, who supervised the work, and all his men deserve the highest praise.'

On 9 March the *Cygnus* arrived from Italy with aviation equipment, hydrogen cylinders and the mooring mast. The mast was assembled on the ground and raised into place with a derrick, tackle, men and mine winches under the supervision of Engineer Lund. When the hangar was covered the covering was painted green. The paint helped to make the hangar wind proof. Just before the *Norge* arrived the mast was completed by the installation of a red painted steel cone which would mate with the reinforced tip on the nose of the airship. The airship base was equipped with spare engines, petrol and oil, spare rudder and elevator blades and an enormous quantity of hydrogen kept under a pressure of 100 atmospheres in steel cylinders. A shipment of hydrogen was landed from the *Hobby* and consisted of 900 cylinders weighing 140 tonnes. The *Knut Skaaluren* delivered 3,900 cylinders weighing 625 tonnes to Ny Alesund.

While the work was progressing at Ny Alesund Höver was working on the placing of the masts in southern Norway. Höver made a careful inspection of weather records and, after a two week inspection, chose Vadsöy near the town of Vadsö for the northern mast. The mast arrived at Vadsö on 26 March and was ready for use by 26 April. Gas, petrol, oil, ballast and spare parts were made available at Vadsö. The Oslo mast was built by local contractors but the docking-basket swivelling-mount had to come from Italy. It was located at Ekeberg Flats and was not ready until shortly before *Norge* arrived there on 14 April.

While all this was going on Amundsen and Ellsworth were doing what all explorers had to do; they were raising money. In a letter dated 27 October 1925 they proposed, and had accepted, an exclusive contract with the *New York Times* for articles by them about the expedition. The contract price was $55,000 with $19,000 payable on signature of all the parties, $18,000 when the airship arrived at Spitsbergen and $18,000 when the expedition was completed. If the flight did not reach within approximately 50 miles of the North Pole the last amount was not payable and the total due was reduced to $37,000.

When Amundsen gave the first lecture of his American tour in Washington, Ellsworth attended and was introduced to the Chairman, 37 year-old Commander Richard E Byrd Jnr, United States Navy. Byrd was a courageous and determined man who was also well connected politically (his father had been Speaker of the Virginia House of Delegates and his brother was Governor of that state and then a United States Senator). Byrd was an aviator who saw that aviation had great potential as a tool for exploration, particularly in the Arctic and Antarctic. He was a 1912 graduate of the United States Naval Academy. He had suffered a serious injury during a sporting event while at the Academy and struggled to graduate and to perform his duties as a line officer. The injuries eventually lead to his retirement on three-quarter pay. Academy graduates were in demand as soon as America entered the Great War in April 1917 and Byrd was recalled to duty and learned to fly. He specialised in navigation, air navigation in particular. This skill was utilised when he was appointed to plan the flights of three NC (Navy Curtiss) flying boats which attempted a west to east crossing of the North Atlantic. The crossing was to be made in stages and surface units of the navy were allocated to support the flights. Byrd was aboard NC 3 on the first two stages of its flight to assist in the navigation. These stages were from Long Island to Halifax and from there to Trepassey in New Foundland. Only the NC 4 completed the flight across the Atlantic although the crews of the other two aircraft survived. He had a lucky escape after being assigned to the crew of the large rigid airship R 38 (its USN designation was ZR 2) which was being built for the USN in Britain. Byrd was not aboard when it took off for its fourth flight on 23 August 1921. During turning trials at high speed the airship broke up in the air and burst into flames, killing all but five of the 49 men aboard. Only one of the 17 Americans aboard survived. In January 1924 Byrd was assigned to a planned flight from Alaska to Svalbard by the US navy's first rigid airship, the USS *Shenandoah*. The flight was cancelled and Byrd's next significant aviation assignment was with the MacMillan-Byrd Expedition of 1925. This was Donald MacMillan's ninth Arctic expedition and the separate MacMillan and Byrd expeditions were combined for efficiency. One of the aims of the expedition was to prove that short-wave radios could provide reliable communications over long distances during daylight and from the 'Auroreal Belt' above the Arctic Circle. Conventional long-wave radios could not do either. Eugene McDonald, an officer in the United States Naval Reserve, second in command of the expedition and President of the Zenith Radio Corporation was in charge of the radio experiments. The communications segment of the expedition was an unqualified success. Byrd commanded the aerial part of the expedition, three Loening biplane amphibians powered by inverted liberty engines of 400hp. The expedition operated over the north-western region of Greenland and the adjacent Ellesmere Island. The flying was hazardous because of sudden gales, unlandable terrain, icebergs and navigational difficulties caused by the Magnetic North Pole being so close. One of the sailors assigned to the expedition was Floyd Bennett who was a mechanic and also an experienced and skilful pilot. The names of Byrd and Bennett would enter the history books because of the flight they would make towards the North Pole in 1926. By the end of operations 50 hours of flying had been done, much of it over terrain never before seen by man. The final flight was over the Greenland ice cap, the first of its kind. Byrd flew at 7,000ft, the service ceiling of his aircraft, and could see about 100nm in all directions. Operations were concluded on 19 August 1925 and Byrd returned to the United States determined to return to the Arctic with an aeroplane with much longer range than the Loening. He asked Ellsworth and Amundsen about their experiences operating from Kings Bay in Spitsbergen, particularly about take-off conditions on the ice of the bay. He was told that the ice would be thick enough until the end of May. At that point he planned to explore to the north-west of Spitsbergen in search of Crocker Land (which had been reported by Peary but did not exist).

Amundsen had mixed with leading public men and women for as long as he had been an explorer and the 1925 flight and the drama of his return from the dead had brought fresh fame and attention. On 21 October 1925 Amundsen went to the White House with Elmer H Bryn, the Norwegian Minister to the United States. Amundsen dressed in formal attire including tail coat, striped trousers and gloves. He had the knack of looking and dressing the part whether he was in the Arctic or the home of a President. He was introduced to President Calvin Coolidge and the event was covered by many reporters and photographers.

In March 1926 Amundsen and Ellsworth were faced with an unanticipated problem; the Italian government asked for a further $15,000 (on top of the $75,000 already agreed) for insurance. The $15,000 premium for a flight of a few weeks, from Italy to Alaska, is a measure of just how risky the flight was perceived to be. Amundsen and Ellsworth agreed to pay the insurance by way of a loan by Ellsworth to the Aero Club (which had some financial interest in the flight). When the premium was paid it had grown to $20,000. The Italians now wanted the expedition to be named the Amundsen-Ellsworth-Nobile Polar Expedition. Amundsen agreed to this and, somewhat naively, thought that this would not receive any publicity once they had left Italy.

The expedition had evolved from a Norwegian-American flight with an Italian airship and pilot to (at least in the eyes of the world) a Norwegian-

American-Italian expedition which could not have taken place without Italian technological and aeronautical expertise. Amundsen took pains to make it clear that he was the expedition leader and while Nobile was captain of the airship, Amundsen had the final say. For example, Amundsen reserved the right to overrule Nobile if Nobile wanted to turn back at the Pole rather than continue to Alaska. It was agreed that Amundsen, Ellsworth and Riiser-Larsen would consult with Nobile if such a decision had to be made.

As well as Nobile, his five Italian airshipmen and Amundsen and Ellsworth, the crew was to consist of Riiser-Larsen as First Officer and Navigator, the Swedish meteorologist Finn Malmgren, the Norwegian radio expert Birger Gottwaldt, the Russian radio-operator Olonkin, and Norwegians Oscar Wisting, Oscar Omdal, Emil Horgen and journalist Frederick Ramm of the newspaper *Tidens Tegn*. Naval aviator Bernt Balchen had been sent ahead to supervise final preparations at Ny Aleşund. Bernt Balchen and Amundsen's nephew Gustav S Amundsen (an officer in the Norwegian Naval Reserve) would be carried if the airship had sufficient buoyancy at the moment of departure from Kings Bay. Gustav had wanted to go on one of his famous uncle's expeditions since he was a child and had been turned down each time he raised the matter. The first time he asked he was so young that Amundsen simply told him:

'Go back and eat more porridge and then we will talk about it'

When Gustav was older he had his father intervene but was no more successful. Amundsen said:

'I will not agree to have any relations on such expeditions, where we are on board the same vessel for ages. The consequences are too big.'

Riiser-Larsen intervened on Gustav's behalf during the preparation for the 1926 flight. By this time Gustav was a mature adult and an officer in the Norwegian Naval reserve. He clearly had skills of use to the expedition and his uncle accepted him and had him start work with the expedition on 1 January 1926. Two months later he was sent to Italy for training with the other Norwegian members of *Norge*'s crew. It was intended that Gustav be a quartermaster; one of the crew who steered the airship with the rudder or elevator wheels. By the end of February all the crew were there except Finn Malmgren; the Swedish meteorologist and Birger Gottwaldt; the German radio expert. The trainees were quartered in the same boarding house. Nobile made them welcome and showed them around the factory in Rome. The airships were designed and the components manufactured in the factory and sent to Ciampino airfield to be assembled in the large airship hangar there. An airship for Japan was in the process of construction and the Norwegians used the opportunity to study the details of the components and the process of assembly. Gustav wrote that the truck drivers who took them to and from Ciampino were as fast and frightening as Nobile.

Gustav's opinion of the drivers bears a striking resemblance to Riiser-Larsen's opinion of Nobile's driving technique. Gustav wrote that the journey was something between a motor-trip and a flying trip along the Via Appia. The hangar at Ciampino was big enough to house two full-sized rigid airships. The hangar and the rigid airship *Esperia* were part of the reparations Germany paid to Italy as provided in the Treaty of Versailles signed on 28 June 1919. *Esperia* was one of two small, streamlined and fast passenger airships built by Zeppelin and operated by DELAG, the airline, mainly on internal services in Germany. Her sister ship was *Nordstern* which went to France and was renamed *Mediterranee*. The hangar had been built for the Imperial German Navy at Seddin in what was then German Pomerania. Also in the hangar was Nobile's diminutive semi-rigid *Mr. Norge* was being worked on by a large team of mechanics and riggers and order was emerging from apparent chaos on the floor of the airship hangar.

The handover of the ship was a major event and took place on 29 March 1926 at Ciampino near Rome. Amundsen and Ellsworth were in attendance. Dr Rolf Thommessen signed on behalf of Norway and Benito Mussolini on behalf of Italy. Part of the ceremony was a long speech from Mussolini. Mrs Riiser-Larsen then broke a bottle of champagne over the N1s bow, there was a roll of drums, and the Italian flag was replaced by a large silk Norwegian flag and the ship officially became *Norge* (Norway). By the time the ship was handed over it had been extensively modified and test flown. Ellsworth described some of the major changes with these words:

'Great changes had been made in the *Norge* during the winter, the main effort had been to get rid of unnecessary weight and thus increase her fuel capacity. She had been a veritable air yacht with a big luxurious cabin. This cabin had been replaced with another, much smaller, which was little more than a light cage with canvas and celluloid walls. The nose of the ship had been strengthened and ringed for operation from a mooring mast.'

The ship had a keel of tubular steel, hinged in places, from nose to tail. The keel was covered with the same doped fabric as the control car and was translucent. A narrow walkway along the keel allowed the crew to move about and have access to the nose, control car and the engine cars. There were three Maybach engines of 230hp each. One was mounted on struts below the keel well aft and at the same level as the control car. The other two (the wing cars) were mounted out to port and starboard of the keel about halfway between the control car and the rear engine car. The wing cars were mounted higher than the control and rear engine cars. Each engine drove a two-bladed, fixed-pitch, pusher-propeller. Each engine had adjustable louvres to regulate airflow to the radiators. All the engines could be reached from the keel. The wing cars were reached by narrow walkways. Fuel tanks, ballast sacks, provisions and emergency gear were distributed along the keel. Anything and anyone falling from the walkway would probably fall through the fabric cover and out into space. On its flights from Ciampino the *Norge* was walked out by a handling party of about 200 men. The airship was beautiful and of impressive size. It was 106m long, almost 20m in diameter and contained 18,500m$^3$ of hydrogen. It was doped silver all over and the name *Norge* in large black letters on both sides. Its Italian registration had been I-SAAN. This had been replaced by its Norwegian registration N 1 (coincidentally it was registered with the same letter/number as the Italian designation). Its size can be gauged from the photographs showing the ship surrounded by the hundreds of tiny figures of the ground crew. The ship was inflated with inflammable hydrogen because helium was very expensive and only produced in the United States. Helium was heavier than hydrogen and if the *Norge* had been inflated with it, it would not have had the lifting capacity, and therefore range, to complete the flight.

*Chapter Ten*

# Learning to Fly: Ciampino

*February–March 1926*

Riiser-Larsen was the only one of the Norwegians qualified to fly an airship and even he had limited experience of the N1 (soon to be re-named *Norge*). He had flown in her once and had flown with Nobile in *Mr* at least once. This was a 1,000m³ semi-rigid designed by Nobile and said to be the smallest airship of this class ever built. Nobile used it for developing handling techniques to be used on full-sized airships. The expedition would require him to land N1 without a trained ground crew and after a demanding flight of up to 75 hours. He often landed and took off from a nearby lake. He enjoyed flying and it was great sport as well as serious research.

After a brief course on theory of lighter-than-air flight provided by Captain Valini they joined with the Italians in flying the N 1 on training flights. The first of these flights took place on 26 February. They were driven to the airfield at the usual 'breakneck' speed and they arrived to find many journalists, military officers, photographers and spectators in attendance. On the first flight the airship carried 25 men without a problem because only a small amount of fuel was required for a local flight in fine weather. Early in the flight gauges in the control cabin showed a pressure in the envelope that would have split it open. Of course this meant that an accident, fatal to all on board, was seconds away. It turned out that the instrument was defective and the pressure was within safe limits. The instruments of this era were faulty often enough to cause problems, and the crew of a non-rigid or semi-rigid airship had to continually monitor the pressure of the lifting gas. If the pressure was too low the airship's envelope would deform and the airship become uncontrollable. If the pressure was too high the envelope would split open.

This first flight had lasted 8 hours and 30 minutes, a short flight for an airship. From then on, weather permitting there were daily training flights. On one of these flights the nose and its fabric was torn when the airship was driven against the entrance to the hangar when it was being walked out in a cross-wind. It was soon repaired but confirmed that an airship should not be brought in or out of a hangar when there was a significant wind at an angle to the hangar. An important part of the training was docking at the mast, managing the ship while it was at the mast and undocking. Using the mast was a new experience, even for the experienced Italian crew members.

N 1 was leading edge technology in 1926 and it was complicated. On the North Pole flight 16 men were aboard and 13 of them were required to fly and navigate *Norge*. The Norwegians had a relatively short time to learn the necessary skills and establish good working relationships with their Italian counterparts. They attended a brief ground school before the flying started and had to absorb some fundamental concepts. A key concept for them to understand was that an airship is a steerable balloon and behaves like one. If all engines are stopped it has to be flown like a balloon. To go up ballast is dropped (sand or water with anti-freeze in it). To descend gas has to be valved. Buoyancy will change with changes of temperature. If the gas is warmed by the sun it will expand and create more lift, and the balloon or airship will rise. If the gas cools the reverse happens. A power-off landing involves careful valving of gas. Once on the ground no one leaves the airship or balloon without orders. If someone jumps out of a balloon's basket it makes it light and it will lift off. The same applies to an airship. If a strong wind is blowing, a rip panel (or panels) will be torn out to dump the gas and the lift. Until this had been done the envelope acts like a sail and drags the balloon or airship downwind.

Another key concept was that a balloon (or an airship with the engines stopped) drifts with the wind. There is no relative wind past the envelope. A passenger in a balloon flying in a gale can read an open newspaper in the basket because of this fact. A free ballooning airship or a balloon cannot be steered. All that can be done is to rise or descend into winds which may differ in strength and direction with altitude.

The training flights started with the engines of N 1 being warmed up in the hangar. The pilot would 'ballast up', a misleading term meaning 'check the buoyancy'. Ballast would be loaded or unloaded to leave the airship in about neutral buoyancy. Then the ground crew of 200 would hold on to the control car and rear engine car and to ropes hanging down from the full length of the airship on both sides. They would need to exert a slight up or down force to stop it rising or falling. An officer with a megaphone would shout orders and the airship would be walked out onto the airfield. In light winds this was not a problem but things could get tricky. A gusty wind or one blowing at an angle to the axis of the hangar required the ground crew to use their strength and weight in an intelligent and co-ordinated way. An airship on the ground in a gusty wind would drag hundreds of men back and forward and from side to side.

If the ship was light some of the men might be lifted into the air and sometimes men holding on too long would fall from high enough to be killed or injured: if and when to let go was a matter of fine judgement. If the cross wind was too strong the airship stayed in the hangar.

Just before take-off the captain checked buoyancy. If the airship was heavy about 100kg of ballast was dropped to make it light. The captain would take off by leaning out of the control car door and ordering 'let go'. N 1 would slowly rise into the air while the mechanics in the engine cars started the three Maybach engines. After that the captain aimed to make the flight without dropping ballast to climb and without valving gas to descend. He would climb and descend dynamically with the up or down elevator.

For a short flight about 80 per cent of the volume of the envelope was taken up with hydrogen and 20 per cent with air in fabric containers inside the envelope called ballonets. As the airship climbed the pressure dropped and the hydrogen expanded and squeezed the ballonets so the air was forced out of them and out into the free air. When the airship descended, and increasing pressure contracted the hydrogen, air was admitted into the ballonets. That way the total volume was always 100 per cent. The reason for doing this was that N 1 was a 'pressure airship' and needed to have its envelope 100 per cent full and at a pressure greater than the atmospheric pressure to keep its shape. If the pressure fell too low and the envelope became less than 100 per cent full the airship would lose its shape and go out of control. N 1 was a semi-rigid with a steel tube keel along its underside and this helped it to retain its shape but managing gas volume and pressure was essential throughout a flight.

The airship was flown from the control car located under the envelope towards the nose. In it were the captain, rudder coxswain, elevator coxswain, navigator and radio operators in their separate cubicles. The rudder coxswain stood holding the rudder wheel in the front of the control gondola. The compass was sluggish in its response to changes of heading so the rudder-man picked a point on the landscape or cloudscape to steer towards. He would note the compass heading from time to time after the compass settled. The elevator coxswain stood on the starboard side of the gondola holding the elevator wheel and facing out to that side. The cruising height was about 1,000ft and this height was maintained by turning the wheel clockwise (up elevator producing a pitch up and a gain of height) or anti-clockwise (down elevator producing a pitch down and a loss of height). In front of the elevator-man were the wires controlling the gas valves on top of the airship. On the port side of the control car the captain stood keeping a general eye on the flight. The engine telegraphs were located above him. The captain could order each engine started or stopped and the rpm to be set when it was running. The engines (or one of them) could be run in reverse and this was sometimes done when landing. The radio room was partitioned off in the rear of the gondola. The airship had been fitted with aerials built on to the envelope and with an aerial with a weight on its end that trailed about 200ft from the control car in flight. It was wound in for landing. In poor visibility a crew member might be instructed to watch the aerial and yell out if it twitched on contact with the surface. On long flights a radio operator and a technician were aboard. The radio operator sent position reports and received weather information from as many stations as possible. All flight operations are weather dependent, airship operations more than most. For this reason a meteorologist was to be carried who would update his forecasts as information came in. There was a toilet and a ladder led from this space to the keel. The radio would also be used to send news reports from the journalist on board to newspapers that provided the expedition with financial support. Another use for the radio was to provide directional bearings to radio stations. These were handed to the navigator. The navigator worked at his chart table with the tools of his trade; including charts, sextants, chronometers, parallel ruler, pencils, drift and groundspeed meter, magnetic compasses, sun compass, logbooks and sight reduction tables. On a long flight the navigator was the busiest member of the crew and had very little time to relax.

The keel was a triangular structure of tubular steel covered in doped fabric. It was made of sections hinged to allow some flexing under flight loads. The keel was where the petrol tanks, oil tanks, survival gear, tool boxes and ropes and cables for ground handling were stowed. Walkways proved access from the keel to the side engines and a ladder led down from the aft section of the keel to the rear engine. Mechanics were in each engine car when it was running or being repaired. Gustav S Amundsen observed that the noise made conversation difficult and there was a strong draft through the car with the engine running and the radiator shutters, at the front, open. Right forward there was a ladder for use by a rigger who would climb out and up, over the nose, and on to the top of the envelope to check the gas valves. The envelope was divided into 10 compartments for the hydrogen. Each compartment had its own group of valves on top of the envelope. The valves could be operated manually from the control car or automatically when gas pressure exceeded a set value. Each group had a cover over it to prevent ice forming on the valves. If ice formed on a valve it might jam open or closed with drastic results. Also in the keel were three coiled ropes for hauling down and a fourth that was under the control of the captain and was used to shackle to the mooring mast cable if the airship was to be docked to it. In the keel there were 32 tanks hung up in the gang-way in pairs. For the legs of the positioning flight to Svalbard the front and rear pairs contained water ballast and the remaining 28 were filled with petrol. If maximum range was required all 32 were filled with petrol.

The airship was slightly light at take-off but as the airship picked up speed the slipstream cooled the gas making the ship heavy. The captain would order 3° to 6° of up elevator to produce dynamic lift. The sum total of static lift from the gas and dynamic lift from the airflow over the hull equals the weight of the ship and it maintains height. This kind of adjustment continued throughout the flight as the static lift changed with changes in temperature and volume of the hydrogen gas. If the airship is light, down elevator produces negative dynamic lift off the hull, which is subtracted from the static lift and the airship again maintains height. Maintaining height in this way was standard practice but did increase the total drag of the airship and the cruising speed was reduced and so was the range.

On a long flight the crew members spent some time on and off watch. When off watch they could sleep if conditions permitted it. There were no bunks or cabins on *Norge* and sleep had to be sought on the narrow gangway in the keel with a lifebelt for a pillow and only a raincoat for bedding. The gangway was constantly in use and sleep was fitful. The engineers monitored

*Norge* in flight. The Norwegian flag flys from the tail and the Italian from a weighted line below the control car.

the engines in flight. In the keel crew members managed the petrol and oil so that each engine received enough, and so that the fore and aft trim of the airship stayed about neutral.

Before landing the captain would check the buoyancy by stopping engines and noting if the airship rose or fell. A skilled coxswain could tell a lot about the buoyancy from the way the airship responded to the elevator wheel but it was safest to stop engines and let the variometer tell its story. Neutral buoyancy was ideal as the landing could take place without dropping ballast or venting hydrogen. If the wind was too strong or gusty for a landing the airship would stay airborne at low power until the wind dropped. If the wind was ok for a landing but too strong to be walked into the hangar the ground crew would have to wait for a lull and hold on to the ship out on the airfield until one came along.

On the flight to Svalbard the airship would use the mooring masts designed by Nobile and built at Oslo, Vadso and Kings Bay. These high masts had been developed by Major Scott in Great Britain and studied by Nobile on a visit to that country. Their purpose was to enable the airship to be refuelled, resupplied and maintained if there was no hangar or if the wind strength and direction prevented the airship from entering the hangar. A mast had been constructed at Ciampino so the crew of N 1 could train on it. Nobile had to train himself and the crew because the Ciampino mast was the first to be built in Italy and he had no experience of flying to and from them.

The masts were 'high' masts about130ft tall. Ground crew and airship crews had to climb and descend a series of ladders to get up and down them. The technique for mooring to the mast was for a cable from the winch at the base of the mast to be led up to the top, through a swivel arm, and out through the hollow centre of the cone. From there it was dropped to the ground and hauled about 300m downwind of the mast. The airship approached the mast from the downwind side, at about twice the height of the mast. The engines could be reversed and this would be done to take the speed off the airship or if it looked like over-running the mast. A wire was dropped from the centre of the reinforced nose of the airship. The airship then dropped some ballast forward to compensate for the extra weight of the cable from the mast, which it must pick up. The cables were shackled together and the airship was slowly winched towards the mast until the point of the reinforced nose of N 1 fitted snugly into the cone at the top of the swivel arm. The nose was then locked to the cone and a rope was attached to the nose to strengthen the connection. A gangway was lowered from the nose of the airship and connections for gas, petrol and water were made. N 1 was free to swivel through 360° while moored, so it always pointed into wind. The docking cable was released and coiled in the bow of the airship. On a training flight the crew stayed on board until the airship undocked. On the flight to Svalbard part of the crew could disembark but some of the crew remained aboard throughout the stay because the ship needed to be 'flown' while at the mast.

To undock the order 'unhook' was given and the officer in the tower complied. The next order was 'slip the rope' and the hemp rope holding the nose was slowly paid out. The captain checked that the ship was slightly lighter than air then ordered 'cut' and the rope was severed and N 1 floated away and upwards from the mast and the engines were started. Captain and crew used the Ciampino mast on a number of the training flights.

When the airship was walked into its hangar it was normal airship practice to take on ballast before each passenger disembarked. In the hangar the airship had enough ballast aboard to make it slightly heavy and it was tied down. An airship always had a crew member or members standing by to monitor its buoyancy.

On a long flight the airship would take-off 100 per cent full of gas and operate at an altitude of about 1,000ft for as long as it could. If they were forced to climb the airship would reach 'pressure height'. Above pressure height further gas would expand and increase pressure to the point where gas had to be valved off to avoid splitting the envelope. The need to avoid going

The Norwegian flag flys from the tail of *Norge*.

over pressure height meant that airships usually had to go around rather than over mountains. This was a significant limitation on where they could go and added to the distance to be flown.

Airships were every bit as complicated as aeroplanes, possibly more so in the 1920s. The captains and crews had to be well trained and vigilant, stay safe and do the job. With the large aircrews, ground crews and maintenance crews, hangars, masts, workshops and gas generating plants airships were capital intensive and labour intensive to operate.

As the hand-over date, 29 March 1926, got closer the Norwegians and Italians were shaking down into a good crew.

*Chapter Eleven*

# Positioning Flight

## *Ciampino–Pulham–Oslo–Gatchina–Vadso–Kings Bay, 10 April 1926–7 May 1926*

As soon as the handing over ceremony was complete Amundsen and Ellsworth set off for Norway by rail and ship. They would join *Norge* at Kings Bay and be aboard for the great flight from there to the North Pole and across the Arctic Ocean to Alaska.

For the flight to the Pole and beyond to take place the *Norge* had to be delivered to Kings Bay. The airship was too complex to dismantle at Ciampino, ship to Svalbard, and re-assemble at Kings Bay. The only practical way to get the airship to its base was to fly it there. The flight was to be in stages. From Ciampino the ship would fly to Pulham in Norfolk, in the south-east of England. The Royal Air Force had an airship base there with two hangars, an airship mast and supplies of fuel, oil, ballast and food. A large ground crew could be summoned to walk the *Norge* in and out of its hangar and there were facilities for the repair of airships and their engines. The radio station at Pulham provided communications and navigational assistance with its direction finding capability. The next leg of the flight would be from Pulham across the North Sea to the mast at Oslo to give the inhabitants of the Norwegian capital a view of the ship. The expedition had gained permission from the Soviet Union to use the facilities at Gatchina near Leningrad (now known by its old name of St Petersburg) and the next leg was Oslo-Gatchina. Gatchina was chosen because it had the northern-most airship hangar. The plan was to hangar *Norge* until good weather was forecast for the balance of the flight and Vadso and Kings Bay were ready for *Norge*. From Gatchina the flight was across Finland and the Baltic Sea to Vadso in the far north of Norway. The final leg was from Vadso across the Barents Sea, past Bear Island to Ny Alesund on the southern shore of Kings Bay on the Island of Spitsbergen where a complete airship base was waiting for them.

On 6 April 1926 the crew were notified that they would be departing at
10:00 on the following day. A large crowd, including Norwegians living in
Rome, came to Ciampino to see them off. Also there was Mussolini, with a
sticking plaster on his nose; he had been nicked by a bullet in an assassination
attempt the previous day. Luggage was weighed and loaded, flowers were
presented and goodbyes said. They waited for the start but a bad forecast
delayed the start. Bags were unloaded and the crew returned to Rome. Weight
and lift are always on the mind of the captain of an airship and Nobile was
no exception. He told the Norwegians that their baggage was too heavy and
there was a negotiation that ended with the Norwegians allowed to carry
one, very small, bag each. Just before the flight a case containing specially
made flying suits arrived for the Norwegians. The suits had been made to
measure in Berlin for each of the Norwegians. They were of a windproof
material and lined with lamb's wool. With each suit was a helmet and gloves
made of the same material. The case was taken away and was next seen in
Spitsbergen. The Norwegians would have to make a flight to the Arctic in the
casual clothes that they had worn to the airfield. Finally, on 10 April 1926 and
before a smaller crowd, they departed. At 09:00 Nobile ordered the *Norge* to
be walked out of its hangar at Ciampino. Watching were representatives of the
Norwegian Aero Club, the Norwegian Legation and many of the men who
had built *Norge*. At 09:30 Nobile lent out of the control car door and ordered
'let go'. Nobile was using the normal technique for launching a large airship
and had adjusted the ballast so that the airship was a few hundred kilos light
and the *Norge* slowly rose into the air while the mechanics in the engine cars
started the three Maybach engines. The Norwegian flag flew from the tail
cone and the Italian flag from a weighted line below the control car. The
route chosen allowed the airship to avoid high ground. The shortest route to
Pulham (a great circle) would have taken the airship across the Alps but this
had to be avoided to conserve gas and therefore lift. This was because a climb
would have meant that gas would have to be valved off to avoid the expanding
gas tearing the envelope open. The route was an indirect one which took the
airship north-west to the southern coast of France before turning on track
for Pulham. Nobile flew across Rome and then west towards the Tyrrhenian
and Ligurian Seas and past the island of Corsica. He had intended to follow
the Rhone up the middle of France but the forecast from Finn Malmgren,
the meteorologist, suggested that an alternative route would be wise. At
18:00 they crossed the coast of the south of France. The airship flew across
south-western France and turned northward near Bordeaux. If they had
encountered strong head winds they could have landed at the airship base at
Rochefort to refuel.

The stern of *Norge* sticking out from a hangar. Airship hangers were the biggest buildings of their day (1910–1940). *Norge* was enormous: 106 m long, 18.4 m in diameter and 25 m high from the bumpers under the control and rear engine cars to the top of the envelope. The envelope contained 18500 m 3 of hydrogen. This is one of the few photographs which gives a sense of how big the airship was. The size of airships had a positive effect on the imaginations of many and contributed to their popularity.

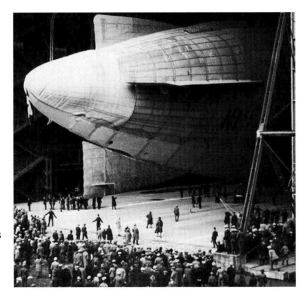

The crew was Nobile as captain, Riiser-Larsen as first officer and navigator, with the rest of the crew being a mix of Norwegians and Italians, plus Malmgren from Sweden. The *Norge* also carried Mercier, a French airship captain, to help navigate the ship if they had to divert to a French airship base. Major George Herbert Scott (who had helped to train Riiser-Larsen as an airship pilot a few years earlier) was aboard to help with communications and navigation in Britain. At 22:00 they crossed the brightly lit city of Bordeaux and shortly afterwards encountered headwinds. At times the ground speed dropped to just over 20kt.

They flew on throughout the night using two of the three motors, each turning over at 1,200rpm, giving an airspeed of around 43kt. This was the most economical airspeed and gave the maximum range. The groundspeed varied as the headwind component of the wind increased or decreased.

At 07:00 on the morning of 11 April the airship left the north coast of France near the city of Caen. The Norwegians aboard felt the cold keenly but the Italians had fur-lined coats so the decision by Nobile to deny the Norwegians the overalls, gloves and helmets delivered to the airship at Ciampino was the subject of considerable resentment. At 15:00 Norge arrived over Pulham to find a crowd of 3,000 people waiting for them. The landing did not take place until 17:00 and Crown Prince Olav, son of King Haakon VII, was there to greet them. Also present was the Air Minister as a representative of the British government. After landing the airship was walked into one of the hangars and berthed alongside the British rigid airship, R 33, the sister ship of R 34 which had made the double crossing of the North Atlantic back in 1919. *Norge* had covered about 1,080nm in 30 hours at a ground speed of around 36kt. They had been airborne for about 32 hours and were very tired.

The crew was shown to a barracks where they could sleep and were provided with food and drink. During the flight they had subsisted on chocolate, biscuits, one thermos of coffee each and water. Early next morning the Norwegians encountered a cultural difference between them and the Italian crew members. The Italians were awake and very vocal at a time when the others would have preferred silence followed by a quiet breakfast and a cup of coffee. During the stay they mixed with the crew of R 33 who were disappointed that the stay was not longer. The only member of the crew not welcome was Nobile's dog Titania who was locked up in quarantine for the duration of the stay.

The flight plan had included a stay at Pulham for about a week but the weather for the next two legs of the flight, to Oslo and Gatchina, was good so they started to prepare *Norge* for flight as soon as they had had a night's sleep and a meal. The ship had its hydrogen gas, petrol, oil and food replenished. Just before departure the chief coxswain of R 33 said that his crew would come and get them if they were forced down during their flight. Between 00:00 and 01:00 on 14 April *Norge* lifted off from Pulham bound for Oslo. Oslo was about 500nm away and the flight would take about 12 hours if there was nil wind and precise navigation, both conditions being unlikely.

'The city was en fete'. *Norge* over Oslo on 14 April 1926 before docking at the mooring mast built outside the city for the flight of *Norge*. This was the only time the mast was used. Norge carried 20 passengers and crew on the Pulham-Oslo leg of its flight to Svalbard. Passengers included the Norwegian naval attaché to Great Britain.

There were 20 persons on board including the Norwegian naval attaché to Great Britain.

Shortly after crossing the English coast and flying out over the North Sea the conditions became hazy and a crew member was placed with a bright light shining downwards to give some warning if they descended too low. An altimeter is accurate only when set to the ambient air pressure. This varies and if the pressure decreases the altimeter will over-read, the reverse being true if the pressure increases. It was best to assume that the altimeter was not accurate when flying in poor visibility. The flight continued through fog and when *Norge* emerged from it the navigator identified its position as being over Jylland, just south of Limfjord in Denmark and some miles south-east of the planned track. They changed course to port and again encountered fog which obliged them to climb above it and fly in a clear blue sky with the top of the pure white fog bank reflecting the sunshine. The air was perfectly still and they experienced several hours of a dream-like flight disturbed only by the knowledge that they could not see the surface and could not estimate their drift and groundspeed. *Norge* left the fog behind and, reaching the coast of Norway south of Oslo, they saw flags flying and many faces looking up in every town and village they passed over. After a flight of around 12 hours they arrived over Oslo and circled to give the citizens of the capital a good view of 'their' airship. The city was 'en fete' with crowds on every street, every park and many rooftops. Norwegian flags were flying in abundance. The mooring mast was at Ekeberg and *Norge* approached to make its first docking to a mast since training at Ciampino. A cable from the winch at the base of the mast led up to the top, through a swivel arm and out through the hollow centre of the basket. From there it was dropped to the ground and hauled about 300m downwind of the mast. The airship approached the mast from the downwind side, at about twice the height of the mast. A wire was dropped from the centre of the reinforced nose. The airship then dropped some ballast forward to compensate for the extra weight of the cable from the mast it must pick up. The cables were shackled together and the airship was slowly winched towards the mast until the reinforced nose of Norge fitted snugly into the red painted cone at the top of the swivel arm.

A gangway was lowered from the nose of the airship and connections for gas, petrol and water were made. *Norge* was free to swivel through 360° while moored, so it always pointed into wind. It was 15:00 and it was a little over 14 hours since departure from Pulham. The docking cable was released and coiled in the bow of the airship. Part of the crew remained aboard throughout the stay because the ship needed to be 'flown' while at the mast.

*Norge* approaching the mooring mast at Oslo on 14 April 1926.

King Haakon was on hand to greet the flyers and congratulate them on their achievements so far. It had been intended that *Norge* would stay at Ekeberg until late on the morning of 15 April but the forecast was for bad weather so the Norwegian crew members only had two hours leave to visit their homes, friends and families.

At 01:08 on 15 April Nobile ordered the airship was unhooked from the mast; the rope was paid out and then cut. *Norge* was light and slowly rose into the air while the engines were started. Norge shaped a course for Gatchina airfield, near Leningrad, about 650nm away to the east. They had promised to fly over Stockholm and Helsinki on the way to Leningrad. Fog was encountered soon after the departure and the sky was hazy so the sun could not be 'shot' to provide a line of position. The navigator could not estimate the drift without sight of the surface and *Norge* passed to the south of both capital cities. They had no navigational information from the wireless for some hours and could not communicate with the Soviet stations. When the fog cleared they were over land and thought it was northern Finland but, after changes of course and following a railway line, they read a sign at a station which said 'Varga', a town on the border of Estonia and the Soviet Union. It was 14:00 and they were south of the Gulf of Finland and not north of it.

Riiser-Larsen had visited Leningrad and Moscow in January 1926 and had no trouble finding Gatchina once the railway station was located on the map. They changed course to the north and at 21:30, in pitch darkness (there was a power failure on the ground) they landed at Gatchina. The landing party formed a v with the apex into wind and *Norge* approached upwind. The party of soldiers walked *Norge* into a hangar while Radio Operator Olonkin (a Russian) translated the orders given by the officer in charge of the soldiers. The hangar was a wooden one which had been in poor condition but had been refurbished especially for the visit of *Norge*. They were struck by the distinctive cap/helmets with the pointed top that the soldiers wore their yellowish capes and high boots. There was deep snow lying on the ground and it was very cold. *Norge* had flown 641nm in 17 hours at an average ground speed of 38kt.

They were transported on horse-drawn sledges to a building in the grounds of the old Imperial Palace of Gatchina. The accommodations were spartan but adequate and they got the sleep they craved after the long journey from England, they had been awake for most of the last 48 hours. Nobile had been awake for 60 hours. They had a long stay at Gatchina while they waited for a favourable weather forecast and confirmation that facilities at Vadso and Kings Bay were ready to receive them. Each crew member was issued with a pass and they soon found that the Soviets took security seriously. The hangar was surrounded by barbed wire and guards armed with rifles with fixed bayonets. A visit to the hangar required presentation of the pass several times and leaving the hangar the same process in reverse order. Members of the crew were in the hangar to look after *Norge* at all times, the aeronautical equivalent of the nautical 'anchor watch'. When Italian technicians arrived at Gatchina they shared this duty. There was great interest in the airship and an estimated 10,000 people passed through the hangar on the first Sunday after its arrival. The crew used their time to visit the art collections in the Hermitage in Leningrad and saw a performance of the Ballet Esmeralda. On 22 April word was received that Vadso was ready to receive the airship but two days later they heard that Svalbard would not be ready until 2 May. Nobile wrote that at that point Amundsen telegraphed him with a proposal that the flight be delayed until June on the grounds that there would be less chance of icing at that time of year. Nobile rejected that suggestion and the expedition proceeded as planned.

On 5 May 1926 at 04:30 the crew turned out and at 09:30 *Norge* was airborne. The ship flew over a Leningrad that looked beautiful from the air and then steered for Lake Ladoga and Lake Onega. The air was more turbulent than at any other part of the flight and the airship pitched and rolled continuously although none of the crew was airsick. The picked up the Murmansk railway and followed it towards the White Sea. At 16:40, just south of Kirkenes in Norway the crankshaft of the port engine broke and *Norge* continued on two engines. They arrived at Vadso, circled over the town, and by 06:40 on 6 May the airship was moored to the mast (located on the centre of a small island) and Nobile and crew were welcomed by the Italian ground crew including the inimitable Rossi. Rossi and three Italian workmen had erected the mast (constructed in Italy) in just 20 days. Nobile wrote that the flight had taken 21 hours and had covered about 730nm at an average ground speed of 35kt.

Nobile ate a meal at the Governor's house, which was decorated with Italian flags, and the crew were given as much coffee and food as they could consume by the townspeople. There were reserve motors at Vadso but Nobile elected to fly the Vadso-Kings Bay leg on two engines. He preferred to proceed while the weather forecast was good rather than change engines, by which time the weather might deteriorate.

At 15:00 *Norge* unhooked from the mast and set off, following the coast as far as Vardo, and then setting a course for Bear Island. A sighting of Bear Island would give them a positive fix and would be a departure point for the second half of this flight. Soon after leaving the coast the weather turned stormy with whitecaps on the sea and rain which turned into a heavy snow fall. A snow build-up on *Norge* had been a worry for Nobile but did not happen on this occasion. In 79° north they sighted a huge iceberg and at 21:45 *Norge* sighted Bear Island and passed to the east of it. At 11:58 one of the two remaining engines stopped with 'a broken cross-head' and for two hours they had to fly on one. The damaged engine was partially dismantled and the (very hot) parts were carried over the narrow walkway to the keel gangway where they were worked on. The mechanics re-assembled the engine and got it running. The decision to start on a long over-water flight in the Arctic with only two out of three engines running was surely an error of judgment on Nobile's

*Norge* at Kings Bay.

part but he got away with it, just. He had been on his feet for 31 hours when *Norge* left Vadso and fatigue was probably a factor in the decision to proceed without installing a replacement engine. After being awake for 40 hours Nobile slept briefly in a sleeping bag given to him by Norwegian naval officers at Vadso. Lippi, at the helm, was first to sight Spitsbergen and at 02:20 on 7 May the airship crossed the coast. They encountered fog soon after reaching Spitsbergen and made contact with Kings Bay with the wireless. At Kings Bay they sent up a small tethered balloon to mark the airship base but the fog dissipated and the base was clear before the airship arrived. At 06:40 *Norge* entered Kings Bay and Nobile saw the buildings, mast and hangar.

While *Norge* had been making its flight work had continued at Kings Bay to finish the mooring mast and to ensure the airship would find a completely equipped airship base when it arrived. On 21 April 1926 the *Knut Skaaluren* arrived at Ny Alesund with passengers including Amundsen, Ellsworth and 26 year-old Bernt Balchen, a pilot and mechanic in the Norwegian navy. Amundsen was a friend of the Balchen family and Bernt had been introduced to him in 1912, soon after his return from the Antarctic and the South Pole. Balchen (then 12 years old) wanted to be a polar explorer and said as much to Amundsen who responded with his usual amused tolerance. Balchen's parents were mortified by their son's presumptuousness in addressing the great man. Later Bernt's mother told him that Amundsen was the last Viking. Amundsen's mother had said the same thing when Amundsen was training for a life as an explorer. Balchen had studied forestry and then enlisted in the French Foreign Legion during the Great War before joining the Norwegian Army and being sent to Artillery School. After the Russian Revolutions of 1917 a civil war broke out in Finland, which had declared its independence. Balchen joined the Finnish White army which defeated the Finnish Red army. On one occasion his horse was shot from under him and he was left for dead on the battlefield. While recovering from wounds he trained hard to represent Norway at boxing in the 1920 Olympics although he was not included in the team. In 1921 he was accepted for flight training with the Norwegian Navy. He met Amundsen again in 1925, when he was at Kings Bay with the Norwegian floatplanes sent to search for the missing North Pole expedition, and Amundsen recruited him for the 1926 expedition. Just before coming to Svalbard in 1926 he had been selected for the 50km country race in the International Ski Derby at Holmenkollen and wrote that this was 'the highest ambition for a Norwegian'. In his autobiography, Balchen was open about the admiration he had for Amundsen. There was already a monument at Ny Alesund to commemorate Amundsen's epic 1925 flight.

No sooner had the *Knut Skaaluren* arrived than a two-day gale and blizzard produced snow up to the second storey of the mining company's buildings. The narrow gauge railway was under two metres of snow, and another way of getting the supplies from the wharf to the hangar and mast (a distance of about 2,500m) had to be found. Balchen repaired a tractor owned by the mining company. The tractor and a pony also owned by the company worked long hours to move cargo from the pier to the site of the hangar and mooring mast. The Norwegian Navy gunboat *Heimdal* was there to assist the expedition and its sailors worked on carrying cargo to the site. The biggest crate weighed several tonnes and the tractor broke its drive shaft towing it. On opening it Balchen and the others found lighting equipment including a large searchlight. At Ny Alesund the sun rises on 7 April and sets on 10 September so this equipment was redundant.

The mooring mast was 130ft high, the highest structure in the Arctic. It would not be usable until the red painted metal cone, that the nose of the airship docked into, was attached to its top. The sun was up 24 hours a day and shifts worked around the clock. Balchen was a skilled mechanic and after the tractor broke its drive shaft he manufactured and fitted a new one.

At 10:00 on 29 April the smoke of a ship was seen and the radio operator at Ny Alesund picked up a message from the ship. It was the *Chantier*, the expedition ship for Commander Richard Byrd's attempt to fly to the North Pole and back. At 14:00 the ship entered the bay and Balchen watched as it made its way through the 'blue and iridescent green cakes of ice which have been calved by the crumbling glacier at the head of the bay'. There was every chance that Byrd and his pilot would make the first flight to and from the North Pole. Amundsen always played down the competitive nature of the activities of the two expeditions. He always wrote that since Peary had already been to the Pole in 1909 there was no value in being the first to fly there. The Norwegian members of Amundsen's expedition did not see it that way; they had a strong loyalty to Amundsen and saw Byrd as an interloper in what should be a Norwegian effort to get to the Pole from Norwegian territory. Balchen described Amundsen as he was at Ny Alesund waiting for the Byrd expedition vessel to drop anchor:

'His face is expressionless and we cannot read it. Beneath the thick tufts of
his eyebrows, white as hoarfrost, his eyes in their deep sockets are hidden
in shadow. His cheeks are leathery and folded into hard creases, with a fine
network of wrinkles spreading out from the corners of his eyes like a map of
all the dog trails he has run. The most prominent feature of his face is the thin
arched nose, which gives him the look of an eagle. It is a face carved in a cliff,

the face of a Viking. We wait for him to speak, but he pivots on his skis without a word and strides back to the headquarters building.'

The *Chantier* asked for permission to dock but Captain Tank-Nielson of the *Heimdal* refused as he was taking on coal and water and there was only room for one ship at a time. Tank-Nielson explained that *Heimdal* had to be ready to sortie if *Norge* had to force land. His instructions from the Norwegian government were to be available 24 hours a day for rescue work, if this became necessary.

The *Chantier* dropped anchor 300m out and immediately started to discharge its cargo, including the Fokker tri-motor to be used for the flight to the North Pole. The crew was mainly volunteers, students and lawyers working for no pay, who had signed on to be part of the great adventure. Life boats were lowered and four were rafted together. It snowed as the crew tied the boats together in two pairs, nailed on beams and then planks to deck over the life boats. Pieces of ice, of various sizes, drifted past as they worked. The 14.56m fuselage was swung out over the raft and lowered on to it. The next item was the massive one piece wing. The 21.71m wing was lowered on to the fuselage and bolted in place. The sailors in the boats slowly rowed the raft through the drifting ice to the shore. A fifth lifeboat was tied to the front end and sailors in it fended off the larger icebergs. Movie cameramen from the Pathé news organisation could not get close-up shots from the ship so they set up their cameras on floating ice. The crew had improvised a slipway at the ice-edge and a pair of wheels under the plane. The plane was rolled carefully ashore with four men on each side of the fuselage and another 15–20 men pulling on ropes.

As soon as Byrd arrived there was a conflict between cameramen covering the two expeditions. Each expedition had given exclusive rights to one organisation but that meant that rival organisations were trying to prevent film being shot of 'their' expedition's activities while doing their best to get footage of the rival expedition. It was a hopeless situation but caused considerable friction until all involved saw that there was no way of preventing the 'other-side' from capturing some images they were not entitled to.

On 30 April the red-painted eight-ton steel cone was winched to the top of the mooring mast by a diesel powered winch and fixed in place. Everything was now ready for the arrival of *Norge* and Nobile was informed by radio.

A day and a half after all pieces of Byrd's aeroplane had been rafted ashore it had been assembled. The aeroplane was a Fokker F VII (a) 3/m with three uncowled wright whirlwind radial engines, each of 200hp, with one in the nose and one on a pylon beneath each wing. The aircraft was mounted on skis, one large ski under each wing engine and a small ski under the tail. The aircraft, with its one piece, thick section wooden wing was an early production model of a design which was to be used successfully all over the world. The air-cooled radial engines were a new design and were reliable and efficient by the standards of the day. The machine was beautiful in a functional sort of way. The fuselage, tail and engine nacelles were painted royal blue and the wing was clear-varnished wood. The aircraft was named the *Josephine Ford* (Edsel Ford was a major sponsor of the flight and the aircraft was named after his daughter) and the words 'Josephine Ford Byrd Arctic Expedition' were painted in white on both sides of the fuselage. The flight was an advertising opportunity for the manufacturers of the airframe and engines. Photographs and movie footage featuring the aircraft would be shown around the world. The Fokker name was painted on both sides of the fuselage, the leading edge of both wings and in huge letters below the wing. 'Wright "whirlwind" engines' was painted on both sides of the nose and on the outboard side of each of the nacelles housing the outboard engines.

The expedition also had a Curtiss Oriole (a single engine biplane two-seater with open cockpits) of the type carried by Amundsen's *Maude* in 1922–23. The ground was snow covered and a firm runway was prepared by shovelling and patting down snow. Soon after the arrival of the *Chantier*, Balchen struck up a friendship with Byrd's pilot Floyd Bennet. Bennet was a warrant officer in the USN who had been on the MacMillan-Byrd Expedition to the Arctic in 1925 and was both a mechanic and a skilled pilot. Balchen found him to be approachable and modest.

Balchen saw Lieutenant Oertell waxing the bottoms of the skis fitted to the Fokker and told him that they would not glide easily and suggested a change. The hard crystalline snow at that time of year would stick to the wax and rub it off. The skis needed to have a mixture of pine tar and resin burned into them with a blow torch. His advice was ignored and the machine was started for its first test run. The Fokker had trouble accelerating and news film shows it lumbering along at about 30kt before yawing suddenly to port and stopping. When the undercarriage was dug out from the snow it could be seen that the left ski was broken. At this point Amundsen, very sportingly, offered Balchen's services to Byrd.

Balchen had experience of flying on skis in the Norwegian winter and knew what type of ski worked and what didn't. The second time Balchen's advice and expertise was accepted with gratitude. At Balchen's suggestion the skis were reinforced with hard wood strips cut from some lifeboat oars from the *Chantier*. Members of both expeditions worked together creating the new, stronger, skis.

On 6 May Kings Bay received a wireless message that *Norge* was at the mast at Vadso and would depart for Spitsbergen in a few hours. The wireless station had been picking up messages sent by *Norge* on its way north and heard the exchange of signals with Bear Island as the airship passed it. At 05:00 on 7 May Radio Operator Olonkin on *Norge* signalled that the airship was over the head of the Bay and Höver called out the landing party. The weather was now clear and at 06:00 the men waiting at Kings Bay spotted *Norge* approaching from the south-west. The airship circled the base and then the handling guys were dropped and the airship sank into the hands of the ground crew. The wind was light, 'the smoke from our pipes went straight up', and so the airship did not have to dock at the mooring mast and could be walked into the hangar with the ground crew holding on to the ropes. The ground crew was surprised when a sudden gust dragged the airship sideways and the ground crew with it. After control was regained Nobile alighted to be greeted by Amundsen and Ellsworth. The band from *Heimdal* played the national anthems of Norway, Sweden, the United States and Italy. The crew was honoured with 'three times three cheers'. Amundsen, Ellsworth and Nobile walked over to the manager's house while the ground crew walked carefully to the hangar, bringing the airship with them. The crew was cold

*Norge* at Kings Bay with the mooring mast to the right. The Norwegian flag flew from the stern throughout the flight from Italy to Alaska.

after the flight and the housekeepers Berta and Klara made cup after cup of hot, strong coffee for them.

Balchen joined the others in the office to find them in the middle of a dispute about what to do next. Nobile, supported by Ellsworth and Riiser-Larsen, wanted to leave as soon as the airship has been supplied with fuel, oil and gas. They want to be first to fly to the North Pole and only by leaving as soon as possible would they be able to beat Byrd. They are also aware that Hubert Wilkins and pilot Ben Eielson were in Alaska waiting to start their flight to the North Pole and on to Svalbard. The Wilkins expedition had a single engine Fokker and a Fokker tri-motor like Byrd's. Accidents with both aeroplanes would mean that Wilkins could not attempt the North Pole flight in 1926 but the knowledge that the *Norge* was only one of three expeditions attempting to fly to the Pole increased the pressure on Nobile and the others. *Norge* needed to have its damaged engine replaced and extra fuel tanks installed. This work kept it in its hangar for at least three days. Amundsen was in charge and he would not do anything hasty. Balchen heard him say:

'We will not be rushed, we will take every precaution, we will leave only when the ship and the weather are right……Our flight is not a race. Its purpose is bigger than that. We're trying to chart a shorter route to the new world, and the North Pole is just a point we will pass on the way.'

Amundsen put it this way in *First Flight across the Polar Sea*:

'…Byrd's object was the Pole only, whilst in our plans the Pole was merely a station on the way. We agreed then to make all necessary preparations quietly and steadily, so that nothing would suffer on account of hasty work.'

If Amundsen could have been first to fly to the North Pole he would have but his restraint, in the interests of safety, was admirable. On 8 May 1926 the weather forecast was favourable and just after midday Byrd and his pilot Floyd Bennet said their goodbyes, started the engines and taxied out only to find that a rise in temperature had made the snow sticky. Balchen advised them to wait a few hours for an expected drop in temperature to make the snow icy again.

Some hours later, after the snow had become icy Byrd and Bennet took off and disappeared on a heading of due north. If Amundsen was disappointed at this development he hid it well.

When they return from the flight Amundsen was the first to greet and congratulate them and kissed Byrd and Bennet on both cheeks. Byrd and

Bennet were carried on the shoulders of *Chantier*'s crew to a celebration aboard the ship. Amundsen never expressed any doubt about Byrd's claim to have reached the North Pole although there are serious doubts in many people's minds. Balchen's diary notes take-off at 00:37 on 9 April 1926 and return at 16:07 the same day, for a total flight time of 15 hrs 30min and Byrd had spent 15 minutes circling the Pole. Balchen thought that they could not have done it in the time they were away. Bennet did all the flying and Byrd (out of sight in the Fokker's cabin) all the navigating so only Byrd knew if they really reached the Pole. Weather conditions, including estimates of the wind encountered, make an out and back flight in the time recorded unlikely. Also unlikely is Byrd's claim to have continued on to the Pole when he could see oil leaking from one of the outboard engines. The heavily loaded Fokker could not have remained in the air had that engine failed. Balchen later flew the *Josephine Ford* all over the United States, sharing the piloting with Floyd Bennet, and came to know as much about the plane's performance as anyone. This knowledge confirmed his suspicion that Byrd turned around about 150nm south of the Pole.

When Balchen submitted the manuscript of his autobiography shortly after Byrd died it included an assertion that Byrd could not have been to the Pole with facts and figures in support. The best cruising speed with skis was 74kt. The greatest distance that could be made good (assuming nil wind) in Byrd's stated time of 15 hours 17 minutes was 1,131 nautical miles. The return distance is 1,330 nautical miles. The Fokker could not have flown further than to 88° north.

The debate about Byrd's claim went on long after he was dead and a detailed analysis of Byrd's written record has confirmed that his claim to have reached the North Pole was false. History has judged Byrd's flight to have been a heroic failure, redeemed by his later real achievements in the Antarctic. The diary in which Byrd made his navigational calculations only became available for inspection long after his death but when it did it confirmed that his claim was false. An article written by Dennis Rawlins and published in the *Polar Record* in 2000 provided a careful analysis of Byrd's diary and established beyond reasonable doubt the falsity of Byrd's claim. Amundsen was too mature to buy into the doubts and always said that he accepted Peary's claim to have walked to the Pole in 1909 as well as Byrd's 1926 claim to have flown there. After his flight Byrd gave Amundsen some of his navigation instruments including a sun compass, escorted *Norge* for the first hour or so of its flight to the Pole and made the *Josephine Ford* available in case *Norge* was forced down on the ice of the Arctic Ocean.

Shortly after Byrd's return *Norge* was ready and the only issue was whether or not all the crew could be taken. Nineteen men were available and keen to make the flight including Bernt Balchen and Gustav S Amundsen. The structure of the airship had been made as light as possible during the modifications made at Ciampino to give it the maximum disposable lift. Weight was so important that Nobile had every crew member weighed. The ship needed to carry fuel for at least 75 hours at 43kt. All weight going aboard the airship was carefully tabulated by Balchen. Basic physics would decide how many men would be carried. The airship's lift increased with each degree the temperature dropped and with each increase in atmospheric pressure. If the temperature is low and the barometer is high the airship will lift more than on a warm day with a low barometer. These variables change by the hour and so a decision on who can fly had to wait until just before take-off. Balchen wrote later that Nobile wanted to carry dress uniforms for each Italian member of the crew but Amundsen ordered them to be removed. The uniforms are destined to be part of the post-flight controversy.

During the wait for departure Amundsen skied 20km every day to keep fit. Balchen did the same and, at Amundsen's request, taught the Italians the basics; if *Norge* was forced down all aboard would need to know how to ski. Balchen picked a shallow slope and watched as his pupils fell over time after time or slide out of control to thud into the wall of the hospital building.

On the evening of 10 May *Norge* was ready and Nobile made a final decision. Three of the crew must remain behind. Balchen was one of them and Gustav S Amundsen another. Radio Operator Genadii Olonkin had an ear infection and had to be replaced by Norwegian Frithjof Storm-Johnsen. Olonkin had been aboard *Maude* with Amundsen on the voyage through the North East Passage and Amundsen was loyal to his men. This time there was a suggestion that the 'ear infection' was a cover story and an excuse to exchange Norwegian Storm-Johnsen for Russian Olonkin.

Although the sun was above the horizon 24 hours a day there was a time of day when the air was at its coolest and most dense giving the airship its greatest lift. This was about 01:00. Nobile decided to take off late on 10 May but at 23:00 there was a strong wind across the entrance to the hangar and he postponed the departure. He decided that the ground crew were to be available at 04:00 and set 05:00 as the take off time. The ground crew and Amundsen, Ellsworth and Riiser-Larsen appeared between 07:00 and 08:00. By Nobile's account Amundsen, Ellsworth and Riiser-Larsen had compromised the flight by not being available at the earlier time set by him. Amundsen ignored this accusation and wrote in his autobiography that Nobile was in a state of great indecision and only Riiser-Larsen's intervention got the airship out of the hangar and the flight started. There is little doubt that the temperature rose steadily and Nobile had to valve-off gas three times and unload about 200 kilos of petrol. The wind got up again and at 08:00 Riiser-Larsen and Horgen picked a lull and *Norge* was walked backwards out of the hangar with a horizontal fin narrowly avoiding a scrape on the wall.

When Amundsen wrote about the interaction of Nobile with Riiser-Larsen before *Norge* was walked out he had this to say:

> 'Here again Nobile demonstrated his conduct in an emergency. We were to have yet further demonstrations on the flight.'

Just before take-off Nobile weighed off the airship and loaded some tins of petrol and sand ballast, at a total weight of about 75 kilos.

Last to board was Amundsen with a roll of charts under his arm and Balchen described him thus:

> 'He pauses at the bottom of the steps, and the meteorologist hands him a final weather reading. He studies it, and lifts his carved face for a moment to the sky, weighing his decision. It is a face that lived a thousand years ago, and will live a thousand years from now. I continue to see it in my mind long after the *Norge* becomes only a silver dot in the north.'

*Chapter Twelve*

# Hour of Gold

## *Svalbard–North Pole–Alaska, 11–14 May 1926*

On 11 May 1926 the headline of the Italian newspaper *Il Piccolo* read:

'Under an Italian flag, in the spirit of fascism, *Norge* sails in the polar sky!'

Newspapers in Rome and Oslo printed special editions to mark the departure of *Norge* from Kings Bay, bound for the North Pole, Polar Ocean and Alaska. The editor-in-chief of Oslo newspaper *Aftenposten* had travelled to Rome to report on the Italian response to the expedition and wrote that more newspapers were sold on the day of departure than were sold during the black shirt 'March on Rome' of 1922.

At 09.50 on 11 May 1926 Nobile had ordered hands-off and *Norge* rose slowly into the air leaving the ground crew and the settlement of Ny Alesund below. The engines were started, the engine telegraphs set at 1,200rpm and the airship steered for the western end of Kings Bay at an altitude of between 1,200 and 1,350ft. The people turned into dots and the buildings of the settlement, the green hangar and the 130ft mooring mast with its bright red cone got smaller and smaller. Spectators at Ny Alesund watched the airship dwindle to a dot and then disappear into the north-west.

Amundsen biographer Tor Bomann-Larsen makes the point that the flight received worldwide press coverage but that it had important political overtones for Italy and Norway. Both were young nations with something to prove to the world.

*Norge* cruised beneath a cloudless blue sky with the snow covered mountains of Spitsbergen reflecting the bright sun. There were 6,959kg of petrol and a proportionate amount of oil aboard. The configuration giving the greatest range was 1,200rpm on two engines with the third stopped. On two engines *Norge* cruised at an airspeed of about 43kt and could stay airborne for about

*Norge* being walked backwards out of the Kings Bay hangar on the morning of 11 May 1926.


75 hours. In still air *Norge* could cover about 3,225nm. At first the port and rear engines were running. The rear engine was used throughout the flight with the port and starboard engines each running about 50 per cent of the time. The airship was slightly light at take-off but the slipstream cooled the gas making the ship heavy. Nobile ordered 3° to 6° of up elevator to produce dynamic lift. The sum total of static lift from the gas and dynamic lift from the airflow over the hull equals the weight of the ship and it maintains height. This kind of adjustment would continue throughout the flight as the static lift changed with changes in temperature and volume of the hydrogen gas. If the airship is light down elevator produces negative dynamic lift off the hull which is subtracted from the static lift and the airship again maintains height. Maintaining height in this way is standard practice but does increase the total drag of the airship and the cruising speed is reduced and so is the range. At Cape Mitre *Norge* turned on to a heading of 360° and steered directly for the North Pole.

In 1961 Nobile wrote this about the start of the flight:

'I felt deeply happy: the malaise and weariness that had oppressed me on the previous evening and during the night had vanished as if by magic. How light I felt! A few hours previously I had been shivering with the cold; now I would have liked to take off my furs.'

By 10:00 the sky had clouded over and they flew over Danes Island where Andree, Fraenkel and Strindberg had taken-off in 1897. The mystery of their disappearance would not be solved until 1930.

There were 16 passengers and crew aboard *Norge*. There were eight Norwegians, six Italians, one American and one Swede. Roald Amundsen and Lincoln Ellsworth spent most of their time in the control car observing. The journalist Frederick Ramm also spent his time sitting in the control car writing his dispatches. During the early part of the flight he was able to file by having his reports sent by wireless. This was the first time a journalist had been able to report while a major aviation expedition was in progress. His newspapers published his stories while the airship was still in the air. A three day flight gives plenty of time for that kind of thing. Thirteen of the sixteen men took an active role in flying and navigating the airship. In the front of the control car Emil Horgen was at the rudder wheel and Oscar Wisting at the elevator wheel. Umberto Nobile monitored the flight and gave orders as circumstances dictated. Hjalmar Riiser-Larsen worked at the navigation table. Birger Gottwaldt looked after the wireless set and helped the navigator by providing bearings to the wireless station at Kings Bay. Frithjof Storm-Johnsen operated sent and received messages in Morse code for as long as reception allowed. Finn Malmgren updated his weather forecasts with data received by wireless from time to time. Natale Cecioni worked in the keel supervising the operation of the engines and helped Ettore Arduino to regulate the distribution of the fuel. Attilio Caratti worked in the port engine car, Vincenzo Pomella in the starboard and Ettore Arduino and Oscar Omdal took turns in the rear engine car.

The rigger and helmsman Renato Alessandrini moved about inspecting every part of the airship. One of his jobs was to inspect the gas valves on top of the ship. It was essential that they be checked to make sure they were functioning and were properly seated. If they were damaged by ice they would not seal cleanly and gas would vent continuously and destroy the airship's buoyancy with fatal results. To get to the top of the ship Alessandrini climbed to the top of the keel which finished at the nose, out through a hatch, up steps on the outside of the nose and along the top of the envelope checking each valve along the way. The top of the ship was soft. Anyone walking along the top had to time his steps to avoid producing a wave in the outer cover which might pitch him off. Gustav S Amundsen wrote that one long step followed by two short steps damped out the movement of the gas in the envelope. Anyone outside on the envelope experienced the sub-zero air and the wind chill of the 40kt-plus slipstream.

By 10:35 they were over Amsterdam Island and at 10:44 over the edge of the pack ice. They sky had been overcast for a time but now they left the clouds behind them. For the next few hours Nobile checked the groundspeed from time to time and changed altitude to benefit from the most favourable wind strength and direction. First he checked the ground speed by timing the passage of the airship's shadow against a mark on the ice. *Norge*'s groundspeed was 29kt. Nobile descended to 600ft and timed the shadow again. This time the groundspeed was just over 37kt. On the ice below the crew saw a white fox and then bear tracks. A little later they saw some white fish in pools on the ice. The sun shone from a cloudless sky and reflected off the ice sheet. Nobile ordered a climb to just over 3,600ft and checked the groundspeed again. This time he used a Goerz drift-meter. If the surface was clearly visible and the airship was in stable flight, this instrument would give an accurate reading of drift, port or starboard of course, and groundspeed. The wind had changed and the groundspeed at this altitude was almost 45kt so he maintained this altitude for the next eight hours. The speed and the clear weather contributed to high morale aboard at this stage of the flight. In 83°N they saw bear tracks. This was the last sign of life for almost two days.

Nobile wrote:

'Everyone was excited at the thought that in a few hours we would reach the Pole. The sunlight on the vast ice-field gave it a semblance of life, so that no-one on board felt that we were flying over a desert, no one was oppressed by that enormous desolation. Why, then–was it simple and easy as this to go to the Pole?'

At 18:45 the port engine stopped due to icing but was soon started again. The sky clouded over, cleared for a time in 88° north and then, at 22:15 *Norge* flew into snow and then fog. Ice formed all over the ship in minutes. Nobile had been flying low but climbed to 2,000ft and then 3,000ft to get out of the icing. When the sun was visible sextant sights were taken to determine the latitude. The bright clear sky and shining ice was far behind them and everything in sight was a 'pearly grey shade' and looked 'sad and solemn'. At 89°N the temperature was –10°C outside and –4°C inside the control car. The temperature in the control car was below zero centigrade for the entire flight.

Throughout the flight Riiser-Larsen had been working at his chart table on the navigation. Conditions inside the control car were infinitely better than in the open cockpit or crowded cabin of most aeroplanes. The navigator had a large chart table, plenty of room for his instruments and no slipstream to freeze or distract him. As well as logbooks, charts, pencil, protractor, parallel rule, sextant, sight reduction tables, chronometers and magnetic compasses *Norge* was equipped with a sun compass, Goerz drift sight and with radio direction finding. The radio equipment was also used to receive time signals to check the chronometers which were an essential aid in determining longitude.

As the airship neared the Pole Riiser-Larsen took sun-sights at frequent intervals. At 00:50 on 12 May Nobile started to lose height and had the national flags readied for dropping. At 01:30 GMT on 12 May 1926 Riiser-Larsen shot the sun and confirmed that they were at the North Pole. Nobile had the engines throttled back and *Norge* drifted quietly over the ice at 600ft. The flags of Norway, United States and Italy were dropped on the spot. They had reached the spot which had exercised the imaginations of geographers and explorers for centuries, although, in truth, there was nothing to distinguish that spot from any other on the vast ice field covering the Polar Ocean. Cooke, Peary and Byrd had all claimed to have reached the North Pole but careful review of the evidence confirms beyond reasonable doubt that Amundsen and his companions were the first to reach the spot. The careful navigation possible on an airship meant that the logbooks and other records of the flight provided clear and unchallengeable

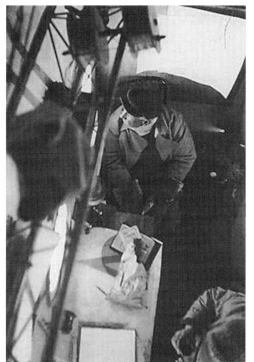

evidence that Amundsen, Nobile and the others had reached the Pole. Oscar Wisting had been with Amundsen's party when they reached the South Pole on 11 December 1911 so there were now two men who had been to both Poles.

Amundsen's role was an observer during the flight. The

Amundsen sitting in the control car of *Norge* during the flight to the North Pole and Teller on the north-west coast of Alaska which took place 11-14 May 1926 and took 70 hrs 40 min. Amundsen was the expedition leader and joined the airship at Kings Bay. The flight would not have taken place without his prestige and his acceptance of the risk inherent in a long flight over the Arctic Ocean.

agreement made before the flight was that Nobile would be consulted if any major deviation from flight plan was being discussed but Amundsen, Ellsworth and Riiser-Larsen would have the final say.

Without Amundsen's hard earned prestige there would have been no flight and if the airship had been forced to land on the ice he would have become leader in reality and not just name. He was open about his role on the flight:

> 'Naturally I had the easiest task of all on board. The others did the work of keeping the ship going, and going to the right objective. My function was solely that of the explorer, watching the terrain below, studying its geographical character, and especially keeping an alert eye out for any signs of a possible arctic continent.'

Amundsen sat in the cabin wearing enormous overshoes stuffed with senegrass as insulation, divers' gaiters and red and white gloves.

From the North Pole all directions are south. Norge headed south following the 158° meridian west of Greenwich which would take them to the north coast of Alaska at about Point Barrow. From the Pole onwards the sun was often obscured and the surface and the sky were grey with yellowish gleams as the sun tried to shine through the overcast. The wan light showed up irregularities in the pack. At 08:30 on 12 May Nobile noted that the sky had been blue for some hours and he noted from time to time how morale was always higher when the sun was out and shining on the ice. They had been airborne for just short of 24 hours and had almost 48 hours to go. The radio was not operating and if they had gone down on the pack they would have been on their own in every sense of the word. Even if radio communication was available they could not expect rescue as there were no facilities for rescue from the unknown reaches of the Arctic Ocean.

By 09:00 *Norge* was at 85° north and in a fog that persisted until 82° 40'. In the fog the airship iced up and 'ice projectiles were thrown against the sides of the ship'. Fortunately the ice caused rents in the fabric covering the keel rather than the envelope containing the hydrogen. The crew were busy sticking patches on the damaged sections using a special adhesive called emaillite. The fog not only caused anxiety about damage to the airship but meant that the surface was out of sight for long periods of time. This meant that they could not be sure what was or was not below. Finding land or confirming that it was not there was a major goal of the expedition and it was disappointing that they did not have a continuous view of the surface. Gottwaldt showed Nobile the radio antenna which was sheathed in ice and could not send or receive even if all the equipment was functioning.

By 15:37 the ship was in equilibrium in spite of having used 2½ tonnes of petrol and oil. *Norge* may have lost some hydrogen but this probably meant that the ship was carrying about that weight of ice. There was no way to de-ice the ship and about this time Alessandrini, the rigger, could not inspect the gas valves on the top of the ship because it was coated in ice and anyone walking on top would have slipped off. The airship flew out of the fog and the ice started to melt. Some of the pieces fell into the propellers and were thrown against the ship. Rents were torn in the side of the ballonets that Alessandrini could not reach to patch. Nobile ordered the side engines throttled back to limit the damage. *Norge* was driven on by the rear engine which could operate at normal revs because it was below the centre line and was out of the way of the falling ice.

The crew must have been anxious that ice would cause major rents in the envelope. If they lost gas they could compensate for some of the lost static lift by flying dynamically. They would lose some airspeed and range doing that and there was a limit to how much lift could be produced that way. There was also a real risk that the propellers would be damaged. Falling ice could chip them and the out-of-balance forces could tear them from the engines. Ice forming directly on the blades could have the same effect. They flew on hour after hour with their fates in the balance.

Between 80° and 79° north the fog opened out and they could see the surface from time to time. For the first time in hours they could calculate the groundspeed and estimate the drift. The wind had freshened and changed direction and they were drifting 13° to port. Doctor R A Harris, of the United States Coast and Geodetic Survey, had predicted that large land masse(s) would be found in the zone that *Norge* was traversing. Although they had no continuous view of the surface they could see enough to be sure that no large landmasses were in the area. From 21:15 onwards fog was encountered and Nobile climbed to 3,500ft to stay out of it and the associated icing.

Nobile described the scene when they flew out of the fog and in sight of the surface:

'Magnificent scenery, the Polar regions, just as I imagined them. The surface of the limitless sea of ice-all white-seems veiled in a transparent whitish mist. Here and there the whiteness is streaked with blue-that tenuous shade of blue, so characteristic of the ice.

The vast expanse of frozen sea, with its shadows, dark patches, embroidery of blue, was truly fascinating. From time to time there appeared long serpentine channels, dark grey in colour; and once, what looked like a wide black river, its banks formed by layer on layer of blue-sprinkled ice.'

The ice on the airship decorated it so that it 'toned into the arctic landscape'. The engine cars, solar compass, drift meter, the metal rings of the mooring-ropes and every other part were picked out in ice. A piece of ice cut a rent a metre long in the envelope and Cecioni told Nobile that they were almost out of emaillite glue.

At 06:45 on 13 May the coast of Alaska was sighted and at 07:35 *Norge* crossed the ice edge, the strip of water between ice and coast, and was over land after almost two days flying of the ice of the Polar Ocean. The rocky hills were coated with ice and snow with occasional outcrops of rock showing darkly. Nobile order a turn to starboard and *Norge* followed the coast. At 08:40 they came to Wainwright which was familiar to at least two of the airship's crew. Amundsen's second Junkers F 13 had been stored there, with Omdal looking after it, in the winter of 1922–23. Flight trials had ended in an accident and a dose of reality had caused Amundsen and Omdal to give up their planned flight to the North Pole and on to Svalbard. Amundsen told Nobile where they were and, working back, it was clear that the landfall had been made just west of Point Barrow. They had passed so close to Nome that they had been seen from there and word of *Norge*'s arrival had been telegraphed south. A note was dropped at Wainwright and this was duly reported in the *New York Times*. Nome was just under 400nm away by a great circle course and a direct flight would have taken about 9 hours in nil wind but circumstances dictated that they follow the coast and be airborne for almost another day before landing. The mountains between Wainwright and Nome were high and not well mapped, visibility was poor and the weather deteriorating so there was only one way to proceed.

As *Norge* flew south-west along the Alaskan coast the weather deteriorated and Nobile described what followed as the most difficult and dangerous part of the flight. *Norge* carried all the charts that they had been able to locate and the one for this part of the flight was not detailed or particularly accurate on the positions and heights of the mountains of north-west Alaska. Poor visibility over the sea was not a great problem but close to land and overland they could encounter high ground unexpectedly if their navigation was inaccurate. Without sight of the surface the wind speed and direction could change and they would not know it. Without a view of the sun the sextant could not be used to provide a line of position. High winds over rugged terrain caused turbulence. The airship pitched and rolled and gained and lost 150ft at a time in the turbulence. Above all everyone on board was very tired after days of little sleep and great mental strain. Nobile's logbook of the flight

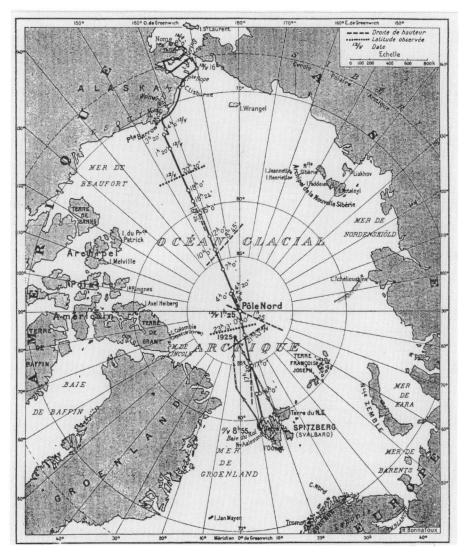

Chart of *Norge*'s flight from Svalbard to Alaska by way of the North Pole 11 May to 14 May 1926. The flight took 70 hours 40 minutes and was the first undisputed journey to the North Pole and the first journey across the Polar Ocean by any means. The dotted line is the 1925 flight in the Dornier Wal flying boats N 24 and N 25 towards the Pole on 21-22 May 1925 and the return of N 25 on 15-16 June 1925.

had little detail for this part of the flight because he was preoccupied with the demands of flying minute-to-minute in poor visibility and being uncertain of *Norge*'s position. He reconstructed the flight from memories and brief notes. *Norge* entered fog for a time and was over land when it emerged but it was featureless and no one knew where they were but guessed near Kukpuk.

Fog rolled in again and Nobile climbed to pressure height in an attempt to out-climb it. He was still in fog at 3,500ft and dared not go higher because gas would have to be valved-off and ice might form on the valve seals jamming the valves open. When they flew out of the fog and in sight of the surface they saw frozen sea. A little later they saw the ice turn into a white capped ocean and Nobile estimated that they were north of the Bering Strait over the Chukchi Sea and close to the Russian shore. Nobile ordered a course of just north of east to take them back to the Alaskan side and in due course they sighted the settlement of Kivalina. Riiser-Larsen asked Nobile to climb above the clouds so that he could get a sun-sight with his sextant and Nobile complied. The sun was so high Riiser-Larsen could not take his sextant observation from the control car window. He climbed into the keel, walked to the nose and went out the hatch and up the ladder to the top of the ship. After the sight had been taken the airship would not descend and at 5,400ft *Norge* kept climbing in spite of gas being valved-off continuously. The ship was trimmed nose up and had to be level or nose down before the engines and elevator would do the job. Nobile ordered three crew members including Gottwaldt into the nose to trim the airship nose down. They did so after some initial confusion and Nobile was able to descend flying dynamically to overcome the excess lift. Ellsworth wrote in *Beyond Horizons* that all crew members except Nobile and the helmsmen on the rudder and elevator had to go into the nose and take petrol tins and boxes of pemmican with them before the nose would go down and they could descend dynamically although he was writing 10 years after the event and probably had the details wrong.

Riiser-Larsen's sight gave latitude of 67° 5' north confirming that they were near Kivalina. Nobile was on the elevator wheel and Riiser-Larsen maintained a lookout out forward in the poor visibility. Riiser-Larsen saw that they were descending and called out to Nobile to raise the nose. Nobile wrote that he and Riiser-Larsen were working as a team and Riiser-Larsen called out and gestured towards the wheel simply to alert him to the proximity of the ground. *Norge* avoided diving into the surface by only a few feet.

They cruised along at about 600ft. Nobile noted that even the reliable Wisting closed his eyes from time to time while at the elevator wheel. Once *Norge*'s position had been fixed Nobile ordered a course that took the airship along the northern coast of the Seward Peninsula and then south around Cape Prince of Wales in the general direction of Nome. Nobile was exhausted and handed over the elevator wheel to the tireless Riiser-Larsen and sat down to rest.

They wind was behind them as they flew westward along the coast. They reached Cape Prince of Wales at 03:30 on 14 May having averaged a ground speed of 65kt since leaving the Shismaref Inlet. This was the highest groundspeed noted on the flight. The sky had blackened and *Norge* was now making little headway into a headwind. The rest of the flight would have been comparatively straightforward but they would have had to be awake and alert for hours more. Nobile and the rest of the crew were exhausted and he elected to make a landing at the small settlement of Teller.

The landing presented a great challenge as there was no trained ground crew to receive them. The problem was that, like all airships, *Norge* was at the mercy of the wind the moment it touched down. It took a trained crew to assist *Norge* to dock at a mast and about 200 men to walk the airship in and out of a hangar. He discussed the landing with Riiser-Larsen. The airship was regarded as expendable and Riiser-Larsen proposed getting the whole crew into the control car and cutting away the fabric and leaving both sides open. As soon as they touched down eight could jump out to port and eight to starboard. This was a sensible idea that would probably have worked although the airship would, relieved of their weight, then have risen and drifted off. Nobile decided to attempt a landing. He had selected the frozen lagoon as his landing place. The strong wind may have been an advantage as there would be air flowing around the control surfaces even when his ground speed dropped to zero. He would maintain steerage way until he touched down. He ordered the landing bag readied. It was a fabric tube 30cm across and 7m long with anchors at one end and a rope attaching it to the airship's bow at the other. It was weighted with spare containers of food and weighed about 275kg. When it was dropped on to the surface the weight kept it flat and the anchors dug in and held the airship nose to wind. As he approached to land he valved gas to make the ship heavy and a small group of men grasped the rope. *Norge* touched, rear engine car first, and then control car, bounced a few feet and settled. Nobile held the valves open and ordered all crew members to stand fast. He stood by the door of the control car so no crew member could exit until *Norge* was heavy. Holding the valves open he ordered the crew to disembark one at a time. Nobile sent Alessandrini aloft to cut the rip-panels which let the gas out rapidly and avoided the wind blowing the airship around as if it was a sail. He had Cecioni sever the walkway from the keel to the port engine car so that it was not driven into the keel as *Norge* rolled on to its side. *Norge* settled onto its port side without further damage. It was 07:30 GMT on 14 May 1926 (20:30 13 May 1926 local time). The landing is probably one of the outstanding examples of airmanship of the airship era. The flight itself is one of the greatest ever made in an airship. The airship had been airborne for 70 hours 40 minutes. Nobile noted that *Norge* had flown 2,763nm at an average ground speed of 39kt. Amundsen wrote this of the landing:

On the morning of 14 May 1926 Nobile made a perfect landing at Teller in Alaska. There was no trained ground crew and he relied on a 'landing sack' to act as a sort of sea anchor to keep *Norge* facing into wind while the airship touched down. He ordered the rip panels opened to spill the gas as quickly as possible. This photograph shows *Norge* deflating as planned.

Another view of *Norge* deflating at Teller on 14 May 1926.

'But for the bump against the air fender [below the control car] causing us to spring some metres in the air, we should scarcely have noticed the landing, so finely was it done.'

They had completed the first flight to the North Pole, the first journey of any kind across the Polar Ocean and the first flight from Europe to the Americas by way of the Pole. Although Byrd's claim to have made the first flight to the North Pole denied Amundsen, Ellsworth and Nobile that particular honour in their lifetimes, the other achievements brought them fame, publicity and, in Amundsen's case renewed recognition as a successful explorer of the Arctic.

## Chapter Thirteen

# Enough Credit for Everyone

*Teller–Nome–Seattle–Rome–Oslo, 1926*

A journalist made a very accurate and acute observation. He wrote that at the moment of the landing everyone on board deserved and would be given the appropriate credit for the achievements of the flight. Any squabbling between them over who had contributed the most could only diminish the respect and affection given to them. It was not a zero sum game although that term was not known in 1926. Credit to one participant did not reduce the credit given to another.

The whole population of Teller came to welcome them although they showed no particular surprise at being visited by the first airship to fly to Alaska. In his autobiography Ellsworth wrote:

'For two days we had been reduced to gnawing at blocks of chocolate and frozen bricks of pemmican for food. We were even suffering pangs of thirst, since long ago the coffee and tea in our thermos flasks had frozen solid….the good women of Teller had rushed to their cook stoves……hot dinners were ready for us. Too exhausted to do more than mumble our thanks, we gorged and then tumbled into beds to sleep, most of us, for 20 hours or more.'

Amundsen recorded a more spiritual moment after arriving at Teller with the journey complete and all the participants on American soil, alive and well:

'Honour be given to whom honour is due. Let us then be of one mind in giving to Him the honour Who on several occasions on this venture clearly and distinctly held His Hand over us and protected us. Let there be no disputed as to who amongst us was the best. We are all so pitifully small, if God the almighty does not help us.'

Teller was an outpost on the Alaskan frontier. There had been settlements in the area for some time but Teller was established in 1900 after the discovery of gold at the Bluestone Placer Mine, about 25km to the south. At the height of the gold rush Teller had a population of about 5,000 and was a major trading centre. In 1926 the population was about 250, over 90 per cent of whom were Native American. The main activities in 1926 and in 2009 were subsistence hunting and fishing.

Nobile and crew spent 18 days dismantling *Norge* so that it could be transported by ship back to Italy. Disagreements surfaced almost immediately. Nobile complained about some events soon after the arrival. One of the Norwegians saw him watching the others at work on the airship and told him he should be working not just supervising. He chose to take offence and said that he had been insulted. Ellsworth advised him to forget about the 'insult'.

Amundsen and Ellsworth looked at their writing contracts for the first time and realised it committed them to write 75,000 words for the *New York Times*. An exchange of telegrams confirmed that the newspaper held them to their contracts. They left the others behind and travelled to Nome where they hired a room and got down to work. In three weeks Amundsen, Ellsworth, Riiser-Larsen, Malmgren and Ramm wrote a total of 80,000 words. They sold tins of petrol for $10 each (for use and for souvenirs) and swatches of fabric from the envelope of *Norge* where taken by (rather than purchased) for souvenirs. Ellsworth wrote about anything local that was interesting and sent the stories to the *Times*. He visited several of the mining camps and wrote about them.

President Calvin Coolidge sent this telegram to King Haakon VII:

'I desire to offer your Majesty and the people of Norway my congratulations on the success which has attended the bold undertaking of this hardy and intrepid descendant of the Vikings. It is a matter of great satisfaction that one of my countrymen should be associated with him in this daring and courageous exploit.'

A similar one was sent to the Italian King who had had flown in *Norge* and listened to a lecture by Riiser-Larsen on the proposed flight.

Amundsen would also be honoured by Congress of the United States. Congress ordered a silver medal struck to mark the flight and awarded to Amundsen. The obverse showed a radiant North Star with a female face over a map of the edge of the Arctic Ocean. Around its edge were the words:

'For his courage sagacity and perseverance in the transpolar flight in the dirigible Norge May 1926'

The reverse of the medal showed *Norge* flying over the North Pole with these words around its edge:

'Awarded by the Congress of the United States to Roald Amundsen'

Nobile had intended to travel to Japan from the United States to supervise the assembly and flight testing of one of his airships which had been sold to the Japanese government. Mussolini (air minister as well as prime minister of Italy) saw the propaganda value of the flight. It could, if handled the right way, enhance the reputation of fascist Italy amongst Italians living abroad and the world generally. He promoted Nobile to General and instructed him to embark on a long tour of the United States. Interest in the flight was high and Nobile

Amundsen and Riiser-Larsen at Nome Alaska after landing at Teller on 14 May 1926.

received 'an avalanche of telegrams'. Nobile spent much of his time at Nome writing articles for the Italian newspaper *Corriere della Sera*.

Photographs of Amundsen, Ellsworth, Riiser-Larsen and Nobile taken at Nome shortly after the completion of the flight show four relaxed and happy individuals. Amundsen in particular looks like a man who has done what he intended to do and now intends to enjoy himself. They are the only photographs which the author has seen showing Amundsen smiling broadly. In 1927 Amundsen wrote:

'For I am here confiding to the reader that I consider my career as an explorer closed. It has been granted to me to achieve what I set out to do. That is honour enough for one man.'

It reflects credit on Amundsen that in the autobiography he took pains to praise his old comrade Oscar Wisting and to write how much pleasure he (Amundsen) took from having Wisting with him at both the South and North Poles.

On 17 June the expedition members boarded the *Victoria* bound for Seattle. After two days delay caused by ice, a stop on at Falsepasse in Aleutian Islands, and some unpleasant weather they arrived in Seattle on 27 June. Nobile was greeted by a boat flying the Italian flag and crowded with men and women singing in Italian. Ellsworth watched Nobile, wearing the uniform of a General in the Royal Italian Air Force, giving the fascist salute and acknowledging the applause. The expedition broke up with Ellsworth staying in America, Amundsen going home to Norway and Nobile going on tour in America as ordered. Nobile summed up the expedition in these words:

'Our names were henceforward linked together in the history of Polar exploration. Together we had crossed the Arctic; together our flags had dropped upon the Pole. Each of us had contributed his own share to the success of the enterprise. Amundsen, who had first thought of it, had brought the prestige of his past exploits; Ellsworth had made it a practical possibility by putting up his share of the expenses; I had born the responsibility of preparing the ship and superintending the flight from Rome to America. Our widely divergent life-paths had run together for a while; but know at Seattle they branched off again….I was never to see Amundsen again, though once more his name was to be linked with mine.'

At each stop on Nobile's tour of America he gave speeches and lectures to large crowds of Italian immigrants. In Washington Nobile was invited to meet President Calvin Coolidge. He took his dog Titina who proceeded to misbehave on the Presidential carpet. Coolidge laughed the incident off and treated it as an ice-breaker.

Nobile was treated like a hero and the press coverage of these events irritated Amundsen and Ellsworth. They saw the speeches and the coverage as claiming a priority for himself and the Italian members of the crew to which they were not entitled. To Amundsen, Nobile was a hired pilot and all kudos was due to Amundsen, Ellsworth and to Norway. Amundsen and Ellsworth felt that the more credit that Nobile and the Italians got, the less was due to them. In the expedition book, *First Flight across the Polar Sea*, published in late 1926, he did not use the official title of the expedition which was the 'Amundsen-Ellsworth-Nobile Polar Flight'. Nobile's contract allowed him to contribute a section on technical and aeronautical matters to the book but this did not happen. Amundsen, Ellsworth, Riiser-Larsen, Gottwaldt, Hover, Gustav S Amundsen and Finn Malmgren all contributed.

Amundsen and the other Norwegian crew members arrived back in Norway on 12 July. They were guests of the town of Bergen and found that every house was flying the Norwegian flag, the steamships were sounding their whistles and were dressed overall with flags and the officials of the town were there to greet them. There was a formal dinner and a ball. There were flowers, cheers and speeches. When they set sail in the *Stavangerfjord* for Oslo they travelled as guests to the steamship company. As they passed Haugersand the locals 'sent out a large fleet of all kinds of craft with music and cheering'. The ship stopped at Stavanger for a few hours and there were banners depicting Amundsen's achievements from the North West Passage in *Gjøa* to the flight of the *Norge*.

At Christiansund they were woken and welcomed by Leif Dietrichsen with a huge bouquet of roses. Aircraft from the army and navy flew over their ship. At Oslo the weather was clear and sunny with flags flying and streets crowded as Amundsen and the others were driven through the capital in open limousines. Speeches were made and acknowledged and the reception was concluded by an audience with the King and Queen. Members of the expedition had decorations conferred on them and the naval officers received promotions.

Back in February 1926 Amundsen had signed a book contract with a publisher in New York. The book was to be an autobiography and was appropriate because he had made it known that the 1926 expedition was his last. His career over Amundsen set to writing his autobiography. Amundsen was an experienced and successful author. His books included a two volume account of the *Gjøa* expedition through the North West Passage in 1903–1907, a two volume account of the Antarctic expedition of 1910–1912 which had included the attainment of the South Pole and the 1925 Polar Flight. He had also written countless magazine articles and scripts for his lecture tours. The book emerged as *My Life as an Explorer* and was published in 1927 in a number of languages.

Amundsen found it difficult to 'settle down' and seems to have written the autobiography in a state of mild depression. He had never married but had enjoyed the company of a number of women over the years including some who were still married at the time. His career, which took him away for years at a time and also required a great deal of travelling to lecture and raise funds, had made him a glamorous but difficult man to have a relationship with. There was to be a final relationship and he would have married but for the events of mid 1928 in the Arctic near Svalbard.

He covered an extremely rich and complex life in a book of only 282 pages. It was notable that he referred to, but did not name, the leader of the 1897–1899 expedition which had given him his first taste of exploration in high latitudes. He did write warmly of the men, mostly Norwegian, who had been with him and made his achievements possible.

Amundsen had been lukewarm towards Nobile in *First Flight across the Polar Sea* but was positively hostile in his autobiography. When Amundsen came to write his autobiography in 1927 the events were fresh in his mind and the wounds still raw. Amundsen's career had lasted 30 years and yet he devoted 103 out of 282 pages in *My Life as an Explorer* to the *Norge* expedition. He even had Riiser-Larsen contribute an appendix in the autobiography devoted to corroborating his criticisms of Nobile. He alleged a number of events in the flight which portrayed Nobile as a hysterical incompetent saved only by the intervention of the Norwegian Riiser-Larsen.

The controversy emerged soon after the landing of the *Norge* in 1926 and was still alive when Nobile's *My Polar Flights* was published in 1961. The criticisms varied from the deeply relevant to the slightly childish. For example, the Amundsen faction noted that the Norwegian and American flags dropped at the North Pole on 12 May 1926 were small and purely symbolic while the Italian flag was huge and so big it was difficult to handle in the confines of the control car. Amundsen wrote that Nobile had stood by idly while Riiser-Larsen and Horgen directed the ground crew while they walked the *Norge* out of the hangar at Kings Bay of the morning of 11 May 1926. Nobile's very credible comment was that since the ground crew spoke Norwegian it was sensible of him to give the orders to the two Norwegian officers and let them get on with it. Film of the airship being walked out shows Nobile watching it happen. Nobile wrote that the inexcusable delay by Amundsen and the others caused an operational issue. Although it was daylight 24 hours of the day at Kings Bay the temperature varied. The lowest temperature was at about 01:00 every morning. That was the time when the air was coldest and most dense. An airship's lift (buoyancy) is greatest at that time. In an ideal world the take-off would be made at that moment because the greatest load, including fuel and passengers, could be lifted then. Winds prevented walking out and take-off then but Nobile requested the ground crew for 04:00 and Amundsen and the others for 05:00. Nobile says that there was an unnecessary delay of several hours. During the delay Nobile had to valve off gas three times as the temperature rose and the gas expanded. The lift lost was equivalent to the weight of two heavy men. Bernt Balchen and Gustav S Amundsen, who had contributed so much time, energy and expertise to the expedition, could have flown but for the delay. It seems that Nobile's point is a valid one. There is the matter of the warm flying suits and helmets delivered to Ciampino just before take-off on 10 April 1926. They had been made to measure at some trouble and expense in Germany. Nobile sent them by ship to Kings Bay leaving the Norwegians to make long flights of many hours in inadequate clothing. The reason was that they weighed too much and there was not enough lift for them. Nobile took his dog, which weighed only a few kilograms, with him on the flights. The dog's weight is not important but the symbolic significance of it was. It was poor leadership to insist on carrying dead weight and yet refuse to take the flying suits which would add much to the efficiency and comfort of the crew. When Ernest Shackleton abandoned *Endurance* in the ice off Antarctica in 21 November 1915, he insisted that no unnecessary items be carried on the long and dangerous journey across the ice dragging the boats and supplies they needed to survive. He made his instruction so much more salient by taking out his gold pocket watch and leaving it on the ice. That is leadership, one of the most important skills an explorer should possess. Nobile's virtues did not include the insight required to be a great leader of men. The dog and its symbolic significance were lost on Nobile and it would come back to haunt him in 1928.

Riiser-Larsen criticised Nobile for sleeping most of the way from Vadso to Kings Bay on 6–7 May 1926. More importantly Nobile had elected to depart Vadso with one of the three engines out of action. There were spare engines available at Vadso and the engine could have been changed at the mast. Another motor failed during the flight, something that was a distinct possibility, and for some hours *Norge* flew on one engine. The decision to make a flight across the Barents Sea on two engines was clearly a significant error of judgment and yet does not figure in the catalogue of complaints against Nobile.

When *Norge* was over the Chukchi Sea in the final hours of the flight from the North Pole to Alaska Riiser-Larsen asked Nobile to climb above the clouds so that he could get a sun–sight with his sextant and Nobile complied. At 5,400ft *Norge* kept climbing in spite of gas being valved off continuously. The airship was trimmed nose up and the only way to change that was by shifting weight forward. Nobile ordered three crew members including Gottwaldt into the nose to trim the airship nose down. They did so after some initial confusion and Nobile was able to descend flying dynamically to overcome the excess lift. This incident was also retold by Amundsen who claimed that Nobile was shouting and crying and had lost control of his emotions. Nobile wrote that he may have been showing signs of stress but he was not crying or out of control and that he had to repeat the order because of language issues in an airship flown by a crew who spoke Norwegian, Italian, English and Swedish. Ellsworth wrote that all of the crew except Nobile and the two men on the rudder and elevator wheels had to go into the keel and go as far forward as possible dragging as many containers as they could, before the airship became trimmed nose down. This seems unlikely and adds nothing to the dispute of facts. Whatever the details, Nobile got the airship under control and was entitled to be stressed. No one would be on top of his game after 90 hours with only a few hours of sleep. They were about 60 hours into the flight at that stage and Nobile had had little sleep the day before the take-off. He, more than most of the others aboard, had had to cope with several weeks with many hours flying and few hours of sleep.

Riiser-Larsen wrote that Nobile ceased to function adequately in the final hours of the flight. On one occasion Nobile was on the elevator wheel and Riiser-Larsen was maintaining a lookout out forward in the poor visibility. Riiser-Larsen saw that they were descending and called out to Nobile to raise the nose. Amundsen wrote that Nobile stood as if in a trance and did nothing and Riiser-Larsen had to grab the wheel and apply nose up elevator. Nobile wrote that he and Riiser-Larsen were working as a team and Riiser-Larsen called out and gestured towards the wheel simply to alert him to the proximity of the ground. They were so low that when the airship pitched up, as intended, they looked aft and watched the rear engine car to see if it would hit the ground. Whatever happened, it seems clear that *Norge* avoided diving into the surface by only a few feet. Nobile pointed to Amundsen's technical mistakes when writing about the flight. Amundsen did use the word rudder when referring to the elevator but he was in good company as Wilbur and Orville Wright used 'front rudder' when referring to what came to be described as the elevator. Amundsen claimed that Nobile had been confused and claimed that a line of position could give them latitude and longitude when it could only give them latitude. Who can be sure what happened when all were at the end of their physical endurance? Then there was the issue of the Italian uniforms. Nobile said that the officers' uniforms worn after the flight had been worn under the cold weather gear. Amundsen accused him of carrying the 'heavy' uniforms in spite of the critical importance of minimum weight at take-off. Ellsworth wrote, ten years later, that Amundsen had seen the parcel of uniforms on *Norge* on the day of departure and ordered it removed but this does not ring true. Either they were worn under the cold weather gear or Nobile was dissembling when he wrote about them.

One thing is clear, Amundsen chose to criticise Nobile when Nobile had done no more than respond to Mussolini's lead in emphasising Italy's major contribution to the flight and its success. Doctor Thommessen said that he estimated that Italy had contributed the most to the finances of the 1926 flight, Norway the second greatest amount and the United States (Ellsworth) $100,000, a considerable amount but less than the other two countries.

Eighty-seven years after the flight it is not possible to say what really happened and I am not sure that it is all that important. Riiser-Larsen emerges from the story as an authentic hero, skilful and strong when those attributes were needed and surely posterity owes the others our admiration for their many virtues. Without Amundsen's prestige and courage, Nobile's engineering and piloting knowledge, Riiser-Larsen's navigation skills and strength and endurance and the skills and endurance of the crew there would have been no flight. We do know that Amundsen and Nobile and their crew achieved what no one had achieved before. They had flown to the North Pole, across the Polar Ocean to Alaska, filled in parts of the map which had been blank since the beginning of geography, proved that aircraft were the way of the future and all of them were alive to enjoy the acclaim. Everyone has shortcomings and makes mistakes. Amundsen and Nobile are no exceptions. We should discard the petty controversies and admire them for their energy, imagination, skills and achievements.

On 24 December 1927 came the news that Oscar Omdal was missing over the Atlantic. Omdal had been recruited by Bernt Balchen to be reserve pilot on Richard Byrd's first Antarctic expedition on which he would attempt to fly to the South Pole. The expedition was due to last from 1928–1930. While Omdal was waiting he was engaged to fly a Sikorsky S-36 amphibian named *Dawn* and owned by property developer Francis Wilson Grayson.

The Sikorsky S-36 amphibian *Dawn* owned by Francis Grayson. On 23 December 1927 Oscar Omdal took off from New York bound for Harbour Grace, New Foundland on the first leg of a Trans-Atlantic flight with the ultimate destination Copenhagen. Aboard were Omdal, Grayson, navigator Brice Goldsborough and radio-operator Frank Koehler. No trace of the aeroplane or its crew was ever found.

Grayson had made two previous attempts to fly the Atlantic with pilot Wilmer Stultz and a navigator and radio operator. Both attempts were made from Old Orchard Beach, Maine in October 1927. On the first the aeroplane encountered a strong headwind soon after take-off and was reluctant to climb. Fuel was jettisoned and a safe return was made. On the second attempt the Sikorsky was 500nm east of America when the pilot decided to turn back, much to the annoyance of Grayson. Omdal was a replacement for Stultz. On 23 December 1927 Omdal, Grayson, navigator Brice Goldsborough and radio operator Frank Koehler took off from Curtiss Field in New York bound for Harbour Grace, New Foundland with the ultimate destination being Copenhagen. They reported heavy icing off Boston and the aircraft failed to arrive at Harbour Grace. No trace of the *Dawn* or its occupants was ever found. Aviation was dangerous in those days. Navigator Goldsborough had a son who would die in an aircraft accident aged 20 in 1930.

*My Life as an Explorer* was a bitter and small-minded effort by a man who had deserved every ounce of the respect and affection he garnered from his achievements. Amundsen biographer Bomann-Larsen described this part of Amundsen's life as 'literary suicide'. The book was released in a number of languages but never quite made it to the bestseller lists. Even people who admired Amundsen were shocked by the bitter tone and the lack of generosity of spirit the book displayed. It was as if he had been transformed by retirement, by the knowledge that he would never go on another expedition, would never return to the acclaim he had become accustomed to. Perhaps he felt as Winston Churchill did on being voted out of office as Prime Minister after winning the war in Europe. There is a story, possibly apocryphal that Churchill said 'life is so boring without a war to fight'.

*Chapter Fourteen*

# Our Names Would be Linked One More Time

## *Italy–Svalbard–Arctic Ocean–Norway–Barents Sea, 18 June 1928*

While Amundsen was writing his autobiography Nobile returned to adulation in Italy. There were state banquets and flowers, parades and medals and the promotion to General. In 1961 Nobile would write that he did not read the autobiography until after returning from the Arctic in 1928 although he must have heard of the unflattering comments which it contained.

Mussolini had recognised the propaganda value of the flight of the *Norge* and was receptive to Nobile's next proposal. He wanted to build an improved airship based on the *Norge* and fly it to Svalbard and from there make a series of flights to search for undiscovered lands and fill in the blanks that still existed in the maps of the Arctic. Nobile discussed it with Dr Thommessen, President of the Norwegian Aero Club, and it was agreed that Nobile would have the right to use the mast and hangar at Kings Bay and the mooring mast at Vadso for a period of three years. There was a delay as Mussolini instructed him to complete an airship several times the size of *Norge*, for a non-stop flight from Rome to Buenos Aires in Argentina. This was cancelled and the airship broken up before completion while Nobile was in Japan supervising the assembly of an airship he had designed for the Japanese. He came into conflict with Italo Balbo. Balbo (1896–1940) was a fascist Black Shirt who had helped organise the March on Rome of 1922. In 1926 he began the build-up of the Royal Italian Air Force and he had a great deal of power in the Fascist Government including over aviation matters. Nobile had asked that the big ship be completed for use in the Arctic but Balbo squashed the idea and insisted on the scrapping of the partially completed airship.

A plan evolved to explore the region of Severnaya Zemlya (Nicholas II Land), the northern coasts of Greenland, the Canadian Arctic and the region of the North Pole. There was also to be an ambitious scientific programme involving, inter alia, the study of oceanography, terrestrial magnetism and atmospheric electricity. Scientists were recruited to carry out this programme. As on Amundsen's expeditions, a scientific programme was embarked upon to legitimise the flight and to help raise funds. Part of the plan was to land a number of scientists at the Pole and to retrieve them after they had completed their observations. This required the development of a system of cables, a winch and baskets which would be used while *Italia* remained airborne.

The Italian Royal Geographical Society and the City of Milan provided funding and support. Mussolini and Balbo agreed to *Italia* being used in the expedition. The airship had a lighter structural weight than *Norge* and therefore had a greater useful lift to be used for passengers and crew, petrol and oil and scientific equipment. *Italia* was completed and test flown in the summer of 1927 and the expedition planned for mid-1928. It was to be an almost all Italian expedition so there could be no doubt which country would garner the credit and prestige when it reached its successful conclusion. Nobile finalised a list of 18 men (including himself) and the dog Titina for the flights. Dr Finn Malmgren, the Swedish meteorologist from the *Norge* flight, and Dr Francis Behounek a Czechoslovakian scientist would be the only non-Italians aboard. Nobile arranged for some Alpini mountain troops to be at Kings Bay as part of the ground support in case a rescue from the ice was necessary. For the same reason he requested that some seaplanes be sent to Svalbard. Balbo vetoed Nobile's request that one or two seaplanes be sent to Kings Bay with the *Citta de Milano* which was the support ship.

*Citta de Milano* and *Hobby* departed for Svalbard in March 1928. On 31 March the crew were received by Pope Pius XI who entrusted a large wooden cross to Nobile and asked that it be left at the Pole. *Italia* positioned to Milan and departed from there at 01:55 on 15 April, with 20 people aboard, for Stolp in Germany. *Italia* went by way of Vienna and Breslau through some very rough weather and arrived after a flight of about 1050nm in 29 hours and 55 minutes. Hail had eroded all three propellers and two of the fins were damaged. Materials and mechanics were railed from Italy and 10 days were spent waiting and repairing and reinforcing some of the damaged components.

On 2 May at 03:28 *Italia* departed for Vadso. At 11:30 that day *Italia* was over Stockholm with an escort of aeroplanes from the Swedish Navy. Finn Malmgren recognised his house. *Italia* descended and Malmgren dropped a letter to his mother. The airship was moored to the mast at Vadso 29 hours 52 minutes after leaving Stolp, after a flight through some more bad weather.

Refuelling and gassing up was completed in a few hours but bad weather delayed the start. *Italia* swung port and starboard at the mast while gusts of up to 35kt caused damage to metal tubing at the tip of the stern, which was repaired. After a long wait and rain which saturated the inside of the control car *Italia* departed for Kings Bay at 08:34 on 5 May arriving at Kings Bay after flying over the weather station on Bear Island. On the flight they encountered strong winds and some snow storms while an engine failure meant that only two were available. At 12:45 on 6 May 1928 the landing ropes were dropped at Kings Bay. The landing was made in gusty winds meaning they had to moor to the mast until the weather permitted *Italia* to be walked into the shed. It had taken *Italia* from 15 April to 6 May and 75 hours 58 minutes flying time to fly from Italy to Svalbard. Nobile had been aboard *Italia* continuously since leaving Stolp and had not left the airship for 82 hours when he disembarked in the Kings Bay hangar.

It took four days for the material aboard *Citta de Milano* to be dragged over the snow to the hangar and for the airship to be repaired and for petrol, oil, gas and supplies to be loaded on it. The scientific equipment was checked and the weather map studied before the first flight.

*Italia* took off for its first flight of exploration at 07:55 on 11 May. With 14 men aboard it turned north at Cape Mitre and coasted along Haakon VII Land. A worn wire cable in the rudder circuit was repaired in flight. They turned east at Barren Cape and headed for Moffen Island. Shortly after the turn the weather deteriorated and a violent gale came up with cloud and snow. Ice formed all over *Italia* with snow sticking to the fabric walls of the control car and the airship pitched and rolled in the turbulence. Nobile received reports of deteriorating weather all along the intended route and decided to turn back. *Italia* was soon back in the hangar after a flight of eight hours.

At 13:15 on 15 May *Italia* again took off with 14 aboard for a flight to Severnaya Zemlya. Severnaya Zemlya was of particular interest because only the east coast had been explored and a flight up the west coast would put its major features on the map. The route was north up the west coast of Spitsbergen, north-east along the northern coasts of North East Land and the islands of Francis Joseph Land and then south-east towards Severnaya Zemlya.

Cloud came down and ice formed on the control car, keel and envelope. The icing was serious and the airship became heavy. Nobile descended under the cloud and the ice stopped forming. Ice had formed on the propeller which drove the dynamo to charge the radio batteries. Ice was thrown from it and hit the control car with a noise like a pistol shot. They sighted an island in the Franz Joseph Land group and coasted along the other islands in the group in poor visibility. Course was altered to the south-east to head for the west coast of Severnaya Zemlya.

They had been airborne for 34 hours and the only life seen so far was some black birds and a single bear. The journey had lasted 10 hours longer than expected and had eaten into the reserve of petrol so Nobile changed course to the south-west before reaching Severnaya Zemlya and headed for Cape Zelantya on the northern tip of Novaya Zemlya. *Italia* turned south at the Cape and followed the coast to Cape Nassau then north-west to North East Land and back to Kings Bay. They landed at 09:15 on 18 May; having been in the air for 69 hours they disproved the existence of Giles Land, on the charts since 1707, and made the first crossing of North East Land proving that it was not thickly covered in ice as had been believed. They had covered about 2,080nm and explored 44,700km $^2$ of previously unknown territory.

On 23 May 1928 at 12:30 *Italia* took off with 16 men aboard on a flight which would take it to Cape Bridgman on the north-east tip of Greenland, the North Pole and south-east to North East Land in the Svalbard archipelago. At 00:24 they arrived at the Pole by way of Cape Bridgman after a flight of 19 hours. The plan was to lower several scientists on to the ice to make observations. A winch, an inflatable raft and survival packs had been prepared for this purpose but windy conditions prevented it being carried out. The circled the area for several hours making observations and dropping the cross, the Italian and Milanese flags and a religious medal (the Virgin of the Fire) from the citizens of Forli. For six Italians and one Swede it was the second time they had been to the Pole. With engines throttled back they could all hear *The Bells of San Giusto* playing on a gramophone and causing pangs of home sickness to some. After a cry of 'long live Nobile' from Zappi they set course for Cape Platen on North East Land. It was 02:20 on 24 May. For 24 hours they flew along, sometimes under a clear sky and sometimes under overcast. On the afternoon and in the evening ice formed all over the airship and ice flung from the propellers struck the envelope with sharp cracks causing rents which were found and repaired. There was a strong headwind and for eight hours in the middle of the day their groundspeed was only 32kt. Nobile conferred with Malmgren who recommended increasing the airspeed to get out of the zone of strong headwinds as soon as possible. Nobile accepted the advice and ordered the third engine started. They were under an overcast sky and so could not take a sun sight. The radio aboard *Citta de Milano* gave them a bearing which gave a position line on the chart but not where they were on that line. Nobile ordered a change of course to the west for an hour so that a second bearing from Kings Bay would intersect with the first. That gave an approximate position of about 80nm north of Cape Platen on North East Land although it was a low grade position because lines cut at a shallow angle.

At 09:25 they were flying at 750ft and the elevator wheel jammed and the airship dived out of control. Nobile ordered the engines stopped and *Italia*, which was light, stopped descending at about 250ft and free-ballooned upwards. While the wheel was being repaired Nobile allowed the airship to ascend through the clouds to take a sun sight which gave them an accurate position line. The sun line and the latest radio bearing intersected to show them to be about 155nm north-east of Kings Bay.

At 10:30 on 25 May 1928 they were flying at about 900ft on two engines with a ground speed of around 25kt and estimated that they would arrive at Kings Bay between 15:00 and 16:00 that day although this had not been reported to the base ship. Cecioni was on the elevator wheel and called out 'the ship is heavy'. Nobile ordered the third engine started, 1,400rpm on all three engines and up elevator to check the descent by adding dynamic lift. He ordered Alessandrini onto the top of the ship to check the gas valves on the top of the stern. If they were open it would account for the stern heaviness. Ciocca got the third engine started. The ship was 15° to 20° nose up and was producing about 200kg lift dynamically but the variometer showed a more rapid descent than ever. A crash was inevitable and Nobile ordered the engines stopped to avert fire on impact and told Cecioni to go into the bow to drop the ballast chain. Nobile saw that the port engine was still running and leaned out of the window to shout an order to stop it. Cecioni had trouble freeing the chain, the uneven ice loomed up and there was the noise of the ship smashing into the ice. It was less than three minutes since Cecioni had called out that the ship was heavy.

The control car and rear engine car were ripped off on impact. Nobile found himself lying on the ice amid the ruins of the control car. The airship, lightened by the loss of the control car and the rear engine car, was drifting away and gaining height with the name *Italia* in huge black letters on the silver doped fabric of the side. Petrol or water ballast poured from damaged tanks in the keel. The tattered port side of the control car was still attached to the keel. Part of the crew was drifting away with the derelict ship. On the envelope or climbing up the bow ladder to it was Renato Alessandrini. In the keel or in the port or starboard wing engine cars were Ettore Arduino, Attilio Caratti, Ettore Pedretti, Dr Aldo Pontremoli and Dr Ugo Lago. Vincenzo Pomella was on the ice dead, having been killed instantly by the impact when the rear engine car was ripped from under the rear part of the keel. Lying in the wreckage with Nobile were Dr Finn Malmgren, Dr Francis Behounek, Adalberto Mariano, Filippo Zappi, Alfredo Viglieri, Felice Trojani, Giuseppe Biagi and Natale Cecioni. Some of them were badly injured. Nobile's dog Titina survived on the ice.

Amundsen was in Oslo at a reception for Australian explorer Sir Hubert Wilkins when the news came that *Italia* was missing.

As Byrd and Amundsen waited at Ny Alesund for their chance to be first to fly to the North Pole in 1926, Wilkins was at Point Barrow in Alaska. He had two Fokkers, a single engine F VII that crashed at the conclusion of its first flight and a trimotor F VII 3/m Detroiter, which also was damaged. A journalist helping to push one of the aircraft after it stuck in a snow drift had already been killed after he walked into the arc of one of the propellers. After repairs Wilkins used the aircraft to build up a cache of fuel at Point Barrow. On one of these trips he had made in an impromptu flight in the VII out over the Arctic Ocean 150nm from land. He returned to Alaska in 1927 with two Stinson Detroiter cabin biplanes fitted with 220hp Wright whirlwind engines and mounted on skis. Wilkins and pilot Carl Ben Eielson made two flights out over the Arctic Ocean in them. On the last flight Wilkins and his pilot made an epic march across the ice back to the north coast of Alaska after abandoning the Stinson a long way from civilisation. Wilkins showed his professionalism by landing out on the ice of the Polar Ocean and taking soundings of the depth of the ocean. He even asked for the engine of the Stinson to be stopped so the sounding (by an explosion and stop watch) could be made. The problem was that in the sub-zero temperatures the engine might not start again. It did and they flew on, landed after a loss of power, took off but eventually the engine failed finally and the march to the coast took place. In 1928 Wilkins sold the surviving aircraft and raised enough money to purchase the second Lockheed Vega made. The Vega was a small monoplane, streamlined and efficient, with a long range. Wilkins had planned meticulously and made an important flight from Point Barrow in Alaska to Green Harbour in Svalbard across the Polar Ocean. The flight took about 20hrs and covered a swath of ocean to the south of the flight by *Norge* in 1926 so that he was exploring territory not seen by Amundsen and Nobile. He gained the recognition he been seeking and was honoured wherever he went in the developed world. Wilkins and his pilot Carl Ben Eielson were in Norway on their way home. When Wilkins reached London he would be knighted by King George V and awarded the Patrons Medal from the Royal Geographical Society for exploring much previously unknown territory in the Arctic.

As soon as news of *Italia*'s disappearance was known an emergency meeting was called by the Minister of Defence and included Amundsen because of his knowledge and skill in Arctic survival and Riiser-Larsen as an aviation expert. Harald Sverdrup was there and Defence Minister Andersen-Rysst was in the chair. A comprehensive plan for a Norwegian participation in the search and rescue effort was worked out and put before the Italian Ambassador who passed it on for Rome to consider. Meanwhile Wilkins and Eielson gave lectures and went to receptions at various places in the Norwegian capital. When Riiser-Larsen was told by Count Senni that Mussolini had declined to permit any major Norwegian effort to rescue Nobile and the other survivors he was stunned, as he recorded in his auto-biography 30 years later. It seems that Mussolini did not want to give Amundsen the chance to rescue the man he had criticised so seriously, publicly and recently.

Gradually ships, aeroplanes and men converged on Svalbard to join in the search. On the ice Nobile and his men treated the injuries as best they could. Nobile himself had a broken leg. By great good fortune bags of emergency supplies had been in the control car at the moment of the crash. They were left over from the failed attempt to land men at the Pole. There were firearms and ammunition, food of various kinds, a tent and most importantly a small radio with aerial and batteries. The radio would save the lives of seven of the eight men on the ice. The *Italia* disaster has been the subject of many books, articles and films. One of the books and the movie based on it would be called *The Red Tent*. Originally the tent was white and blended in with the ice. Amongst the items picked up from the wreckage were a number of glass balls filled with red dye. Nobile directed that the tent be dyed with the red liquid from the glass balls to make it stand out from the ice. The balls containing the red dye were carried to help re-set the altimeter. Altimeters are simply accurate barometers calibrated with altitude figures matching the pressure at each altitude. They are only accurate when either the local air pressure is known or when the actual altitude is known and they can be reset. They had been dropped from the airship from time to time. The drop was timed with a stop watch and converted to distance. With the distance known the altimeters could be reset so they were accurate.

It had been arranged that if they failed to return the radio station aboard *Citta di Milano* would listen out on an agreed frequency at certain fixed times. *Italia* would listen out at certain other times to prevent the two stations from blocking each other. They got the radio going and started to transmit a Mayday with their latitude and longitude and information about numbers of crew lost with the derelict ship and survivors on the ice. For many days they got no reply but persisted with the transmissions. They knew from listening out to news broadcasts that their messages were not being received and no one knew where they were or what had happened. After the rescue it became known that the captain of the base ship had made the extraordinary decision to not listen out because if they had crashed they would not have a radio to use. *Citta di Milano* continued to send routine traffic and did not maintain a listening watch. From 25 May to 3 June they transmitted without results. The batteries were gradually going flat. The ice was drifting with the current and on 28 May land became visible. On 29 May a polar bear was shot near the tent and gave them about 190kg of fresh meat.

On 31 May some of the survivors had given up hope of rescue and decided to attempt to walk across the ice to dry land. On that day Italians Mariano and Zappi and Swedish scientist Malmgren left the Red Tent although Nobile would have preferred that all nine survivors stayed at the crash site. Nobile and five others stayed at the crash site. They had navigational instruments and checked their positions from time to time. The ice flow was moving with the currents and winds. Finally, on 3 June, Nikolai Schmidt, an amateur radio operator at Vokhma in the Soviet Union heard the signals and passed on the information to Rome. On 8 June, 15 days after the crash, they were in regular communication with the base ship at Kings Bay and could co-ordinate flights by the search planes. On the ice the survivors updated their position reports every day.

Riiser-Larsen was sent to Svalbard by ship with an aeroplane, a Hansa-Brandenburg two seat seaplane, to join in the search. Amundsen had telegraphed Lincoln Ellsworth in the hope that he would fund a private effort commanded by Amundsen. Ellsworth was lukewarm to the idea and nothing came of it. Probably Ellsworth read the news reports of the many ships and aircraft sent to Kings Bay and, quite reasonably, decided that any further effort was redundant. The rescue effort was improvised and several of the rescuers needed rescuing. Norwegian naval aviator Lutzow-Holm had an engine failure in his Hansa-Brandenburg seaplane and was rescued from Mossel Bay, Spitsbergen by a dog-sled team.

Amundsen did not give up trying to get an aeroplane and crew and it is not hard to understand why. If Amundsen found Nobile, an enemy since the controversy of 1926–1927, he would again be seen as noble and selfless. As he looked for an aeroplane and crew Mariano, Zappi and Malmgren were making an epic march across the ice. By 14/15 June Malmgren was unable to continue and was left behind. He would not be seen again and died alone on the pack ice of the Polar Ocean. Later Mariano and Zappi would say that he asked to be left but the truth would never be known. There were rumours that the two Italians had killed and cannibalised him. There was no evidence of this and the rumours were pure speculation. There was some criticism of the decision to leave Malmgren behind and this was justified.

Eventually Denmark would send the schooner *Gustave Holm* to Kings Bay. From France came the ships *Strasbourg*, *Durance*, *Quentin Roosevelt* and *Pourquoi Pas?*. With them were two Schreck flying boats. From Italy came two Dornier Wal flying boats, a Savoia-Marchetti S 55 flying boat, two Macchi M

18 flying boats and the ship *Braganza*. Norway sent two Hansa-Brandenburg's and two Sopwith Baby seaplanes. Norway also sent ships including the *Hobby* and the coast defence battleship HNoMS *Tordenskjold*. The Soviet Union sent two Junkers F 13s and a trimotor Junkers G 23 on skis. Soviet contributions also included icebreakers; *Krassin*, *Malygin* and *Sedov*. Sweden sent a number of aeroplanes. Eventually there were more ships and planes than were needed. Any effort led by Amundsen would be redundant, as he must have known from reading the newspaper coverage and listening to the radio news. Amundsen had asked Leif Dietrichson to go with him on any search and Dietrichson had agreed. Still he continued to look for a way to participate and found it when he talked to Norwegian Fredrick Peterson, a wealthy merchant living in Paris. Peterson agreed to find him a French aeroplane and crew. A formal approach was made through the Norwegian Ambassador in Paris and it was agreed that a French Aeronavale Latham 47 flying boat and a crew of four would be dispatched from Caudebec en Caux as soon as it could be prepared.

Some time before Amundsen had been interviewed by the Italian journalist Guidici and is recorded as saying:

> 'Oh if you only knew how wonderful it is up there [in the Arctic]. That is where I want to die and I wish death would come to me in a chivalrous way, that it will find me during the execution of some great deed, quickly and without suffering.'

If he found Nobile he would have acted chivalrously and repaired his reputation one more time. If he died in the attempt he would have fulfilled the wish he had disclosed to Guidici. He had every right to take the chance for himself but did he have the right to take his friend Dietrichson and the French crew with him?

Throughout the period of the search for Nobile Amundsen was exchanging telegrams with Bess Magids who was coming to Norway to marry Amundsen. He had never married although he had had a series of important relationships with women. She was due to arrive in Norway from Alaska about the time he set off for Svalbard. The Latham was due to arrive at Bergen on 16/17 June 1928 and he took the night train from Oslo to Bergen on the evening of 16 June. There to see him off were well-wishers including the Italian ambassador. With him were Captain Oscar Wisting and Leif Dietrichson. It was exactly 25 years since he had set out down Oslofjord in Gjoa at the start of his expedition to sail thought the North West Passage. The Latham was waiting for him at Bergen after a trouble-free 13 hour flight from France. He wanted to take both Wisting and Dietrichson with him but there was only room for one.

Latham 47.02 on a beaching trolley at Caudebec-en-Caux. This was the second prototype of the Latham 47. The flying boat was designed for trans-atlantic flights, had an enclosed cockpit and could carry enough fuel for a long range flight.

Dietrichson was a pilot so he went and Oscar Wisting was left behind. At Bergen on 17 June he met the French crew. The captain was Rene Guilbaud. The co-pilot was decorated war veteran Albert Cavelier de Cuverville with radio operator Emile Vallete and mechanic Gilbert Brazy. Later it was written that the aircraft was not suitable for the flight but this does not seem to be correct. The aircraft had twin radial engines of 500hp each, a span of 25.2m, was 16.3m long and an all up weight of 6,886kg. It cruised at around 70kt and had a ceiling of 13,000ft. It had been designed with trans-Atlantic flights in mind. In 1928 there were no aircraft specially designed for operations in the Arctic and the Latham was probably no less suitable than most other aircraft of its class. It had made the long flights from Caudebec en Caux in Northern France to Bergen and from Bergen to Tromso without a problem. Its range was adequate for the Tromso to Kings Bay leg of the flight.

There was one detail which was not the best possible for the Arctic environment. The Latham was a flying boat which stayed afloat by having a waterproof fuselage, the underside of which was shaped to lift the aircraft slightly out of the water as it gathered speed, so that water drag was reduced and it could accelerate to take-off speed. It had floats under the tips of each bottom wing to prevent it capsizing sideways when stationary. Experience had shown that these tip floats were vulnerable if the sea was rough. Flying boats had been lost when a tip float was holed or ripped away and the flying boat, hull still intact, had capsized. They were also vulnerable on landing if it was on ice or snow. The Dornier system of sponsons built into the lower part of

The Sikorsky S-36 amphibian *Dawn* owned by Francis Grayson. On 23 December 1927 Oscar Omdal took off from New York bound for Harbour Grace, New Foundland on the first leg of a Trans-Atlantic flight with the ultimate destination Copenhagen. Aboard were Omdal, Grayson, navigator Brice Goldsborough and radio-operator Frank Koehler. No trace of the aeroplane or its crew was ever found.

Amundsen, Guilbaud and Commandant Moe in Tromso on 18 June 1928

the fuselage amidships had proven to be less vulnerable on water and on ice or snow. Not only had Amundsen's Wal N 25 survived its weeks on the ice, other Wals were building up a reputation for surviving days of drifting on rough seas.

The flew to Tromso and prepared for the next leg which was from there, north-west, over the Barents Sea, past Bear Island and on to Kings Bay in Svalbard where the ships and aircraft searching for *Italia* survivors were based. At Tromso were Finnish and Italian seaplanes also on their way to join the search. There was discussion about whether to wait until the next day (19 June) and make the flight in formation. Amundsen was for pressing on at once. At 16:00 on 18 June 1928 the Latham taxied out and took off bound for Kings Bay. Witnesses later recalled that it seemed to struggle into the air. The water was smooth, almost a glassy calm, and all heavily loaded seaplanes take a long run to 'unstick' from the water in such conditions.

The flying boat headed down the fjord slowly climbing to cruising altitude. At the seaward end of the fjord it turned on to a heading which would take it north-west across the Barents Sea, past Bear Island and on to Svalbard. A fisherman saw the aircraft fly towards a fog bank, apparently climbing before

The Latham 47.02 at Bergen after flying direct from Caudebec-en-Caux in Northern France on 16 June 1928. It was the second prototype of a type designed to fly across the Atlantic. It had a crew of four, Pilot, Co-Pilot Navigator, Radio Operator and Mechanic. It was powered by two radial engines, each of 500 hp and mounted back to back under the centre section of the upper wing and driving four-bladed propellers. As was normal at this time, the propellors were fixed pitched and could not be feathered if an engine failed.

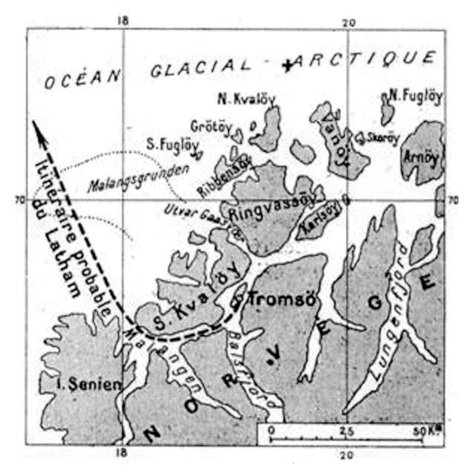

On 18 June 1928 at about 16.00 the Latham 47.02 flying boat with Amundsen, Dietrichsen, Guilbaud, De Cuverville, Brazy and Valette took off from Tromso. It climbed out along the fjord leading to the Barents Sea. It made its departure from the seaward end of the fjord.

it disappeared from view. The Latham broadcast routine messages until about 19:00. No more messages were received and the aircraft did not arrive at Kings Bay.

At first the concern at Amundsen's failure to arrive was tempered by the distinct possibility that Amundsen had chosen to fly directly to the survivors camp on the ice north-east of Svalbard. The survivors were in regular radio contact with *Citta de Milano* at Kings Bay and updated their position at regular intervals as their camp drifted with the pack ice. Amundsen had a reputation for doing the unexpected. In 1903 he had sailed from Kristiania in *Gjoa* in the middle of the night to dodge creditors who might have arrested

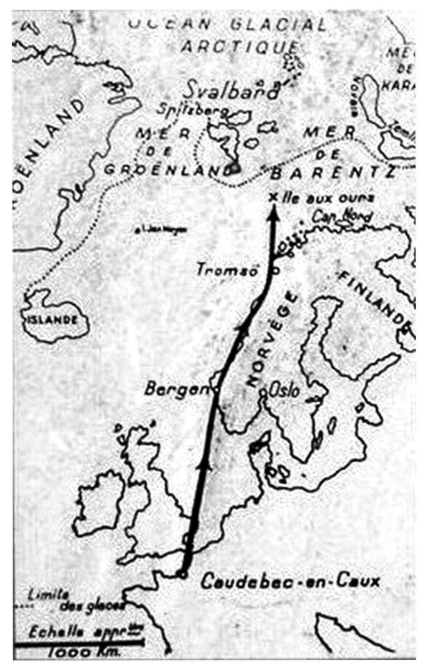

The Latham 47.02 flew non-stop from Caudebec-en-Caux to Bergen in 13 hrs. Amundsen and Dietrichsen joined it at Bergen on 17 June and flew to Tromso. At 16.00 on 18 June 1928 the Latham took off from Tromso. It was sighted by a fishermen heading towards Kings Bay on Svalbard. Signals with the Latham were received until about 19.00. It failed to arrive and the six passengers and crew were not seen again.

the ship. He said he would pay them when he returned (which turned out to be in 1907). In 1911 he sailed from the same port bound for the Bering Strait and the North Pole. At Tenerife he announced that *Fram* was bound for Antarctica and the South Pole. Only two years before he flew out from Tromso Amundsen and his five companions had disappeared into the Arctic Ocean and reappeared 28 days later when most people had believed them dead. The days passed and there was no news of the Latham. It gradually became clear that it had gone down over the Barents Sea. The search for *Italia* survivors was widened to take in Amundsen and his companions.

There were a number of false reports that the six men had been found including one in an Australian newspaper on 4 July saying that they had been rescued by the British yacht *Albion*.

Assuming it had crashed en-route there had to be a cause. Aviation was dangerous in 1928 and there were a number of distinct possibilities. Firstly it is possible that at least one of the two engines had failed. A heavily loaded aeroplane of this type would probably be unable to maintain height even if the other engine continued to run. The Latham's engines drove large four-bladed fixed-pitch propellers that could not be feathered to reduce drag. A fixed-pitched propeller produces an enormous amount of drag in flight when its engine is not running, particularly if it is windmilling in the slipstream. It is a curious fact that a windmilling propeller produces more drag than a stationary one. On one engine there would have been an involuntary descent. The remaining engine would only reduce the rate of descent, flatten the glide and give the pilot time to think and plan a forced landing. A landing on the open sea would have been inevitable. The Latham had no de-icing gear and an ice build-up was likely in cloud or fog. Icing increases the weight, changes the wing profile for the worse and would bring an involuntary descent to the water, hopefully to a controlled landing. In heavy icing the ice could change the shapes of wings and control surfaces so much that the aircraft would go out of control and spin or spiral into the water. Such a crash would not be survivable. Another possibility is that there were navigational problems and they landed after they ran out of fuel, or made a precautionary landing just before they ran out. Flight in cloud or fog deprives the pilot of visual references and blind flying instruments, and pilots trained in their use, are required for safe flight in cloud or with no visible horizon. With inadequate instruments or piloting skills or both a pilot will become rapidly disorientated and spin or spiral into the sea. Such an accident is not survivable. If they spun or spiralled all aboard would have been killed instantly. If they made a controlled landing they would stick with the aeroplane as long as it floated. Flying boats are vulnerable to wind and waves in the open sea so it would be

The six men lost somewhere in the Barents Sea with Latham 47.02 on 18 June 1928.

a distinct possibility that hull would be breached or a tip float knocked off. Either way the flying boat would be likely to sink.

On 20 June Italian pilot Maddalena located the red tent and dropped supplies, much of which were damaged by the drop. On 22 June Swedish and Italian pilots dropped supplies which were recovered and raised the morale of Nobile and the others left after the departure of Malmgren, Mariano and Zappi. On 23 June Swedish aviator Lundborg and his observer landed their ski equipped Fokker CV on the ice and Nobile made a decision that would haunt him for the rest of his long life. He allowed himself to be persuaded that the Italian government wanted him rescued first and flown to the *Citta de Milano*. Nobile would justify his decision by arguing that he consented so that he could co-ordinate the search, which had been chaotic up to date. The Fokker has two open cockpits and normally carries two, a pilot and an observer. Nobile squeezed into the rear cockpit alongside the observer; he took his dog, Titina, with him. He had committed a major error of judgment. He was injured (he had a broken leg) but so had another survivor. He was the captain of the *Italia*. The tradition and the expectation of the public was that he be rescued last. It made matters worse that he elected to take his dog with him. The dog weighed only a few kilos and took up little room yet it was symbolic in the worst possible way. The captain left his crew and his dog was rescued before any of them.

Lundborg returned to the ice flow flying solo so that he could rescue two more survivors but the Fokker flipped on to its back during the landing and he was trapped on the ice at the red tent. On 6 July Swedish pilot Birger Schyberg lands his de Havilland Moth on the ice and rescues Lundborg.

The Soviet Union had contributed several ice-breakers to the search. When *Krassin* left Tromso after coaling the wharf was crowded with people shouting 'rescue Amundsen' and there was a strong feeling that everything possible should be done to rescue him and his comrades. The search for Amundsen eventually became as complex and long running as that for the *Italia*. *Krassin* pushed its way through the pack ice towards the survivors' camp and picked up Mariano and Zappi on 12 July after they had been walking across the ice for 42 days.

Later the same day *Krassin* rescued the five men at the red tent. *Krassin* did not have the coal to make a long search for the six men who drifted away from the crash site in the derelict *Italia* on 25 May. An air and sea search for them was made too late to do any good and no trace of the six was ever found.

A massive search for the aircraft and its occupants had been mounted involving many ships, aircraft and men. Participants included units of the Royal Norwegian Navy. Riiser-Larsen took part in the search aboard *Hobby*.

The vessel had been under charter to an American, Louise Arner Boyd. Boyd was a woman of means who financed and led nine Arctic expeditions, created a unique archive of motion picture and still photographs, wrote a number of books and was awarded many decorations by private and government organisations. She was 41 in 1928 and was on her third expedition to the Arctic. When the news of Amundsen's disappearance reached her she immediately offered the ship, its crew and herself to the search. The *Hobby* searched for ten weeks and sailed about 10,000nm above the Arctic Circle looking at every island or coastline that Amundsen might have reached. Afterwards Miss Boyd was awarded a high Norwegian honour for her efforts. She had also shot 20,000 feet of movie film during the search.

Other units engaged in the search included the French Navy cruiser *Strasbourg* and the Norwegian coast defence battleship HNoMS *Tordenskjold*. On 31 August a fishing boat picked up an item from the sea off the coast near Tromso that was positively identified as coming from the Latham and the *New York Times* for 2 September 1928 ran banner headlines:

**AMUNDSEN PONTOON FOUND OFF NORTH NORWAY COAST;**

**HOPE FOR CREW ABANDONED**
IDENTIFICATION IS DEFINITE
Repairs Prove Relic Found
By Fishing Boat is From
Explorers Plane
FLOAT WAS WRENCHED OFF

The item was a float from under one of the wingtips of the flying boat and was identified from a small repair made to it at Bergen. The struts and bracing wires were still attached to it and the four strut ends show that it was torn from the lower surface of the wing. There was then no realistic hope of finding any of the men alive. There was still uncertainty as to what happened. The float could have been torn off in an out of control spiral or spin into the sea. It is equally possible that a controlled ditching was made and then the float was ripped off by wind and wave as the men struggled to keep their machine afloat. If it had been a controlled ditching they would have had a significantly greater chance of survival if they had been flying a Dornier Wal, as used on the Amundsen-Ellsworth Polar Flight of 1925.

On 13 October an empty petrol tank was found in the sea south of Tromso. It had had its bung stopped with a hastily whittled piece of wood. This is consistent with two scenarios. If they were on the water in the Latham and

A tip float from the Latham was recovered from the sea near Tromso on 31 August 1928. It had been torn off the bottom of a wing tip. It was identified from a small repair made at Bergen on the way north. The only other item found was an empty fuel tank found in October 1928.

could see the tip float about to go they would have sent one or two of the crew out on the opposite wing to provide weight to lift the vulnerable side out of the water. The empty tank could have been hurriedly made waterproof and lashed under the vulnerable side. They would not have been able to take off but it would stabilise the boat laterally and keep it afloat for a time. The other possibility is that the Latham had lost its tip float and was sinking and the crews' only option was to improvise a raft from available components including the petrol tank. They then took to the raft and hours or days later died by drowning or exposure or thirst.

The *Italia* crash had now claimed 17 lives. Foreman Motor Mechanic Vincenzo Pomella was killed instantly when the rear engine car was ripped off in the crash. Professor Aldo Pontremoli, Chief Motor Engineer Ettore Arduino, Motor Mechanic Attilio Caratti, Journalist Ugo Lago, Motor Mechanic Calisto Ciocca and Foreman Rigger Renato Alessandrini drifted off with the derelict *Italia* and died somewhere on the pack ice. Dr Finn Malmgren had died attempting to walk across the ice from the crash site to dry land. Roald Amundsen, Leif Dietrichson, Rene Guilbaud, Albert Cavelier de Cuverville, Gilbert Brazy and Emile Valette had been lost with the Latham on 18 June or soon after. Others had died in September 1928 on an aircraft returning to Europe from Svalbard. On 29 September 1928 an Italian flying boat with a crew of five was flying home from Svalbard across France. As it followed a river it struck wires and crashed into the river. Two of the crew were rescued but Pierluigi Penzo, Tullio Crosio and Giuseppe Della Gatta died in the crash.

On 14 December 1928 the Norwegian people celebrated the seventeenth anniversary of Amundsen's arrival at the South Pole and marked the death of their hero. Flags were flown, speeches made by public men, the national anthem was sung and pupils in their classrooms were told about Amundsen's achievements. The radio stations devoted the entire day to the event. At 12 noon church bells tolled, trams stopped, flags were lowered to half-mast and the whole nation held a two-minute silence. Amundsen was dead but had no grave yet the people accepted that he departed his life in a way that he might have wished for, taking chances in a noble cause in the Arctic that he loved.

## Chapter Fifteen

# Gardens of Stone and an AUV

*Caudebec-en-Caux 5 November 1931, Barents Sea 2009*

mundsen and his comrades had not been forgotten.

On 6–19 February 1929 the cruise ship *Stella Polaris* made a voyage to North Cape, Norway, which would have been Amundsen's last sight of his native land. Aboard was Fridtjof Nansen, Arctic explorer and winner of the Nobel Peace Prize, who made a speech on the first anniversary of Amundsen's death.

The Latham had been built, and had departed from Caudebec-en-Caux which lies on the right bank of the Seine 47km west-north-west of Rouen. On 5 November 1931 a striking sculpture and monument was unveiled at Caudebec-en-Caux with all due ceremony. The centre piece is a three dimensional representation of the forward part of the Latham 47 which flies out of the stone in a climbing turn to the right. The monument is enormous and steps lead from the road up to it. It dominates the location and includes the names of the passengers and crew lost with the aircraft, the dates and places where it flew and two large metal replicas of Aeronavale wings. Elsewhere Guilbaud is remembered with a striking monument consisting of a full length sculpture of him and a cross piece with images of the aircraft and its flight in bas-relief. There is a Rue Gilbert Brazy and a handsome stone column surmounted by a metal bust of him and with a metal bas-relief image of leaves on its front.

At Tromso is a stone and metal marker paid for by the newspaper *Le Temps*, commemorating the events of 1928, and unveiled during a visit of the ship *Stella Polaris* in 1934. Also at Tromso is a monument to the memories of the 17 men who died on the *Italia*, on the Latham and on the way home from the search effort. It was unveiled on 22 June 1969 and Umberto Nobile attended the ceremony.

Amundsen and his companions were not forgotten. This monument was unveiled at Caudebec-en-Caux in 1931. On the 80th anniversary of the unveiling in 2011 there was a ceremony which was attended by the Ambassadors of Norway, Sweden, Russia and the United States, local and national politicians, officers of the French navy and an honor guard.

Captain Roald Amundsen 1872–1928.

On 5 November 2011 the eightieth anniversary of the unveiling of the monument at Caudebec-en-Caux was marked by a major ceremony attended by leading politicians and naval officers and the ambassadors of Norway, Sweden, Russia and Italy. Flowers were placed at the monument, a parade was held and an honour guard of sailors in formal uniforms with white gaiters presented arms.

Images of Amundsen are too numerous to catalogue. At Ny Alesund is a metal bust on a plinth made of stone slabs. The wood and canvas hangar at Ny Alesund vanished many years ago although the foundations are said to be visible. The airship mast, designed and built in Italy, and assembled just before the *Norge* arrived in 1926 still stands. It has not been used since the *Italia* took off on its final flight in 1928. Attached to the base of the mast is a rectangle of metal embossed with images of *Norge*, the flags of Norway, Italy and the United States standing at the North Pole and words including:

'Amundsen-Ellsworth-Nobile Trans-Polar Flight 1926

Honouring a glorious achievement of human endeavour'

It was placed there by the Italian Air Force and gives Nobile the equal recognition that he has always deserved. The mast at Vadso survives and has a plaque with a picture of *Italia* and text (in English) explaining its significance. There is a museum including a mock-up of the interior of the control car of an airship.

Since Amundsen's death there has been a steady stream of books and magazine articles published about him, his men and his rivals. Learned papers have been published analysing issues including whether or not Byrd reached the North Pole on his flight of 9 May 1926.

In the early 1930s a fishing vessel operating near Bear Island may have snagged and pulled to the surface an engine from Amundsen's plane but it slipped back into the sea.

In 2004 a group of aviation historians tried to search the seabed where the Latham may have gone down but bad weather caused the search to be abandoned. On 21 May 2007 the frigate *Roald Amundsen* was commissioned in the Royal Norwegian Navy.

On 24 August 2009 the vessels HNoMS, *Tyr* and CGV *Harstad* sailed from Tromso for the Barents Sea near Bear Island to conduct a search of the seabed for the remains of the Latham 47. The expedition was organised by a German film company and lead by New Zealander Rob McCallum. *Harstad* was the recently commissioned first of a new class of offshore patrol vessels operated by Remoy Management for the Norwegian Coast Guard. *Tyr* is a mine sweeper equipped to locate small sea mines and has located World War Two wrecks including the German battleship *Scharnhorst* and the submarines *U-864* and *U-735*. It carries the Hugin 1000 Autonomous Underwater Vehicle (AUV). The search area was defined after reviewing the evidence of the cruising speed of the Latham and the time that radio messages ceased. It also relies on the reported catch of wreckage by a fishing boat in this area in 1933. This is approximate at best and the water is about 400m deep in that area. The wood and metal structure of the Latham will be gone but the search team hoped that the twin engines will have survived. The Hugin 1000 would be sent down to conduct a sonar search. The AUV is autonomous, can operate for 18 hours at a time and has sonar that can resolve an image down to 5cm in size.

If Hugin found anything the Scorpion ROV would be deployed to obtain high resolution images. After some weeks of searching, some of it amidst cold green seas, the ships returned having found nothing of interest. The Norwegian Navy was pleased that the Hugin 1000 performed perfectly. It is significant that interest in Amundsen and his fate is great enough to justify the expense of such a search and the financing provided by the documentary company.

In 2010 the major documentary film *Roald Amundsen: Lost in the Arctic* by Rudolph Herzog and covering the 2009 search was aired on television.

*Gjoa* and *Fram* are preserved in Norway as museum ships. The remains of *Maude* (renamed *Bay Maude* by the Hudson's Bay Company) lie in the Canadian Arctic and there are plans to return her to Norway and restore her. There is a Farman 'Longhorn' of the type used by Amundsen for the test for his aviator's certificate in 1914, preserved in the Norwegian Museum of Science and Technology in Oslo. N 25 was sold in Great Britain and then to Germany. She made many great flights and was donated to the Deutsches Museum in Munich in the early 1930s and was destroyed in an allied bombing raid in 1944. On 25 July 2012 a reproduction N 25 was unveiled in the Dornier Museum in Friedrichshafen.

The mystery surrounding the time, place and circumstances of Amundsen's death after 18 June 1928 foreshadowed the mystery of the disappearance and death of Amelia Earhart and navigator Fred Noonan, which sprang to life on 2 July 1937 near a spot in the Pacific Ocean called Howland Island. They were heroes, celebrities and role models in their own countries. They were both engaged in difficult and dangerous overwater flights. They had both taken chances and had failed to survive the risks. There is an enduring mystery in both cases. Many are interested in solving each mystery and each mystery has developed a life its own.

One hundred and forty-one years after his birth and 85 years after his death Amundsen continues to exert a strong force on our curiosity and emotions.

# Epilogue

## Bernt Balchen (1899–1973)

After *Norge* had completed its flight to the North Pole and Alaska he was recruited by Richard Byrd and travelled to the United States with him. Balchen was co-pilot to Floyd Bennett when he flew the *Josephine Ford* on a tour of more than 50 cities, after which they delivered the Fokker to the Henry Ford Museum. Recruited by Anthony Fokker as a test pilot he flew in the Arctic repairing and maintaining the Fokker Universals used as bush planes. He was co-pilot to Bert Acosta on Richard Byrd's flight in the Fokker *America* from New York to Paris on 29 June-1 July 1927, ditching on the Normandy coast when Paris was covered in fog. He went to Antarctica on Byrd's first expedition of 1928–1930 and flew him to the South Pole on 28 November 1929. He was technical advisor to Amelia Earhart and prepared her Lockheed Vega for her 1932 Atlantic flight. After spending time on aviation matters back in Norway and Finland he returned to North America. After the German occupation of Norway he negotiated the setting up of Little Norway in Canada. This was a base in Ontario where 2,500 aircrew and ground crew were trained for the Free Norwegian Forces. He joined the United States Army Air Forces and set up bases in Greenland for use as staging posts for aircraft being ferried from the US to Europe. Later in WW II he set up organisations to fly Norwegians out of Sweden and supplies and men into Norway. He stayed in the USAAF after the war and reached the rank of colonel although Richard Byrd blocked further promotion for personal reasons. When asked why Byrd did this he said 'I know that he did not fly to the North Pole and he knows I know.' Assignments included the 10th rescue squadron operating across the far north of Alaska and Canada. In May 1949 he flew a Douglas C-54 from Fairbanks, Alaska to the North Pole and on to Thule in Greenland which made him the first man to fly over both Poles. He retired from the USAF (which had come into being in 1947) in 1956. After retirement he remained active in aviation working for, or with, organisations such as Hughes Aircraft,

General Dynamics Canadair and Electric Boat. He died in 1973 in New York having received many honours including the Harmon Trophy, Distinguished Service Medal, Distinguished Flying Cross, Air Medal and a Knighthood of The Royal Norwegian Order of St Olav.

## Floyd Bennett (1890–1928)

Bennett had joined the USN in May 1917 and learned to fly. He flew on the Byrd-Macmillan Arctic expedition in 1925. After Byrd's polar flight of 1926 he returned to the United States and was awarded the Medal of Honour. He flew the *Josephine Ford* (with Bernt Balchen as co-pilot) on a tour of more than 50 cities in America. He worked with Byrd on the proposed transatlantic flight in the Fokker tri-motor *America*. Badly injured during a practice flight, he was unable to make the flight to France. He developed pneumonia and died on 25 April 1928. Two airports and a USN destroyer were named in his honour. Richard Byrd named the Ford Tri-motor used in the first flight to the South Pole after him.

## Richard Byrd (1888–1957)

After the North Pole flight of 1926 he flew the Atlantic as navigator of the Fokker *America* on 29 June-1 July 1927. He then turned his attention to Antarctica and navigated the Ford Tri-motor *Floyd Bennett* to the South Pole on 28 November 1929. He made five expeditions to Antarctica; 1928–30, 1933–35, 1939–40, 1946–47 and 1955–56. He died a retired Rear Admiral in 1957.

## Odd Dahl (1898–1994)

After the Maude expedition he went on to a long and distinguished career as a physicist in the United States and Norway where he was a pioneer in the use of nuclear energy. When he died in 1994 he was the last survivor of Amundsen's men.

## Hjalmar Riiser-Larsen (1890–1965)

He had been promoted to Captain after the Norge expedition and went on to have an outstandingly eventful and successful life. He flew a Hansa-Brandenburg seaplane from Svalbard on searches for the *Italia* survivors and then joined the search for Amundsen. He led the Louise Boyd search aboard the *Hobby* which spent 10 weeks and steamed 10,000nm looking for Amundsen and his companions. He flew a Hansa-Brandenburg and a Lockheed Vega in Antarctica in 1929–1930 while using the ship *Norvegia* as a base. He returned to Antarctica in 1933–1934 to make some surface explorations. In 1933 he became director of the aviation company DNL. He stayed in this job, gradually expanding the airline network until he returned to the Navy in 1939. After the Germans occupied Norway he went to North America becoming a Rear-Admiral and head of the Norwegian Air Forces joint command. He later became a Major-General in command of the Air Force when the naval and army aviation was merged in 1944. After the war he was forced to resign from the air force. He played a big part in arranging the merger of all Scandinavian airlines into SAS and was regional director until his retirement in 1955. He received many honours from many countries and died in Copenhagen in 1965.

### Lincoln Ellsworth (1880–1951)

In 1928 he was awarded a gold medal by Congress for his 1925 and 1926 polar flights. He made four expeditions to Antarctica between 1933 and 1939 using his ship *Wyatt Earp* and made a Trans-Antarctic flight in 1935. He was awarded a second gold medal by Congress in 1936 for his Antarctic flight and is said to be the only person to receive the award twice. He wrote his auto-biography, *Beyond Horizons*, in 1937.

### Trygge Gran (1888–1980)

Gran had been a Major in the RFC and RAF in the Great War and was awarded the MC and DFC. During World War II Gran collaborated with the Quisling regime and was sentenced to 18 months imprisonment after a trial in 1948. He devoted the rest of his life to writing.

### Umberto Nobile (1885–1978)

Returned to Italy from Svalbard to a hero's welcome but received official blame for the loss of members of *Italia*'s crew and for abandoning them on the ice. He resigned his commission in protest. He spent 1931–36 in the Soviet Union designing airships. He returned to Italy then spent time in the United States, teaching aeronautics at Lewis University in Illinois. After World War II he was restored to rank, given back pay from 1928 and promoted to Lieutenant

General. He spent much of his life after 1928 justifying his actions of 1928. He died in 1978. His story has been told in books, the film *The Red Tent* and in a permanent exhibition in the Italian Air Force Museum at Vigna de Valle.

## Oscar Wisting (1871–1936)

Wisting had been first mate and then first officer of Amundsen's *Maude* for most of 1918–1925. For much of the voyaging he had been acting captain. After going to the North Pole in *Norge* he spent much time working on *Fram* to preserve her as a museum ship. He often spent nights aboard *Fram* after a day's work and died in his old bunk on the night of 3/4 December 1936 only a few days before the twenty-fifth anniversary of the arrival at the South Pole. Hjalmar Riiser-Larsen gave the speech that Wisting had intended to give on the anniversary. Mount Wisting, at the head of the Amundsen Glacier in the Queen Maude Mountains in Antarctica is named after him.

# A Note on Sources

The most important sources for Amundsen's career in aviation are his account of the North Pole flight of 1925, *My Polar Flight* (1925), and of the *Norge* flight to the North Pole and Alaska, *First Flight Across the Polar Sea* (1926). Each book was written soon after the events when events were fresh in the mind and each include material from other participants. They were written and published so rapidly that they were not proofread carefully and the dates and times are not always consistent and it is not always clear whether local time or Greenwich Mean Time is being used. Nobile's books *My Polar Flights* (1961) and *With Italia to the North Pole* (1930) provide useful narratives of the *Norge* and *Italia* flights that are particularly valuable as they are from the pen of the man who designed both airships and was captain on both flights. *My Airship Flights* includes measured responses to accusations by Amundsen and Riiser-Larsen that Nobile performed badly when preparing the *Norge* flight and towards the end of that flight.

Bowman-Larsen's quirky and revealing biography *Roald Amundsen* (2006) is my favourite Amundsen biography. He has the advantage of being Norwegian and able to read the sources not yet translated from that language. Amundsen's *My Life as an Explorer* (1927) is useful and revealing in a way that was unintended. Harald Sverdrup's biographical article is particularly useful as the author spent several years with Amundsen aboard *Maude*.

I have pieced together Amundsen's aviation activities 1909–1924 from various sources including internet pages, which have been carefully compared with published sources, and I have used those that seem to be consistent. Newspapers have been used sparingly and carefully as they are often unreliable as to the spelling of place-names and names of people. They also often contradict each other on facts; for example, the Junkers F 13 crash in April 1922 is variously ascribed as being caused by a hail storm, engine failure, or running out of petrol, and the list of persons on board the aircraft is incomplete and names are misspelled.

National Geographic Society maps have been useful. The Arctic map published by the Society in February 1984 was particularly useful as it used a polar projection and included all places relevant to the story on one sheet.

DVDs containing flawless copies of the 1925 and 1926 flight documentaries, *Roald Amundsen-Lincoln Ellsworth's Polar Flight* (1925) and *The Airship Norge's Flight across the Arctic Ocean* (1926) were a delight to watch and provided much detail not in the books.

For navigational details I have relied on whatever skills and experience I have acquired in 3,000 plus hours flying as a commercial pilot and flying instructor.

*French Aircraft of World War One* by Davilla & Soltan provided technical details of the Farman aircraft in which Amundsen passed the flight test for his aviator's certificate in 1914. Van Der Mays's *Dornier Wal: A Light Coming over the Sea* is a useful and interesting account of the aircraft used in the 1925 expedition. The Van Dyke Collection of airship plans provided useful details of *Norge*. Maynard's *Wings of Ice* includes important quotes from the suppressed parts of Balchen's autobiography in which he explained why he knew that Byrd had not flown to the North Pole as he had claimed.

Grierson's *Challenge to the Poles: Highlights of Arctic and Antarctic Aviation* (1961) is still essential reading and the best account of aviation in high latitudes 1897–1954.

# Annotated Bibliography

## Part One: Books & Journal Articles

Allen, Richard S. 'Amundsen's Aircraft 1922–1925' *Skyways: The Journal of the Early Airplane 1920–1940*, No. 70, April 2004. pp 49–52
This article provides details of the Curtiss Oriole biplane and the two Junkers F 13 monoplanes used by Amundsen.

Allen, Richard S 'Fokker's JOSEPHINE FORD Part 2' *Skyways: The Journal of the Early Airplane 1920–1940*, No. 67, April 2003. pp 37–46.
The biography of the Fokker F VII 3/m monoplane used by Richard Byrd and pilot Floyd Bennett on their attempt to fly from Spitsbergen to the North Pole and return on 9 April 1926.

Amundsen, Roald Engelbregt Gravning, *My Life as an Explorer*, London: Heinemann, 1927 (281pp, ill)
Amundsen's autobiography (With contributions by Hiljmar J. Riiser-Larsen, Leif Dietrichson, Friedrich Ramm, and Lincoln Ellsworth) *My Polar Flight*, London, Hutchinson, nd (ca 1925) (292pp, ill)
An account of the 1925 Amundsen-Ellsworth North Pole Expedition which was written within two months of the end of the expedition and rich in detail and anecdotes and with contributions by all the major participants. (With contributions by Lincoln Ellsworth, Joh Hover, Hiljmar J. Riiser-Larsen, Gustav Amundsen, Finn Malmgren and B L Gottwaldt) *The First Flight across the Polar Sea*, London, Hutchinson, nd (ca 1927) (274p, ill, charts)
A detailed account of the Amundsen-Ellsworth-Nobile airship with contributions by all the major participants except Nobile.

Andree, S A. *Andree's Story: The Complete Record of His Polar Flight 1897. From The Diaries and Journals of S.A. Andree, Nils Strindberg, and K Fraenkel, Found on White Island in the summer of 1930*, New York, Viking Press, 1930 (xvi + 389pp, ill, plans, maps)
A complete account of the first attempt to fly to the North Pole.

Balchen, Bernt *Come North with Me: An Autobiography*, London, Hodder & Stoughton, 1959, 318pp, ill, maps
Balchen was a leading Arctic aviator who was connected to both Byrd and Amundsen and has useful insights into the veracity of Byrd's claims to have reached the North Pole on 9 April 1926.

Barr, William, 'Imperial Russia's Pioneers in Arctic Aviation', *Arctic*, Vol 38 no. 3 (September 1985) pp 219–230

Bomann-Larsen, Tor. *Roald Amundsen* Brimscombe Port, History Press, 2006 (xvi & 384 pp, ill, bibliog, index)

Originally published in Norwegian in 1995 and particularly useful as it draws on archival material not available to earlier biographers.

Bowen, Stephen. *The Last Viking: The Life of Roald Amundsen, Conqueror of the South Pole*, London, Aurum Press, 2012 (xxii + 357pp, ill, maps, index)

A recent biography which concentrates on Amundsen's surface expeditions.

Bowers, Peter. 'Dr Dornier's Flying Whales', *Wings* June 1973 pp 50–65

Byrd, Richard E. *Skyward*, New York, Jeremy P. Tharcher/Putnam, 2000 (xviii & 331pp, ill)

An autobiography (originally published in 1928) of the American naval officer who claimed to have flown from Svalbard to the North Pole and return on 9 May 1926.

Capelotti, P J. *The Wellman Polar Airship Expeditions at Virgohamna, Danskoya, Svalbard*, Oslo, 1997, Norsk Polarinstitutt (101 pp, ill, index, bibliog)

Corn, Joseph P. *The Winged Gospel: America's Romance with Aviation*, 1900–1950, New York, Oxford University Press, 1983 (x & 177pp, ill, index, bibliog)

An insightful book about the popularity and significance of aviation and aviators in the first 50 years of aviation in the United States.

Dear, I C B & Peter Kemp (Editors). *The Oxford Companion to Ships and the Sea* (2nd Edition), Oxford, Oxford University Press, 2005

This book provides much valuable information on the ships which supported Amundsen's aerial expeditions.

Ellsworth, Lincoln. *Beyond Horizons* New York, Doubleday, 1937

The autobiography of the man who helped to finance the Amundsen flights of 1925 and 1926 and who participated in them.

Ferguson, William Paul. 'The Canadian Junkers: An Arctic Odyssey'. *Air Enthusiast Quarterly*, Number Three, nd. pp 109–112

Grierson, John *Challenge to the Poles: Highlights of Arctic and Antarctic Aviation: 1897–1954*, London, Foulis, 1964 (695pp, ill, maps, bibliography)

This book is a detailed survey of the first 57 years of aviation in the Arctic and Antarctic. There is little on Russian and Soviet activity because it was written at the height of the Cold War and the Soviet Union would not release the information.

Grierson, John. *Sir Hubert Wilkins: Enigma of Exploration*, London, Robert Hale Ltd, 1960 (224pp, ill, maps)

A biography of the explorer who tried to fly to the North Pole before Richard Byrd and Roald Amundsen but achieved notable firsts later in his career.

Davilla, James J. & Arthur M Soltan. *French Aircraft of the First World War*, Stratford, Flying Machines Press, 1997 (vi & 618 pp, ill, maps, bibliog, index)

Gunston, Bill. *The Cambridge Aerospace Dictionary*, Cambridge, Cambridge University Press, 2002 (741pp)

This book is the best modern technical dictionary of aviation in English.

Hayes, Derek. *Historical Atlas of the Arctic*, Seattle, University of Washington Press, 2003

Huntford, Roland. *The Last Place on Earth: Scott and Amundsen's Race to the South Pole*, London, Abacus, 2000 (528pp, ill, maps)

Originally published as *Scott & Amundsen* this is a good biography of Amundsen down to 1912 with many insights into his background and personality.

Khoury, G. A & J D Gillett (editors). *Airship Technology*, Cambridge, Cambridge University Press, 1999 (xiii & 545pp, ill, bibliography)

This is the only modern book on the subject. The chapter on airship piloting by David Burns is particularly valuable.

Mabley, Edward. *The Motor Balloon "America"*, Brattleboro, Stephen Greene Press, 1969 (95pp, ill)

A well-written account of Walter Wellman's airship expeditions including the 1906, 1907 & 1909 polar attempts.

Maynard, Jeff. *Wings of Ice*, Sydney, Vintage Books, 2010 (viii & 296 pp, ill,)

Maynard's book is a well-written and entertaining account of the first flights to the North and South Poles. It also contains an interesting and objective analysis of Byrd's claim to have flown to the North Pole. It mainly concentrates on Byrd and Wilkins.

Mills, William James (Ed). *Exploring Polar Frontiers: A Historical Encyclopedia*, Santa Barbara, ABC Clio, 2003, 2 volumes (629+pp, maps)

A very useful encyclopaedia which includes background on many of the men active in Arctic exploration in Amundsen's lifetime.

Nobile, Umberto. *My Polar Flights: An Account of the Voyages of the Airships Italia and Norge*, London, Muller, 1961 (288pp, ill)

An account by the Italian who designed and piloted the airships *Norge* and *Italia*.

*With the Italia to the North Pole*, London, Allen & Unwin, 1930 (358pp, ill, maps)

An account of the 1928 flights by *Italia* and the crash and rescue by the designer and captain of the airship.

Pool, Beekman H. *Polar Extremes*, Fairbanks, University of Alaska Press, 2002

Biography of Lincoln Ellsworth who helped finance and participated in Amundsen's 1925 and 1926 flights.

Rawlins, Dennis. 'Byrd's Heroic 1926 North Pole failure' *Polar Record* Vol 36 (196): 25–50 (2000)

Rawlins's careful analysis of the navigational notes kept by Richard Byrd on his flight towards the North Pole on 9 April 1926.

Sverdrup, Harald. "Roald Amundsen, Biographical Sketch" *Journal of the Arctic Institute of North America* 12, no. 4 (1959)

Stroud, John. 'Junkers F 13: The Pioneer from Dessau' *Air Enthusiast* Number 16, August-September 1981, pp 66–77

Taylor, H A & Peter Alting. 'Fokkers Lucky Seven' *Air Enthusiast* Number 12, April-July 1980, pp 24–35

Fokker F VII 3/m including Byrd's.

Thoren, Ragnar. *Picture Atlas of the Arctic*, Amsterdam, Elsevier, 1969 (xii & 449pp, ill, maps, bibliography)

This book provides a comprehensive geographical context to Amundsen's flights in the Arctic.

Van Dyke, Herman. *The Van Dyke Collection of LTA Plans and Drawings (with commentary)*, Auckland, LTA Institute, 2010 (viii + 167 pp, ill)

A useful collection of airship plans with technical notes. Includes *America* I & II and *Norge*.

Van Der Mey, M Michiel.  *Dornier Wal: A Light Coming Over the Sea*, Firenze, LoGisma Editore, 2005 (222pp, ill, maps, bibliography)

A well-illustrated history and technical introduction to the flying boats used by Amundsen in 1925.

Ventry, Lord. *Airship Saga: The History Of Airships Seen Through The Eyes Of The Men Who Designed, Built And Flew Them*, Poole, Blandford, 1982 (192pp, ill, glossary, bibliography)

A collection of articles by airship pioneers including Hjalmar J Riiser-Larsen's account of his training as an airship pilot and navigating *Norge* on her 1926 flight. The book is particularly useful because it includes stories collected by the editor from pioneers long before the publication date.

Walker, Percy B. *Early Aviation at Farnborough: The History of the Royal Aircraft Establishment; Volume 1: Balloons, Kites and Airships*, London, McDonald & Co, 1971 (xvi + 283, ill, app, index)

The man-lifting kites designed by Einar Sem-Jacobsen for Amundsen were almost identical to the ones designed and tested by Anglo-American S.F. Cody. This book examines the Cody kites in detail and depicts them in drawings and photographs.

Wohl, Robert. *The Spectacle of Flight: Aviation and the Western Imagination: 1920–1950*, London, Yale University Press, 2005 (416pp, ill, bibliography)

An account of the social impact of aviation from the end of the Great War to the beginning of the Korean War.

Wright, Monte Duane. *Most Probable Position: A History of Aerial Navigation to 1941*, Lawrence, University Press of Kansas, 1972 (xi & 281pp, ill, glossary, bibliography)

A well-researched and readable account of air navigation in the first 40 years of the 20th century.

## Part Two: DVDs

*The Airship Norge's Flight Across the Arctic Ocean*, National Library of Norway, 2012. A pristine print of the documentary made in 1926 and re-released in 2012.

*Roald Amundsen-Lincoln Ellsworth's Polar Flight 1925*, Norskfilminstitutt, 2010. A pristine print of the documentary made in 1925 about Amundsen's 1925 flight towards the North Pole and re-released in 2010.

*Frozen Planet*, 3 DVDs, BBC Earth, 2011. This documentary series provides a clear picture of the environment of the Arctic and Antarctic.

## Part Three: Maps

*Arctic Ocean*, Washington, National Geographic, February 1983

*Alaska*, Washington, National Geographic, January 1984

*Russia*, Washington, National Geographic, January 1993

## Part Four: Internet

(Date accessed in brackets)

**archives.gov/publications/prologue**
Summer 2010, Vol 42, No. 2 Women of the Polar Archives: The Films and stories of Marie Peary and Louise Boyd (29.01.2013)

**aviation-safety.net**
23 December 1927 Sikorsky S-36

**buehlfield.info.info/amundsen/north-pole**
Brief summary of Amundsen's efforts to reach the North Pole (16.09.2012)
Crash of the Elizabeth (16.09.2012)
Amundsen (23.10.2013)

**ecole.nav.traditions.free.fr**
Albert Cavelier de Cuverville (02.02.2013)
Rene Cyprian Guilbaud (01.02.2013)

**europeanairlines.net.no**
The 'Junkers Spitzbergen Expedition (1923)' (20.10.2013)
Timeline of civil aviation in Norway (15.10.2012)

**foxnews.com**
Norway resumes search for Roald Amundsen's plane that vanished 81 years ago (12.01.2013)

**frammuseum.no**
Odd Dahl (06.11.2012)
Leif Dietrichson (01.02.2013)
Hjalmar Fredrik Gjertsen (31.01.2013)
Oscar Omdal (23.10.2013)
Hjalmar Riiser-Larsen (18.11.2012)
Martin Ronne (09.09.2012)
George Herbert Scott (01.01.2013)

**km.kongsberg.com**
Hugin AUV used in search for Amundsen's airplane (12.01.2013)
Search for Amundsen ends without findings (21.01.2013)

**news.bbc.co.uk**
Hunt on for explorers lost plane (09.09.2012)

**Wikipedia**
Airship Italia (29.01.2013)
Alaska (21.01.2013)
List of Arctic Expeditions (02.02.20130
Floyd Bennett (05.01.2013)
Brusilov Expedition (25.01.2013)

Richard E. Byrd (21.12.2013)
Frederick Cook (04.10.2012)
Demographics of Alaska (25.01.2013)
Brice Goldsborough (31.01.2013)
Trygge Gran (01.02.2013)
Frances Wilson Grayson (30.01.2013)
Haakon VII of Norway (20.10.2012)
Latham (24.01.2013)
Latham 47 (24.01.2013)
Edward Maitland (30.12.2013)
Umberto Nobile (18.12.2013)
Ny Alesund (05.01.2013)
Oskar Omdal (23.10.2013)
Robert Peary (04.10.2012)
R33 class airship (01.10.2013)
Hjalmar Riiser-Larsen (18.11.2012)
Lincoln Ellsworth (06.02.2013)
Roma (airship) (18.12.2012)
MNoMS Tyr (N50) (03.02.2013)
Sikorsky S-36 (01.02.2013)
Teller, Alaska (21.01.2013)
Melvin Vaniman (09.10.2012)
Wainwright, Alaska (21.01.2013)
Ernest Willows (12.11.2012)

## Part Five: Newspapers

*Brisbane Courier*
*Cornell Daily Sun*
*Der Spiegel*
*Flight*
*New York Times*
*Pittsburgh Press*

*Appendix One*

# Glossary of 1920s Aviation Terms

Technology and the language used to describe it evolve continuously. By the mid-1920s the language of aviation had matured. The words defined below are used as they would have been used by people familiar with the flight operation of aeroplanes and airships in the period covered in the main part of this book (1922–1928). Where I refer to earlier aviation (particularly; 1909–1914) I have avoided using earlier, less precise terms.

**Aeroplane**  Powered heavier than air aircraft; a landplane (wheeled undercarriage), seaplane (floatplane or **flying boat**) or amphibian (wheels and floats or wheels on a flying boat hull).

**Aileron** Control  surface hinged to the rear of each **wing tip** in an aeroplane and providing control in **roll**.

**Aircraft**  All aircraft are either **aerodynes** (heavier than air) such as aeroplanes and gliders or **aerostats** (lighter than air) such as balloons and airships.

**Airship**  A lighter than air aircraft with propulsion (engines and propellers) and steering (rudder and elevators). In this period most airships were inflated with hydrogen gas. There were three main types of airship; non-rigid, **semi-rigid** and rigid. The *Norge* and *Italia* were both **semi-rigid** and were inflated with hydrogen.

**Angle of Attack**  The angle between the **chord line** of the wing and the **relative airflow**. In the 1920s the word **incidence** was used. **Riggers angle of incidence** is the angle between the chord line of the wing and the fore and aft line of the fuselage.

**Anhedral**  The negative angle between the horizontal and each wing in front elevation. The reverse of **dihedral**.

**Ballast**  Water or sand carried by **balloons** and **airships** in a droppable form. Dropped to make the balloon or airship lighter. In an airship water ballast (with anti-freeze added to avoid freezing at low temperatures) was used in several ways: (a) To trim the ship fore and aft (b) To prevent a descent in an emergency (3) To make a heavy ship light for landing.

| | |
|---|---|
| **Ballonets** | Fabric compartments of variable volume inside the envelope of pressure airships, containing air, and used to maintain a constant total volume inside the envelope. Deflated as the gas volume increased with decreasing air pressure as the airship climbed and inflated as the gas volume decreased with increasing air pressure as the airship descended. The *Norge* and *Italia* had at least two ballonets (one forward and one aft). Ballonets were also used to trim the airship the airship fore and aft by differential filling. |
| **Balloon** | A **lighter than air** aircraft without propulsion or steering. Balloons are either **captive balloons** (tethered to the ground) or **free balloons** (free to drift with the wind). Inflated with hydrogen. Free balloons were used for sport and recreation and for the preliminary training of airship pilots. Some primitive balloons inflated with hot air were used for short circus type demonstration flights. |
| **Blimp** | A slang expression for airship. Usually applied to describe a small airship of the **non-rigid (pressure)** type. In the 21st century its meaning has been expanded to include tethered streamlined, balloons with fins. |
| **Captive balloon** | Balloon tethered to the ground. Usually of a streamlined shape and with three stabilising fins. The streamlined types were known as **kite balloons**. Manned kite balloons were used for observation and unmanned kite-balloons were used as an anti-aircraft barrage (barrage balloons). |
| **Centre Section** | The middle one third of the **wing**. In the Dornier Wal the centre section contained the **engine nacelle** with its two engines. |
| **Cockpit** | A station for a crew member in an aeroplane. The Dornier Wal had two open cockpits in the fuselage; (1) bow for the observer/navigator (2) aft of the bow for the pilot. The engineer sat inside the fuselage under the engine nacelle. |
| **Control Car** | An enclosed cabin below the forward part of an **airship's envelope** and containing the captain, navigator, **rudder** and **elevator** men; and the controls, navigational instruments, chart table and radio equipment. Observers and other passengers usually spent their time in this part of the airship. Sometimes called the **control gondola**. |
| **Control Surfaces (Airship)** | Hinged surfaces; (1) **Rudder** (upper and lower or sometimes just the lower) attached to the vertical fins to provide directional control and (2) **Elevators** (left and right) attached to the horizontal fins to provide control in pitch. Each set of controls (e.g. the elevators) moved together. |
| **Control Surfaces** | Hinged surfaces; (1) **Rudder** attached to the fin to provide |

| | |
|---|---|
| **(Aeroplane)** | directional control (**yaw**) and (2) **Elevator** attached to the tail plane to provide longitudinal control (**pitch**) and (3) **Ailerons** (left and right) attached to the trailing edges of the wing tips to provide lateral control (**roll**). The elevators moved together and the ailerons moved differentially. |
| **Dihedral** | The positive angle between each wing and the horizontal when viewed in front elevation. Dihedral is used to provide lateral stability. A wing with a negative angle is said to have **anhedral**. |
| **Dirigible** | A slang expression for airship. Usually used to describe a large airship; like the semi-rigid *Norge* or the rigid USS *Shenandoah*. |
| **Dynamic Lift** | Lift produced by motion of a body (including an **aeroplane's** wing and an **airship's** envelope) through the air. An aeroplane relies entirely on dynamic lift to remain airborne. An airship can produce some of its lift dynamically by flying nose up or nose down, to cancel out the effects of being heavier than air or lighter than air. |
| **Elevator** | Pair of control surfaces hinged to the tail plane (**aeroplane**) or horizontal fins (**airship**) and providing control in **pitch**. |
| **Engine Cars** | Small streamlined units suspended below the **envelope** and each containing; an engine, its radiator and a number of crewmen. The *Norge* and *Italia* each had three engine cars; one on the centre line aft (rear engine car) and one on each side of the centre line about half way between the control car and the rear engine car (wing cars). Sometimes called engine gondolas or engine boats. |
| **Engine Nacelle** | A unit containing the engines. In the Dornier Wal the engines were mounted in tandem in a nacelle in the **centre section** of the **wing**. |
| **Envelope** | The fabric outer cover of a **balloon** or **airship**. Made of one or more layers of fabric and coated to make it gas tight. All envelopes suffered from some degree of permeability. In world war one it was assumed that a non-rigid airship would lose 100 per cent of its original volume each month by diffusion through the envelope although envelopes became less permeable with the development of more efficient materials. |
| **Fin (Aeroplane)** | Vertical surface fixed to the upper rear of the fuselage to provide directional stability. |
| **Fins (Airship)** | Two vertical surfaces fixed to the rear of the envelope (upper and lower) to provide stability in yaw (left and right) and two horizontal surfaces also fixed to the rear of the envelope to provide stability in pitch (nose up and nose down). |
| **Floats** | The undercarriage of a float seaplane. Floatation devices rounded on top and fitted with **steps** underneath to help the floatplane to attain flying speed. Usually two mounted on struts |

|  | where the wheels would be on a landplane. Another common arrangement was one large one under the fuselage and smaller ones under each wingtip. |
|---|---|
| **Free Balloon** | A spherical **balloon** inflated with hydrogen and free to drift with the wind. Manned free balloons were used for sport and recreation and for the initial training of airship pilots. Small unmanned free balloons were used to make observations (from the ground) of the winds aloft. An airship with the engines stopped is said to be **free-ballooning**. |
| **Free ballooning** | An airship with its engines stopped and drifting with the wind is said to be free ballooning. |
| **Flying Boat** | A **seaplane** that uses a waterproof, boat-shaped, **fuselage** to keep it afloat on the water. The Dornier Wal was a flying boat. |
| **Fuselage** | The body of an aeroplane. In a **flying boat** the fuselage is watertight and has a planning bottom similar to that of a power boat. |
| **Gas Valve** | All balloons and airships have one or more valves to vent lifting gas. In a balloon or an airship which is **free ballooning** venting the gas will stop a climb or cause a descent. An airship had emergency valves which automatically vented gas when a certain pressure was reached (and the envelope would rip if the pressure increased further) and **manoeuvring valves** to vent gas to make the ship heavier to maintain height or prepare for a landing. |
| **Heavier than air aircraft** | Aircraft that are lifted by the air moving over the wings during forward flight e.g., **aeroplanes** and **gliders**. |
| **Hydrogen gas** | The lightest of gases. Used to inflate balloons and airships. Inflammable when pure and explosive when mixed with oxygen. The *Norge* and *Italia* were inflated with hydrogen. |
| **Lighter than air aircraft** | Aircraft that are lifted by the buoyancy created by the lifting gas contained in their envelopes e.g., **balloons** and **airships**. |
| **Man Lifting Kite** | A series of winged box kites lifting a single cable and either a seat or a basket for one or two passengers. An observation platform for the passengers for military or civilian use. Heavier than air and technologically quite different from the similar sounding kite-balloon. |
| **Pitch** | The motion of an **aircraft** nose up or down. A movement around its longitudinal axis damped by the tail plane and controlled by the **elevators**. |
| **Pitot Head** | An airspeed indicator works by comparing the static and the dynamic pressure of the air with the static pressure. The **pitot head** faces into the airflow and receives the static and dynamic pressure. The **static vent** receives and provides the static pressure of the air. |

| | |
|---|---|
| **Pontoons** | The undercarriage of a float seaplane. A floatation device rounded on top and fitted with **steps** underneath to help the floatplane to attain flying speed. Usually two mounted on struts where the wheels would be on a landplane. Another common arrangement was one large one under the fuselage and smaller ones under each wingtip. Sometimes used to describe the **tip floats** of a **flying boat**. |
| **Port** | Left. |
| **Pressure Airship** | An **airship** that maintains its shape by maintaining the gas in the envelope at a slightly higher pressure than that of the surrounding atmosphere. **Ballonets** that could be filled with air were fitted inside the envelope to maintain a constant volume as the lifting gas expanded or contracted. Air was vented from the ballonets as the lifting gas expanded during a climb. Air was pumped into the ballonets to compensate for the reduction in gas volume during a descent. **Non rigid** and **semi-rigid** airships are both types of pressure airships. |
| **Pressure Height** | The height at which the lifting gas in an airship fills 100% of the envelope. If the airship climbs above pressure height it has to valve off gas to avoid the envelope splitting open. |
| **Rip Panel** | Part of the envelope of a pressure airship or balloon that will open when a rip cord is pulled and let the gas out with a rush. When a balloon or airship is landed in a strong, gusty wind the envelope acts like a sail is and is blown around until the gas is vented. The quicker the gas is let out the better, hence the rip panel. |
| **Roll** | The motion of an aircraft around its longitudinal axis. **Aeroplanes** roll when the **ailerons** are used. **Airships** have no control to roll them but roll slightly when the **rudder** is used and in turbulence they **pitch**, **yaw** and **roll**. |
| **Rudder** | Control surface hinged to the **vertical fin** and providing control in **yaw** (the nose moves left or right). |
| **Seaplane** | An aeroplane designed to take off and land from water. The main types were floatplanes and **flying boats**. |
| **Semi-Rigid Airship** | A **pressure airship** with a keel along the bottom of the **envelope**. The keel stiffened the envelope, simplifying the maintenance of shape and providing an attachment point for some of the **gondolas**. |
| **Sponsons** | Wing like stabilisers mounted on the hulls of some flying boats and used to keep them upright when afloat. The Dornier Wal flying boats were equipped with sponsons. |
| **Starboard** | Right. |
| **Static Lift** | The displacement of air by a lighter than air lifting gas (e.g. **hydrogen**) produces static lift for **balloons** and **airships**. |

**Step** A seaplane is said to be on the step when the hull lifts partly out of the water during the take-off run and can then accelerate to flying speed.

**Sun Compass** An aid to air navigation. Used to steer a steady heading when the magnetic compasses were unsteady or unreliable due to the close proximity of the magnetic north pole. They were set before take-off and the longitude and time had to be known accurately and the sun had to be clearly visible. The 1925 flight used clockwork drive Goerz sun compasses.

**Trail Rope** A balloon was normally equipped with a trail rope which was carried rolled in a ball and could be dropped with the one end attached to the balloons load ring and used to maintain height automatically while flying low over a smooth surface or water or to cushion the final descent while landing.

**Variometer** An instrument which shows whether an aircraft is climbing or descending and the rate at which it is. Usually calibrated in feet per minute.

**Wing** The large fixed surface of aerofoil section which provides an **aeroplane** with its **lift** and a mounting for the **ailerons**. The Dornier Wal was a **monoplane** (single wing) but the wing was said to be made up of the port (left) and starboard (right) wings.

**Wing Tips** The outer one third of the **port** and **starboard** wings.

**Yaw** The motion of an aircraft around its vertical axis damped by its fin or fins and controlled by its **rudder**.

# Dornier Wal (Whale) Flying Boat

GENERAL DESCRIPTION: Twin engine, monoplane flying boat of all metal construction.

HISTORY: The Wal was designed in Germany by Claudius Dornier (1884–1969) but could not be manufactured there because of the Treaty of Versailles of 1919 which ended World War One and imposed a moratorium on the manufacture of aircraft by Germany. The prototype Wal flew for the first time on 6 November 1922. Both the Amundsen-Ellsworth aircraft were manufactured under licence in Italy by Societa di Costruzioni Meccaniche di Pisa of Marina di Pisa. SCMP manufactured both civil and military versions. The expedition's aircraft were military versions, without armament, and with modifications including; rear gunner's position faired over, extra flight and navigational instruments, and extra fuel tankage.

Constructor's number 19 was completed on 30 January 1925 and was test flown on 5 February 1925. It received the Norwegian civilian registration N 24. It was abandoned on the pack ice on 14 June 1925 in position 87° 44' N & 10° 20' W.

Constructor's number 20 was completed on 19 February 1925 and test flown on 21 February 1925. It received the Norwegian civil registration N25. After the 1925 expedition it was bought by Frank Courtney, re-registered G-EBQO and re-engined with 450hp Napier lions. After two unsuccessful attempts to fly the Atlantic it was re-engined again this time with 600hp BMW Vs. and sold to the German School of Civil Flying (DVS) at Sylt. It was used for a flight across the North Atlantic in 1930 by Wolfgang von Gronau. The German registration was D-1422. In 1932 it was donated to the Deutsches Museum and displayed until destroyed in an allied air raid in 1944.

ENGINES: Two water-cooled Rolls Royce Eagle IXs, each of 360hp. Mounted in tandem on the centre section of the wing with the forward driving a tractor propeller and the aft driving a pusher propeller. The engines shared a single radiator mounted between and above the engines.

PROPELLERS: Two four-bladed, fixed-pitched, wooden propellers, one a tractor and one a pusher.

DIMENSIONS: Span 22.5m, length 17.25m, height 5.2m, wing area 96m².

WEIGHTS: empty 3,560kg, normal maximum take-off weight 5,700kg, take-off weight for polar flight 6,660kg.

PERFORMANCE: Maximum speed 180kmph (98kt), cruising speed 150kmph (81kt), rate of climb 33min to 3,000m (9,842ft), (298ft per min), range (with overload fuel and no reserves or allowance for wind) about 2,400km (1.296nm) . Endurance at 150kmph about 16 hours.

- The only surviving Wal is the *Plus Ultra* which is in the Museo del Transporte in Lujan, Argentina. The *Plus Ultra* was flown from Spain to Argentina by Ramon Franco and his crew in 1926.
- A full size replica of Amundsen's Wal *N25* was unveiled at the Dornier Museum, Friedrichshafen, Germany on 25 July 2012.

*Appendix Three*

# Airship Norge

GENERAL DESCRIPTION: N class semi-rigid airship.

HISTORY: Designed by Umberto Nobile for the Italian Navy. It made its first flight in 1924. Purchased by a Norwegian organisation in 1926 and modified for the flight from Italy to Alaska. The Norwegians took delivery at Rome on 29 March 1926. From 10 April 1926 to 7 May 1926 it was flown from Rome to Kings Bay in stages; Rome–Pulham (England)–Oslo (Norway)–Leningrad (Soviet Union)–Vadso (Norway)–Kings Bay (Spitsbergen) in 100 hours flight time. This flight positioned the airship at Kings Bay for the great trans-polar flight. The non-stop flight from Kings Bay to Teller (near Nome, Alaska) by way of the North Pole took place from 11 May 1926 to 14 May 1926 and the ship was in the air for 70 hours. The airship was dismantled at the landing site and never flew again.

**Flight Log:**

10 April 1926 to 14 May 1926

| | |
|---|---|
| Rome–Pulham | 32 hrs |
| Pulham–Oslo | 14 hrs |
| Oslo–Leningrad | 17 hrs |
| Leningrad–Vadso | 21 hrs |
| Vadso–Kings Bay | 16 hrs |
| Kings Bay–Teller | 70 hrs 40 min |
| Total: | 170 hrs 40 min |

**Technical Information:**

| | |
|---|---|
| Volume | 18,500 $m^3$ |
| Length | 106m |
| Diameter | 19.47m |
| Empty weight | 13,000kg |
| Useful lift | 8,274kg |
| Maximum speed | 61kt |
| Cruising speed | 43kt |

Endurance (at 43kt)          75hrs
Range                        3,225nm

Engines: 3 x Maybach Mb IVa six-cylinder, water-cooled, 250hp (each)
Crew and Passengers (Polar Flight)  16